From the Personal
to the Political

From the Personal to the Political

Toward a New Theory
of Maternal Narrative

Edited by
Andrea O'Reilly and
Silvia Caporale Bizzini

Selinsgrove: Susquehanna University Press

©2009 by Rosemont Publishing & Printing Corp.
All rights reserved. Authorization to photocopy items for internal or personal use, or the internal or personal use of specific clients, is granted by the copyright owner, provided that a base fee of $10.00, plus eight cents per page, per copy is paid directly to the Copyright Clearance Center, 222 Rosewood Drive, Danvers, Massachusetts 01923.
[978-1-57591-129-8/09 $10.00 + 8¢ pp, pc.]

Associated University Presses
2010 Eastpark Boulevard
Cranbury, NJ 08512

The paper used in this publication meets the requirements of the American National Standard for Permanence of Paper for Printed Library Materials Z39.48–1984.

Library of Congress Cataloging-in-Publication Data

From the personal to the political : toward a new theory of maternal narrative / edited by Andrea O'Reilly and Silvia Caporale Bizzini.
    p. cm.
  Includes bibliographical references and index.
  ISBN 978-1-57591-129-8 (alk. paper)
1. Motherhood. 2. Motherhood in literature. 3. Mothers in literature. 4. Mothers—Biography—History and criticism. I. O'Reilly, Andrea, 1961- II. Caporale-Bizzini, Silvia.
  HQ759.F754 2009
  306.874'301—dc22
                                        2009003778

PRINTED IN THE UNITED STATES OF AMERICA

Contents

Acknowledgments 7

Introduction
ANDREA O'REILLY AND SILVIA CAPORALE BIZZINI 9

Part I: Maternal Stories: From Experience to Praxis

Writing as a Practice of Resistance:
Motherhood, Identity, and Representation
SILVIA CAPORALE BIZZINI 37

Narrating the (Lone) Maternal Subject:
The Validation Stories of "Ordinary Women
in Extraordinary Circumstances"
LESLEY PATTERSON 50

White Mothers of Chinese Daughters:
Real Mothers of Real Children
SONYA CORBIN DWYER AND LYNN GIDLUCK 71

"Your Shopping Cart Is Empty":
Social Texts of Single Motherhood
and the Discomforts of Discourse
ANN ELIZABETH WILLEY 86

The Paradox of Separation and Dependency: A Mother's Story
JENNY JONES 101

"My Mum's a Dyke": Maternal Subjectivities in Midlife Transition
from a Heterosexual to a Lesbian Identity
SUSAN KENTLYN 114

The Maternal Autobiography in Performance
BETH OSNES 124

Part II: Maternal Texts: From Narrative to Theory

Maternal Fetters: Motherhood and
Slavehood in Harriet Jacobs's
Incidents in the Life of a Slave Girl
MARY MCCARTIN WEARN   143

The Dialogics of the Sexual-Maternal:
Multiple Births in Gilman and Le Sueur
CAROLINA NÚÑEZ PUENTE   156

The Mother in Mourning as the Subject
of Autobiography in Rosamond Lehmann's
The Swan in the Evening: Fragments of an Inner Life
NÓRA SÉLLEI   170

Implicated in a Color Change:
Darkening the Picture of Jane Lazarre's
Maternal Transracial Memoir
MARTHA SATZ   183

Coalescence in Evolution: Queer Familia
in Cherríe Moraga's *Waiting in the Wings*
R. JOYCE Z. L. GARAY   195

Babies and Boundaries: Mother-Speaking
in Rachel Cusk's *A Life's Work*
CELIA SHIFFER   210

Maternal Subjectivity: A Kristevan Reading
of Anne Enright's Memoir, *Making Babies:
Stumbling into Motherhood*
HEATHER INGMAN   225

The Motherhood Memoir and the "New Momism":
Biting the Hand that Feeds You
ANDREA O'REILLY   238

Notes on Contributors   249

Index   255

Acknowledgments

THE IDEA FOR THIS BOOK WAS CONCEIVED FIVE YEARS AGO OVER coffee in Alicante, Spain, where Andrea was visiting to give a talk at Silvia's University. The book is finally in our hands and we are deeply thankful to the many who midwifed the book's delivery and birth. Special thanks to Andrea O'Reilly's research assistants May Friedman, Cheryl Dobinson, Roni Hoffman, Melissa Nurse, Ayla Lefkowich, Sarah Trimble and Renée Knapp, and to our proofreader and indexer Randy Chase. I am grateful to Sarah Bailey for her belief in this manuscript and to Christine A. Retz for her skill in turning this into a book. Thank you also to the members of the *Association for Research on Mothering*: our thinking on mothering, as always, was enriched and sustained by this splendid community of scholars. Our heartful gratitude goes to the contributors of this volume who sustained and inspired us throughout the long—and at times painful—gestation of this volume.

FROM SILVIA

In the last five years many things have passed and my insights into my own maternal narrative and self-writing have gone through both some adversity and some less difficult moments that have deepened my perspective on what mothering means. I do not welcome all of them, but they belong to life and experience and have made me a more indulgent human being. I especially thank Clarissa Ramos, the friend that shared with me some particularly hard weeks. A special mention to my husband, mostly patient and always supportive, and to my children Claudia and Javier, who have taught me so much about happiness and caring, and also about patience. I am thankful to be able to share my scholarly accomplishments with them.

From Andrea

Special thanks to Renée Knapp, my closest friend and colleague at *ARM* who commiserates and comforts when I need it the most, and to Fiona Green, who mentors and models the best in feminist scholarship and sisterhood. Finally, my love and appreciation to my partner of twenty six years, Terry Conlin, and to our children Jesse, Erin and Casey. Thank you for enabling me—nay, empowering me—to make the personal political in my life and work.

Introduction

Andrea O'Reilly and
Silvia Caporale Bizzini

THE RELATIONSHIP BETWEEN THE CONSTRUCTION OF FEMININE IDENTITY and motherhood theory is a field of research that has aroused considerable interest within feminist cultural analyses of the last thirty years. The scrutiny of the notion of motherhood—as well as the crucial task of exploring the realms in which the ethics of "maternal thinking" becomes a focus of enquiry—has sparked a growing number of critical works (Mitchell 1974; Rich 1976; Chodorow 1978; Benjamin 1988; Corea 1988; Katz 1989; Snitow 1992; Thurer 1994; Ross 1995; Hill-Collins 1997). Since the publication of Adrienne Rich's *Of Woman Born* and, a few years later, of Sara Ruddick's "Maternal Thinking," new ways of understanding who a mother is, along with wider notions of mothering, have arisen. Sara Ruddick offers one of the most important contributions to this through her insights into the social and political meaning of the learning process that lies behind the ethics of maternal care and its application to an innovative way of theorizing citizenship, the individual's responsibility within civil society, peace studies, and the struggle in defense of human rights. Despite the theoretical problems and misunderstandings which have resulted from the interpretation of Ruddick's thinking, the fact is that the American philosopher stresses that maternal caring is not an instinctive part of the female psyche, but an ability that is acquired through learning that, historically, has been assigned to women. Maternal caring is more than mere biological fact; on the contrary, it falls within a relational context that replaces the idea of an innate female caring ability developed within the limits of a nuclear, biological and heterosexual family structure.[1]

This theoretical standpoint epitomizes the intellectual roots of most of the analysis on motherhood carried out since the 1990s, and the aspects that relate it to a shifting notion of mothering (Gilligan

1982; Swigart 1991; Vegetti Finzi 1996; DiQuinzio 1999). The starting point is represented by the analysis of motherhood understood as a social construct whose characterization and role in society adjusts to the field forces defined by the historical period and the needs of the hegemonic groups therein (Nakano, Chang, and Rennie Forcey 1994; Greenfield and Barash 1999; Douglas and Michaels 2004). In this sense, we have to accept that the notion of mothering is not only historically determined, but is, at the same time, subject to both the discontinuities that form the discourse of history—the differences and practices within different cultures—as well as the cultural construction of the concepts of infancy and childhood (Cosslet 1994; Hannisberg and Ruddick 1999). Despite these inspired—and inspiring— intellectual approaches, most of contemporary autobiographical discourse on motherhood limit their exploration of maternity to a "motherhood as experience" perspective. In such, there is a growing tendency to narrate the maternal experience from a standpoint pervaded by a (returning) biologism that rests exclusively on an intimate and ideal/ized perception of mothering and the maternal bond.

In *Narrating Maternity: Theorizing Maternal Subjectivities* (1991), Brenda O. Daly and Maureen T. Reddy argue that in "the limited number of fictional or theoretical texts" that do "begin with the mother in her own right, from her own perspective," few "hold fast to a maternal perspective; further, when texts do maintain this perspective, readers and critics tend to suppress the centrality of mothering" (2–3). Daly and Reddy coined the term "daughter-centricity" to describe the perspective wherein "we learn less about what it is like to mother than about what is like to be mothered, even when the author has had both experiences" (2). The aim of this volume is to consider and call for an explicitly maternal or, more pointedly, a matrifocal perspective that foregrounds the everyday historically and culturally determined experiences of mothering and the intellectual basis of mothering, while resisting claims of a universal, essential, sentimental, normative maternity. Our use of the term "matrifocal" is drawn from Miriam Johnson's discussion of matrifocality in *Strong Mothers, Weak Wives* (1989). Matrifocal societies, she writes:

> tend to have greater gender equality because of the power of a maternal paradigm. In these societies, regardless of the particular type of kinship system, women play roles of cultural and social significance and define themselves less as wives than as mothers. . . . Matrifocality however, does not refer to domestic maternal dominance so much as it does to

the relative cultural prestige of the image of the mother, a role that is culturally elaborated and valued. Mothers are also structurally central in that the mother as a status 'has some degree of control over the kin unit's economic resources and is critically involved in kin-related decision making processes." It is not the absence of males (males may be quite present) but the centrality of women as mothers and sisters that makes a society matrifocal . . . (226)

A matrifocal narrative, borrowing from Johnson's terminology above, is one in which a mother plays a role of cultural and social significance and in which motherhood is thematically elaborated, valued, and structurally central to the plot. In other words—and to draw on Marianne Hirsch, Daly, and Reddy—matrifocal narratives "*begin* with the mother in her own right, from her own perspective," and they "hold fast to a maternal perspective." Drawing upon the writings of Sara Ruddick, a matrifocal perspective as developed in this collection insists that the experience of mothering must be understood as an intellectual, self-reflexive, and philosophical practice, while the institution of motherhood, building upon Adrienne Rich's work, must be viewed as a social and political institution.

In *Of Woman Born*, Adrienne Rich distinguishes between two meanings of motherhood, one superimposed on the other: the *potential* relationship of any woman to her powers of reproduction—and to children; and the *institution* which aims at ensuring "that that potential—and all women—shall remain under male control" (14, emphases in original). The institution of motherhood, Rich goes on to emphasize, has "a history, it has an ideology" (33). Building upon Rich's theoretical formulation, feminist scholars over the last thirty plus years have examined the various ways that motherhood operates as a patriarchal institution to constrain, regulate, and dominate women and their mothering. More specifically, these scholars agree that motherhood is primarily not a biological function; contrariwise, it is specifically and fundamentally a cultural practice that is continuously redesigned in response to changing economic and social factors (O'Reilly 2004a, 2004b, 2006). Similarly, Sara Ruddick argues that mothering is not primarily a natural or biological activity, but rather that mothering demands "that mothers think: out of this need for thoughtfulness, a distinctive discipline emerges" (1984, 24; O'Reilly 2006). Mothers meeting at their jobs, in playgrounds, or over coffee, Ruddick continues, "*can be heard thinking*" (1989, 24, emphasis added). The aim of this volume is to represent mothering-motherhood, both as it is lived and represented: fundamentally and inherently as an intellectual and social site, one that is simultaneously personal and relational, subjective and cultural. In short, this volume advances a new way to read and write the maternal autobiography, one that attends to and accentuates the philosophical and political dimension of motherhood.

The term "motherhood autobiography," as we are using it, refers to mothers' experiences as they are storied and narrated. Part one of the volume examines mothers' stories—their experiences—of motherhood, while the second considers published maternal narratives. The contributors represent and read the motherhood autobiography as specifically a social or political text. More pointedly, and borrowing from the popular feminist slogan, "the personal is political,"[2] this approach to maternal autobiography insists that the personal *is* political. In using the word "political" we refer to a perspective that understands mothering to be an intellectual, philosophical, or self-reflexive activity, and motherhood to be a cultural-political institution. Similar to Mielle Chandler's argument that the word "mother" is best understood as a verb, the writers in this volume see the "motherhood experience" as a position to write from rather than an activity to be written about. Or to use Rachel Blau DuPlessis's concept of "writing beyond the ending," the authors seek to move beyond description to reflection, and from story to theory, in their writings on motherhood. As the contributors move from description to reflection, they also reflect upon, or are self-reflexive about, the ways in which subjectivity is itself formed/informed by discourse. Finally, this perspective insists that maternal subjectivities are not only varied and diverse but that maternal subjectivity itself is multifaceted. In other words, the authors in this collection move beyond normative maternity to explore differences among and *within* individual women in order to challenge the existence of a universal meaning of motherhood and the notion of a fixed and stable maternity. Indeed, in moving the motherhood story from the personal to the political this volume allows for a new reading of maternal autobiography.

Linda Anderson, in her *Autobiography* (2001)—a critical examination of the theories that have defined the autobiography as a literary genre—points out how Felman emphasizes the particularity of the first-person account as opposed to the merely autobiographical account. The first-person account takes shape in the spaces within the textual fabric, in the resistances and hesitations that arise *between* discourses: it recounts the moment and does not require the totality in order to give meaning to a particular life experience. Thus, if as Judith Fetterley declared, "Literature is political,"[3] the autobiographical account symbolizes the need for a re/definition of the ontology of maternity. Through the first-person account, the voice of the mother (understood in the wider sense) may lend a political sense to her personal experience, emotionally intense in both good and bad moments.

In *The Uses of Autobiography* (1995), Julia Swindells stresses that the autobiographical genre represents the need to express outwardly the struggle, tension, defiance, protest, and, in general terms, the conflicts that arise between our consciousness and the surrounding environment and between people and the ideological construction(s) of the world that shape reality. In the same work, Laura Marcus emphasizes how the use of narrative techniques that, although related, have not traditionally belonged to the realm of literature, have given the autobiographical account an element of "literary hybridity" that facilitates—or exemplifies—far more profoundly, the different ontologies of the self that materialize in autobiographical narration. But what do we find when we examine the various collections of autobiographical narrative centred on motherhood? It is striking to find that since the 1990s the majority of narratives about women as the object—but also as the subject—of discourse, have centred their analyses on the relationship between the woman and the newborn baby, and always in conspicuously sentimental terms.

What we need to ask is: Where are the other "mothers"? And the concept of "mothering"? Are all mothers biological? Are they all women? Are they all white, middle-class, middle-aged, heterosexual? Are they all biological mothers, or mothers of young children? In her paper "New Thoughts on 'the Oldest Vocation': Mothers and Motherhood in Recent Feminist Scholarship," Ellen Ross points out that since the second half of the nineties, and as a result of the social changes that shaped the latter decades of the twentieth century, a growing urge to narrate *other* motherhoods seems to have emerged, together with a slow, but inevitable, process of redefinition of the ontology of motherhood(s) (1995, 398). Ross argues that: "In the mid-1990s, much new feminist research . . . has been aimed at uncovering hidden mothers and hearing their long silenced voices" (1995, 402). These good intentions seem, however, to have been lost along the way. In her critique, Ross reminds us that in the nineteenth century, for example, autobiographical narration did not leave aside the most somber and painful aspects of maternal practice, but just the opposite. However, from the beginning of the twentieth century, this type of first-person account loses its connotation of life story and begins to be associated with magazines that publish sensationalist accounts, setting a precedent, so to speak, for the so-called "reality" programs that are now so widespread: "Whereas the nineteenth-century periodicals acknowledged the possibility of an infant's death and validated the mother's mourning for the child, by the early twentieth century they had become silent on this issue and the task of voicing these fears went to the more downmarket *True Story*, which, founded in 1919, regularly published first-person accounts of miscarriages, stillbirths, and infant deaths" (1995, 402).

Ann Snitow cites the experience of the editors of the anthology *Why Children?* (1987) in which an effort was made to include first-person accounts of women who regretted their decision to become mothers. Though they managed to find some of these women, they were unable to persuade them to write about their experiences; this silence is representative of one of the most harmful weaknesses of feminist criticism vis-à-vis the role of the mother, and runs the risk of eclipsing all the profound and complex analyses that have been carried out regarding the ontology of maternity. What happens when we face the death of a child, academic failure, and the problems of adolescence or illness? Where is the voice of the woman who decides *not* to become a mother? And what about the attack by the media and political circles in the United States and Great Britain on mothers who receive state aid in order to live? Where are their life stories and voices? Once again we need to listen to Ross: "Telling the hard things about motherhood has usually been labelled gossip and been confined to women's private conversations on playgrounds, doorsteps, or telephones. But in 1990 I was seeking not feminist books on sick or dying children so much as full recognition of the practice of mothering in its various circumstances—how it is done day by day, its particular skills, its pleasures, and its sometimes great costs" (398).

The chapters in this collection tell "the hard things about motherhood" and push the maternal narrative beyond the private and frequently sentimental "motherhood as experience" paradigm to represent motherhood as the intellectual and political practice and institution that it is. The essays included in this book piece together theory and practice to stress clearly and critically that motherhood—understood as both a cultural and personal construction—requires a profound revision regarding the connections between self and world, experience and ideology. Such a revision needs to be developed at different levels in order to stress the complexity in contemporary ideologies of the cultural construction of maternal identity; it needs to question a totalizing/universalizing representation of the "action" of mothering. As Jana Sawicki reminds us, feminism has not only described the discursive practices that shape contemporary prevailing ideologies ("the outcome of the myriad of micro-practices," Sawicki 1991, 81), but has also defined the discursive nodal points where resistance can be carried out. Motherhood theory and autobiography are, in our opinion, representative of this ideological necessity to renegotiate the notions of "being a mother" and mothering, as well as to stress the importance of mothers as resilient and political agents.

The chapters that make up this volume theorize and narrate maternity against and beyond the descriptive "motherhood as experience" paradigm that characterizes normative views on motherhood and much contemporary writing on motherhood. And in so doing, the maternal autobiographies, as considered in this volume, function as political texts. The chapters reflect and insist upon the specificity of each motherhood experience to challenge the universalizing and essentialist assumptions of normative maternity that define much of contemporary maternal autobiography. The contributors come from a range of countries including New Zealand, Australia, Canada, Great Britain, Ireland, Hungary, and Spain. The maternal identities theorized in section one include single, queer, adoptive, poor, working mothers, mothers of interracial children, and mothers of adult children. The authors studied in the second section on narrative similarly include Chicana, African American, British, Irish, and American mothers, as well as mothers who have suffered from mental illness and grieving mothers whose children have been ill or have died. However, in offering this wide and diverse range of multiple, and often marginalized, maternal voices, the collection does more than represent "other motherhoods"; by illuminating this maternal diversity it shows how motherhood functions as an intellectual practice and social/political site across these differences. As well, the writings span a wide range of literary genres and cover close to a hundred and fifty years of history, from the maternal slave narrative *Incidents in the Life of a Slave Girl* to the popular motherhood memoir *A Life's Work*. Moreover, each text emphasizes the intrinsic political and philosophical nature of motherhood, both as it is lived and represented. In this, they echo Elspeth Probyn's contention that autobiography is "a conjectural document of the self and of the times . . . which arises from the situation *as it comments upon it*" (emphasis added,

1993, 98). Discussing Probyn's statement, Linda Anderson comments further: "The question is recast, therefore, in relation to autobiography becoming not 'what is it' but instead 'what does it *do*'" (2001, 91). In this insistence upon the polity of maternity, not only is motherhood understood to be political, but also, as a result, mothers themselves become political agents or actors. This type of motherhood autobiography, in foregrounding the inherent and inevitable self-reflexive and social dimension of motherhood, makes possible a political resistance to instutionalized motherhood. In moving beyond "motherhood as experience," this political take on autographical motherhood moves the feminist dialogue on motherhood forward; from discussion to critique, or more pointedly, from personal complaint to social change.

Part I: Maternal Stories: From Experience to Praxis

The essays in part I examine maternal autobiography *as it is lived*. However, the writers do not simply aim at giving the reader a universalizing interpretation of the events that have marked the authors' lives as mothers (mothers of older children, adoptive mothers, lone mothers, single mothers, lesbian mothers, etc.); in addition, they aim at transmitting how these women locate themselves between discourses as individuals and, in doing so, how they become resilient subjects. Silvia Caporale Bizzini's essay seeks to describe how the relationship between motherhood, identity, and representation shows how women writers (especially in the case of autobiographical writing) defy, for example, Walter Benjamin's thesis on the impossibility of voicing the historical experience of the oppressed. She points out that the autobiographical and/or literary voice of the mother enables us to understand the social meaning of motherhood and counter stereotypical understandings of mothering, while also considering it in relation to social class, race, or sexual orientation.

The idea of hierarchy in the social negotiation of the definition of maternal subjectivities is addressed—more or less surreptitiously—in most of the essays in the first part of the collection, but is clearly voiced in Lesley Patterson's as well as in Sonya Corbin and Lynn Gidlick's essay. In Patterson's contribution, the conceptual starting point takes into account the parameters of social class and the political meaning of lone motherhood in a social context within which it tends to be vilified.

Lone mothers on welfare, echoes Julie Wallbank, are criminalized by society: "They also often fail to attain the celebrated norms of self-sufficiency and independence. Lone mothers and particularly poor lone mothers are subjected to public scrutiny and placed under some form of state supervision" (2001, 57). Lesley Patterson suggests that mothers negotiate their subject positions within a hierarchy of maternal legitimacy in which not all mothers are equal. With this in mind, this essay describes the concept of "validation stories." The mothers' narratives that constitute the backbone of Patterson's analysis also reveal how lone mothers and their life experiences are ontologically defined as "other" within the same/other dichotomy in the family romance of the hegemonic idealization of the maternal subject. In talking about their lives, validation stories enable these women to position themselves as ordinary women in extraordinary circumstances and thus breach the socially constructed gap between the idealized maternal subject and what actually happens in women's lives.

As stressed above, the reflection on the hierarchy of motherhood is also present in Sonya Corbin and Lynn Gidluck's analysis of adoptive motherhood in relation to reproduction and fertility. In this chapter, the authors interrogate the language surrounding adoptive mothering and challenge the notion that because we did not give birth to our children, we are somehow not their "real" mothers. They focus their attention on a number of interesting topics concerning the ways in which society responds to adoptive motherhood. They insist on how language structures such responses and ideologically constructs attitudes toward interracial adoptive mothers and—once again—the idealized practice of good motherhood, thus demonstrating how the opposition nature/nurture is still powerfully present in our collective imagination. In Barthesian terms, we can affirm that these authors try to come to terms with and narrate their maternal autobiographies in a position that locates them in-between the categories of encratic and acratic discourses.[4] Their experience is voiced between the hegemonic narrative of the "good mother" and the need to narrate their story of mothering within an order of things that cannot fully represent their choices.

The stress on the issue of language that comes to light in Corbin and Gidluck's essay is also present in Ann Elizabeth Willey's contribution. Her personal (contextual) choice to become a single mother situates her in-between discourses and her essay daringly problematizes a particularly thorny issue: the capitalistic logic of "cryobanks" and the ethical discourse that surrounds new reproductive technologies. Willey's experience of maternity has been textually produced in discourses over which she had very little control and that shaped her maternity in ways that she has found herself resisting continuously. In her essay, she explores how her path to single motherhood via anonymous donor insemination was shaped by discourses of lack of fulfillment, illness, commercialism, silence and shame, and traditional maternal images that both accurately described and simultaneously distorted her sense of motherhood and self. In this context, forging a vocabulary and practice of one's maternal and professional self is an ongoing exercise in narrativizing a role that is curiously public and private, external and internal, and individual and communal at the same time. Ann Willey, like Jenny Jones, aims at problematizing the given universal meaning of the mother's tale by giving voice to some of women's anxieties in connection with their perception of who they are as mothers and what mothering means to them.

In her chapter, Jones reflects on how the practice of motherhood is a process that takes shape and acquires different meanings over the years. It is a relational process between the mother and the children, but it is also strongly influenced by social pressures and changing times. Jenny Jones claims that the beguiling narratives, which initially charm and then trick and deceive mothers and non-mothers, continue to be entrenched within white, Western, middle-class culture despite feminist criticism. Through a hermeneutical analysis, she explores the master narratives and her engagement with them. It is through this exploration that she discovered that her voice as a mother of older children had become "constricted and constrained." Jones suggests that the role of master narratives in the self-understanding of one's identity is subject to experience and discontinuities in the time line, and that our response to our children becoming young adults can produce an ontological crisis in the perception of one's maternal identity, which the hegemonic narrative of the good mother does not help one to deal with.

The last two essays in the first part of the collection question the idealized representation of motherhood, and vindicate the cultural richness and variety of those discourses that aim at shaping maternal identities in all their fullness, ambiguity, and complexity, both in the material domain of discourses and in the psychological projection of these. Susan Kentlyn presents her own narrative of transition. Her use of Queer Theory questions the representation of the mother as an asexual subject while seeking to redefine the concepts of maternal "will" and "agency," thus the earthquake and reconstruction metaphor is employed to illustrate the scale and emotional impact of the transformation of subjectivities of both mother and children in this process.

In her contribution, Beth Osnes points out that the maternal autobiographical performance is a discursive site where ideology, consciousness and one's own personal life experience meet and give voice to a unique and altogether different "I." In the telling of autobiographical stories, Osnes simultaneously conveys her belief in the worth of each mother's story as a source from which she can distil her own insight and wisdom. Hearing stories encourages women to claim their voices, to own and operate the portrayal of mothers toward the expression of their own goals and most audacious dreams for the future.

The narratives of this first part of the collection take shape on different levels (ethical, personal, political, etc.) and underline the complex multiplicity of the act of mothering as life experience. With regard to the nature/nurture dichotomy, they speak to the ambiguities of contemporary culture, social tensions, sexual orientation, etc. Some of these narratives are constructed through memory, but also as performance. The backbone of these essays is represented not only by an ethical commitment to the multiple meanings of the act of mothering, but also by a very definite interaction between political and auto/biographical elements which serve to analyse and/or question given maternal models and roles of family, gender or desire in connection with motherhood and mothering. Our narrators define their selves not only as a textual exercise but as individuals positioned within the historical reality of the society they belong to; in this sense, Elaine Tuttle Hansen reminds us that: "in the last three decades . . . It is to be found . . . a rubric that includes non-traditional mothers and 'bad' mothers, including lesbians and slave mothers; women who have abortions and miscarriages; women who refuse to bear children, or whose children are stolen from them; and mothers who are . . . sometimes criminals, murderers, prisoners, suicides . . . or ghosts" (1997, 10). The mother as narrator of her own life story constructs her identity by reflecting and narrating the daily (material) practices of mothering. Referring to this possibility of voicing one's life story and experiences through autobiographical practices, Linda Coleman points out that, "Across the many sub genres, with their varied opportunities and limitations, we discover a fundamental and common strategy for coming to a meaningful understanding of the self and for establishing the needed authority and strength to negotiate or even to subvert external or internalised norms that might silence that self" (1997, 1). In this, we move from individual and private practices of mothering to a social, or more pointedly, a political maternal praxis wherein the personal give rise to a public critique and change on motherhood.

Part II: Maternal Texts: From Narrative to Theory

Part II examines the maternal autobiography as text. However, as with the chapters from part I, the chapters in this section read these private and personal motherhood narratives as profoundly self-reflexive and social texts that make possible a larger understanding of how motherhood functions as a social institution. This in turn leads to theories of motherhood beyond the narratives told. Sidonie Smith and Julia Watson ask in their introduction to *Women, Autobiography, Theory: A Reader*: "Under what conditions can the subject exercise any kind of freedom, find the means to change?" (23). Speaking more specifically on the subject of ideology and agency they inquire: "How does the woman autobiographer negotiate a discursive terrain—autobiography—that has been until recently a primarily masculine domain? How do discourses of identity differentiate the narrative scripts of normative . . . femininity? How does the narrator take up and put off contradictory discourses of identity? How does she come to any new knowledge about herself?" (23). The questions asked by Smith and Watson become more troubling—and troublesome—when applied to mothers as subjects of autobiography. Beginning with Hirsch's *The Mother/Daughter Plot: Narrative, Psychoanalysis, Feminism* (1989), scholars have noted a paucity of maternal autobiographies and commented upon the difficulty, if not impossibility, of writing as a mother (Brenda O. Daly and Maureen T. Reddy, *Narrating Mothers: Theorizing Maternal Subjectivities*, 1991: Maureen T. Reddy, Martha Roth, Amy Sheldon, *Mother Journeys: Feminists Write about Mothering*, 1994; Tess Cosslett, *Women Writing Childbirth: Modern Discourse on Motherhood*; Julia Tharp and Susan MacCallum Whitcomb, *This Giving Birth: Pregnancy and Childbirth in American Women's Writing*, 2000; Patricia Dienstfrey and Brenda Hillman, *The Grand Permission: New Writings on Poetics and Motherhood*, 2003; Jo Malin, *Voice of the Mother*, 2002). And while there has been an increase in the number of maternal autobiographies over the last decade with the emergence of the motherhood memoir, this has done little to facilitate a theory on maternal autobiography since this genre, as noted in the final essay, remains largely limited to the "motherhood as experience" paradigm.

The authors of the maternal narratives, and the scholars who write on them presented in part II, understand mothering to be inherently and inevitably intellectual and motherhood to be intrinsically political and social. More specifically, the authors in section two, whether they write on a nineteenth-century slave narrative or a contemporary motherhood memoir, insist upon differences among and within individual women in order to challenge the existence of a universal meaning of motherhood and the notion of a fixed and stable maternity. Moreover, the authors and contributors in part II see "motherhood as experience"; it is a place to write from rather than an activity to be written about, so as to move from story to theory. Finally, as the authors move from description to analysis, they reflect upon, or are self-reflexive about, the ways in which subjectivity is itself formed/informed by discourse. In each of these themes, the contributors demonstrate how motherhood *and* maternal autobiography are both inherently and profoundly philosophical and political as Ruddick and Rich have theorized. Through this, they show how maternal autobiography, if understood as a political text, can move us beyond narrative to theory in order to facilitate a new understanding of motherhood both as it is represented and lived.

In the essay on Harriet Jacobs's *Incidents in the Life of a Slave Girl* (1861) that opens the second part, Mary McCartin Wearn argues that critics have long noted the distinctly doubled nature of Harriet Jacobs's autobiographical roman à clef. In this abolitionist text, which chronicles the author's slavehood, motherhood, and escape to the free North, Jacobs's narrative voice splits—vacillating between revelation and concealment, between repentance for her perceived cultural crimes and defiance. Wearn explores the doubled nature of Jacobs's text, by specifically examining *Incidents* as a maternal narrative with a clear, political agenda. I will argue that Jacobs's nuanced, multilayered depiction of her own motherhood and slavehood both politically exploits *and* critically deconstructs nineteenth-century maternal ideals. At one level, Jacobs's narrative deploys white, middle-class constructions of motherhood to underwrite her antislavery argument. But just as Jacobs hides her true identity behind the pseudonym of Linda Brent in *Incidents*, so too will she hide a more radical maternal subjectivity under the unthreatening veneer of sentimental motherhood. Examining legible gaps and elisions in the text and focusing on a discernable alternative narrative voice, the chapter explores how Jacobs covertly articulates a more rebellious, politically dangerous maternal subjectivity. Reading the subversive underside of *Incidents*, Wearn reveals how Jacobs acts as an agent of her own liberty by examining and owning the emotional complexities of slave motherhood, and by exposing and undermining the slave state's capacity for transforming the power of mother love into a force of oppression. In this rendition of motherhood, the normative—ahistorical, essentialist, apolitical—view of motherhood is reconfigured to make rage and resistance an integral, if not defining, dimension of maternal subjectivity and experience.

The second essay, "The Dialogics of the Sexual-Maternal: Multiple Births in Gilman and Le Sueur," similarly examines the duality of maternal subjectivity and insists upon a multifaceted understanding of mothering and maternal subjectivity to include, in this instance, the sexual within the maternal. Employing the critical perspective of feminist dialogics, Carolina Núñez Puente develops a comparative reading of the semiautobiographical short stories "The Yellow Wallpaper" and "Annunciation," written respectively by Charlotte Perkins Gilman and Meridel Le Sueur. Puente explores how these authors, through writing on themselves, become subjects for themselves, as well as subjects for their readers with the texts' publications. In this way, the female characters' subjectivities can be said to be dialogical, based on both their own and others' perception of themselves. Furthermore, the introduction of maternity into the public sphere challenges traditional concepts of canonical literature and of motherhood itself. In this, Núñez Puente looks at how the concept "sexual-maternal" functions in these texts to deconstruct not only the "mother/whore" hierarchy, but also that between the "creative" and the "procreative" and its insistence on the vitality of the boundary. The presence of the sexual-maternal in "The Yellow Wallpaper" and "Annunciation," Núñez Puente goes on to argue, causes us to reflect upon the dialogical nature of our identities-alterities, as well as the simultaneous corporeality and spirituality of our bodies-selves. The short stories' reconceptualizations of the "self," as a dialogical "self-in-relations," entail a criticism of Western binary oppositions in a similar vein to that of the "ethics of care." As in the mother-and-child relation, connections, even dependence, are not a liability: they simply sustain life. In general, both Gilman and Le Sueur look for ways to reconcile the individual and the social, the private and the public. In so doing, they show the importance and necessity of recognizing the possibility of the dialogical capacities of all beings—e.g., not only women and mothers—in order to challenge patriarchal binary logic and remake our ways of thinking, feeling, and acting in the world.

As the first two essays of this section problematize normative and normalizing autobiographical constructions of motherhood by narrating the political and sexual-dialogical aspects of maternity, the third essay, by Nóra Séllei on Rosamond Lehmann's only autobiographical writing, *The Swan in the Evening: Fragments of an Inner Life* (1967), gives voice to the censored and silenced voice of maternal mourning. The autobiography covers a wide range of experiences from (mostly traumatic) early childhood memories through her work of mourning to recovery following the death of her daughter Sally. In this way, Lehmann's text as a narrative is driven by a lack (which is always at the core of both mourning and the process of subject formation) that is specific: the loss of the daughter by the mother, which evokes a pervasive cultural image, the mother in mourning, or *mater dolorosa*. Relying on Julia Kristeva's essay *"Stabat Mater,"* a cultural-psychoanalytical interpretation of the mother in mourning, the essay provides a close reading of the narrative of *The Swan in the Evening*, and will claim that in this text Lehmann rejects, or at least rewrites, the traditional discourse of the mother in mourning. Normally, *Stabat Mater* has no story to tell, only tears to shed. In this case, however, instead of repressing and silencing the traumatic event of the death of her daughter, their apparently ultimate separation, the narrator re-creates a cyclical and maternal—even mystical—subjectivity, involving generations of daughters (the text is dedicated to her eldest granddaughter), wherein the autobiographical narrator is both the subject and agent of her narration while, at the same time, is constructed by her intersubjective—and ethical—relationships. Thus, in this text the iconic *mater dolorosa* is turned into the speaking and ethical autobiographical subject of intersubjectivity.

"Implicated in a Color Change: Darkening the Picture of Jane Lazarre's Maternal Transracial Memoir" by Martha Satz likewise considers a maternal perspective that is disregarded and denied in normative constructions of maternity and maternal subjectivity, namely a mother of a biracial child. Weaving her story of being a mother of an interracial daughter with a reading of Jane Lazarre's autobiography, *Beyond the Whiteness of White: Memoir of a White Mother of Black Sons*, Satz explores the "convoluted consciousness" of being a white mother to a black child. To be alienated from most whites and linked to blackness by the strongest of loves, Satz writes, one becomes ensnared in a convoluted consciousness that is akin to Dubois's "double consciousness" in the "anguish of feelings" it invokes. However, Satz, in her reading of *Beyond the Whiteness of White*, insists that Lazarre does more than tell of her journey as a white mother to black sons; in Lazarre's own words, she "used memoir to transcend itself, not only to recall and describe experience but to understand its significance beyond the self . . . the link between an individual life story and the collective story." Satz, in her reading of Lazarre, seeks to do this: reflect upon Lazarre's own maternal practice of a white mother raising black sons while at the same time signalling larger understandings about both race and motherhood in America. More specifically, using Ruddick's concept of attentive love and Dalmiya's thinking on caring relationships, Satz argues that Lazarre's memoir shows us how "a community, however transitory, can be forged between Black and White."

The following essay, "Coalescence in Evolution: Queer Familia in Cherríe Moraga's *Waiting in the Wings*" by Joyce Z. L. Garay, looks at Cherríe Moraga's *Waiting in the Wings: Portrait of Queer Motherhood*. The novel is an intimate rendering of Moraga's pregnancy, the premature birth of her son, Rafael Angel, and the ensuing formation and negotiation of her subjectivity as Chicana, lesbian, mother, and writer. Refusing to deny any part of her self in constructing queer Chicana maternal subjectivity, Moraga continually interrogates and redefines "family." She melds queer consciousness with a definition of family grounded in her Mexican cultural heritage and history, theorizing and actualizing the uncharted territory of constructing and nurturing queer familia. The chapter focuses on Moraga's illustration of the complexities and paradoxes of lesbian motherhood and constructing a family both queer and Mexican. Ultimately, Garay argues that Moraga foregrounds the distinct facets of her maternal subjectivity—Chicana-mother/blood-mother, butch-mother, lover-mother, writer-mother—and fights to bring them together in radical coalescence. This construction of maternal subjectivity and queer familia at once compels provocative discussion of the ways in which Moraga defies simplistic theoretical thinking about both queerness and mother-self.

A central theme of the next essay, "Babies and Boundaries: Mother-Speaking in Rachel Cusk's *A Life's Work*" by Celia Shiffer, is likewise the multifaceted and relational nature of maternal subjectivity. Shiffer argues that Cusk's memoir, as signified by the subtitle "On Becoming a

Mother," is not about parenting but about becoming; it is not about instruction but about comprehension and, most importantly, it is not about raising a child, but about being a mother. In particular, Shiffer argues, Cusk, in her narration of becoming, opposes the hegemonic view of subjectivity that privileges individualism and requires the loss of such in maternity. Motherhood, as Cusk reminds us, is not about the one, nor can it be entirely about the other (as it is suddenly supposed to be). In fact, motherhood cannot recognize such logic of binaries and separations. And so, rather than accept the cultural mythologies of motherhood that oppose the motherself with the individual self, Cusk develops a "self-in relation" model of maternity in which motherhood does not mark the disappearance of self but rather the expansion or branching of self. Moreover, in this telling, Cusk bespeaks the embodied trauma of new motherhood—its psychic and physical pain—and thus disturbs the sentimental and tidy view of motherhood found in the dominant culture. Shiffer concludes that Cusk succeeds in telling a new story of motherhood and speaking a new kind of "I."

Heather Ingman's examination of Anne Enright's memoir, *Making Babies: Stumbling into Motherhood*, similarly explores how normative views on motherhood—in this instance the idealizations of motherhood in Irish nationalist and religious discourse—define Enright's experiences of motherhood and give rise to her critique of normative Irish maternity. More specifically, Ingman argues that by dwelling on the physical aspects of childbirth and early motherhood, Enright, similar to Cusk above, reintroduces what has traditionally been repressed in the Irish Catholic discourse of maternity, namely, the female body. Looking first at the censoring and silencing of the maternal voice in Irish fiction, Ingman goes on to consider, using Kristeva's theory of abject motherhood, how Enright, in dwelling on " the blood, sweat, shit and milk of childbirth and early motherhood," challenges her nation's relegation of maternal subjectivity to the abject and seeks to reclaim the voice of Irish motherhood. Ingman goes on to argue that in the context of the lengthy suppression of maternal subjectivity in the life of the Irish nation, Enright's determined emphasis on her personal experience of the physical realities of motherhood may be said to form a political strategy. In this, *Making Babies* counters not only the idealization of motherhood prevalent in Irish nationalist and religious discourse but also the larger hegemonic script of motherhood that seeks to simultaneously universalize and sanitize the complex and often messy realities of lived motherhood.

The final essay, "The Motherhood Memoir and the 'New Momism': Biting the Hand That Feeds You" by Andrea O'Reilly, examines the emergence of the contemporary motherhood memoir from the perspective of changing ideologies of "good" motherhood. The essay argues that this literary genre is born from a new ideology of motherhood, that which Sharon Hays has termed intensive mothering and Susan Douglas and Meredith Micheals call the "new momism." Beginning with a discussion of intensive mothering and the "new momism," the paper goes on to highlight several themes of the motherhood memoir from the perspective of this new discourse on motherhood. The chapter argues that as this new ideology makes possible a public voice on motherhood, it simultaneously limits what that voice can say about motherhood. More specifically, according to O'Reilly, this discourse ultimately reinscribes, or more accurately, naturalizes and normalizes the very patriarchal conditions of motherhood that feminists, including the motherhood memoir writers themselves, seek to dismantle. O'Reilly maintains that most motherhood memoirs, because of their identification with the new momism, cannot discern, let alone critique, the root causes of mothers' oppression, and concludes that the genre remains one of complaint and not change. Motherhood memoir writers must, according to O'Reilly, offer a critique of the new momism if we hope to move the genre from a rant to a revolution. But to do so, we must do away with the new momism, and its naturalization of gender inequities. Indeed, O'Reilly concludes, memoir authors must bite the hand that feeds them.

Conclusion

In *Writing a Woman's Life*, Carolyn Heilbrun observes: "Lives do not serve as models, only stories do that. And it is a hard thing to make up stories to live by. We can only retell and live by stories we have heard. Stories have formed us all: they are what we must use to make new fictions and new stories" (32).

However, as noted by many scholars there are few maternal stories "to live by." Motherhood, as Marni Jackson observes, "is an unexplored frontier of thought and emotion that we've tried to tame with rules, myth and knowledge. But the geography remains unmapped" (9). "Motherhood may have become an issue," Jackson continues, "but it's not yet a narrative" (3). Perhaps the maternal is, as Hirsch theorizes, unnarratable: Could it be, she asks, that "maternal discourse can exist . . . only on the condition that it remains fragmentary and incomplete?" (185). Indeed, as Sara Ruddick has noted: "It is hard to speak precisely about mothering. Overwhelmed with greeting card sentiment we have no realistic language in which to capture the ordinary/extraordinary pleasures and pains of maternal work" (40). Today, authors and scholars, while acknowledging this difficulty in speaking that which has been censored, distorted, and silenced, struggle to make the maternal story narratable in both literature and theory.

It is our hope that this volume will assist in this endeavor by signalling the need for a political perspective on the writing and reading of the maternal narrative. This perspective begins with the understanding that mothering is a self-reflexive practice and that motherhood is a political and social institution. More specifically the essays seek to show how maternal subjectivities are not only varied and diverse but that maternal subjectivity itself is multifaceted. In other words, we must move beyond normative maternity to explore differences among and *within* individual women in order to challenge the existence of a universal meaning of motherhood and the notion of a fixed and stable maternity. As well, we need to view "motherhood experience" as a position to write from rather than an activity to be written about so as to move the narration from description to reflection. Finally, this perspective asks that we be attentive to the ways in which subjectivity is itself formed/informed by discourse.

However, the essays that comprise this collection do not aim at either being representative of all forms of motherhood or suggest that there is a contemporary way of mothering. Rather, the various maternal perspectives represented in this collection—lesbian, adoptive, lone, working class, and enslaved, among others—are included to emphasize how storytelling becomes a "political" tool across maternal differences. As Hannah Arendt (1998) suggests, storytelling is a way to focus our attention toward the discourse of the *polis*, a public space of dialogue and debate. Writing one's maternal identity is also a way of coming to terms (when necessary) with an external reality that shapes our responses and tries to locate us in a predefinite ontological location. Our point is that we can either accept this location or question it. In other words, as writers we can become agents while narrating and/or fictionalizing our life experience. The aim of this collection is to show how the autobiographical tale is able to interconnect the political meaning of mothering and the private experience in the representation of the maternal ontology of the self in its multiple and complex manifestations. It is our belief that in reading and writing maternal autobiographies in this way we will create "stories to live by" so as to make real the changes we seek in lived motherhood.

NOTES

1. See Marta Fineman, *The Neutered Mother, the Sexual Family and Other Twentieth-Century Tragedies* (New York: Routledge, 1994).
2. Carol Hanisch published a brief paper whose title was "The Personal Is Political" in the Redstockings collection *Feminist Revolution* (March 1969): 204–5.
3. See Judith Fetterley, "On the Politics of Literature," in *Literary Theory: An Anthology*, edited by Julie Rivkin and Michael Ryan (Oxford: Blackwell, 1998), 561–69.
4. "reprenant une vieille notion aristotélicienne, celle de *doxa* (d'opinion courante, générale, 'probable,' mais non 'vraie', 'scientifique'), on dira que c'est la *doxa* qui est la médiation culturelle (ou discursive) à travers laquelle le pouvoir (ou le non-pouvoir) parle: le discourse encratique est un discours conforme à la *doxa*, soumis à des codes, qui sont eux-mêmes les lignes structurantes de son idéologie; et le discours acratique s'énonce toujours, à des degrés divers, contre la *doxa* (quel qu'il soit, c'est un discours *para-doxal*." Roland Barthes, "La division de langages," in *Essais critiques IV, Le bruissement de la langue* (Paris, Éditions du Seuil, 1984), 122.

WORKS CITED

Anderson, Linda. *Autobiography*. New York: Routledge, 2001.

———. *Women and Autobiography in the Twentieth Century. Remembered Futures*. London: Prentice Hall, 1996.

Arendt, Hannah. *The Human Condition*. Chicago: University of Chicago Press, 1998.

Barthes, Roland. *Essais critiques IV, Le bruissement de la langue*. Paris: Éditions du Seuil, 1984.

Bassin, Donna, Margaret Honey, and Meryle Mahrer Kaplan, eds. *Representations of Motherhood*. New Haven: Yale University Press, 1994.

Bordo, Susan. "Are Mothers Persons? Reproductive Rights and the Politics of Subjectivity." In *Unbearable Weight. Feminism, Western Culture and the Body*. Ed. Susan Bordo. Berkeley: University of California Press, 1995. 71–97.

Boulous Walker, Michelle. *Philosophy and the Maternal Body*. London: Routledge, 1998.

Caporale Bizzini, Silvia, ed. *Discursos teóricos. en torno a la(s) maternidad(es)*. Madrid: Entinema, 2005.

Chandler, Mielle. "Emancipated Subjectivities and the Subjugation of Mothering Practices." In *Redefining Motherhood: Changing Identities and Patterns*. Ed. Sharon Abbey and Andrea O'Reilly. Toronto: Second Story Press, 1998. 270–86.

Chase, Susan E., and Mary F. Rogers, eds. *Mothers and Children. Feminist Analysis and Personal Narratives*. New Brunswick: Rutgers University Press, 2001.

Chodorow, Nancy. *The Reproduction of Mothering*. Berkeley and Los Angeles: University of California Press, 1978 [1999].

Coleman, Linda S., ed. *Women's Life Writing. Finding Voice, Building Community*. Bowling Green, OH: Bowling Green State University Popular Press, 1997.

Corea, Gena. *The Mother Machine. Reproductive Technologies from Artificial Insemination to Artificial Wombs*. London: Women's Press, 1988.

Cosslett, Tess. *Women Writing Childbirth: Modern Discourse on Motherhood*. Manchester: Manchester University Press, 1994.

Daly, Brenda O., and Maureen T. Reddy. *Narrating Mothers: Theorizing Maternal Subjectivities*. Knoxville: University of Tennessee Press, 1991.

Davey, Moira, ed. *Mother Reader. Essential Writings on Motherhood*. Toronto: Seven Stories Press, 2001.

Dienstfrey, Patricia, and Brenda Hillman. *The Grand Permission: New Writings on Poetics and Motherhood*. Middletown, CT: Wesleyan University Press, 2003.

Dinnerstein, Dorothy. *The Mermaid and the Minotaur. Sexual Arrangements and Human Malaise*. New York: Harper Colophon Books, 1976.

DiQuinzio, Patrice. *The Impossibility of Motherhood. Feminism, Individualism and the Problem of Mothering*. New York: Routledge, 1999.

Douglas, Susan J., and Meredith W. Michaels, eds. *The Mommy Myth. The Idealization of Motherhood and How It Has Undermined Women*. New York: Free Press, 2004.

DuPlessis, Rachel Blau. *Writing Beyond the Ending: Narrative Strategies of Twentieth-Century Women Writers*. Bloomington: Indiana University Press, 1985.

Fetterly, Judith. "On the Politics of Literature." In *Literary Theory: An Anthology*. Ed. Julie Rivkén and Michael Ryan. Oxford: Blackwell, 1998. 561–69.

Gilligan, Carol. *In a Different Voice: Psychological Theory and Women's Development*. Cambridge: Harvard University Press, 1982.

Greenfield, Susan, and C. Barash. *Inventing Maternity. Politics, Science and Literature 1650–1865*. Lexington: University of Kentucky Press, 1999.

Hannisberg, Julia, and Sara Ruddick, eds. *Mother Troubles. Rethinking Contemporary Maternal Dilemma*. Boston: Beacon Press, 1999.

Heilbrun, Carolyn. *Writing a Woman's Life*. New York: Ballantine Books, 1988.

Hill-Collins, Patricia. "Shifting the Centre: Race, Class and Feminist Theorizing about Motherhood." In *Maternal Instincts. Visioning Motherhood and Sexuality in Britain. 1875–1925*. Ed. Claudia Nelson and Ann Summer Holmes. London: Macmillan, 1997. 56–74.

Hirsch, Marianne. The *Mother/Daughter Plot: Narrative, Psychoanalysis, Feminism*. Bloomington: Indiana University Press, 1989.

Ikemoto, Lisa C. "Lessons from the *Titanic*." In *Mother Troubles. Rethinking Contemporary Maternal Dilemma*. Ed. Julia Hannisberg and Sara Ruddick. Boston: Beacon Press, 1999. 157–77.

Jackson, Marni. *The Mother Zone: Love, Sex and Laundry in the Modern Family*. Toronto: Macfarlane Walter & Ross, 1992.

Jackson, Stevi, and Jackie Jones. *Contemporary Feminist Thought*. Edinburgh: Edinburgh University Press, 1998.

Kenison, Katrina, and Kathleen Hirsch, eds. *Twenty Stories of Contemporary Motherhood*. New York: North Point Press, 1996.

Malin, Jo. *Voice of the Mother: Embedded Maternal Narratives in Twentieth Century Women's Autobiographies*. Carbondale: Southern Illinois University Press, 2002.

Marcus, Laura. "Theories of Autobiography." In *The Uses of Autobiography*. Ed. Julia Swindells. London: Taylor & Francis, 1995. 13–23.

Morell, Carolyn M. *Unwomanly Conduct. The Challenges of Intentional Childlessness*. New York: Routledge, 1994.

Nakano, Glenn, Grace Chang, and Linda Rennie Forcey, eds. *Mothering Ideology. Experience and Agency*. New York: Routledge, 1994.

Nelson, Claudia, and Ann Summer Holmes, eds. *Maternal Instincts. Visioning Motherhood and Sexuality in Britain. 1875–1925*. London: Macmillan, 1997.

O'Reilly, Andrea, ed. *From Motherhood to Mothering: The Legacy of Adrienne Rich's Of Woman Born*. Albany: SUNY Press, 2004b.

———, ed. *Mother Outlaws: Theories and Practices of Empowered Mothering*. Toronto: Women's Press, 2004a.

———, ed. *Mothers and Sons. Feminism, Masculinity and the Struggle to Raise Our Sons*. London: Routledge, 2001.

———. *Rocking the Cradle: Thoughts on Motherhood, Feminism and the Possibility of Empowered Mothering* (with a Preface by Sara Ruddick). Toronto: Demeter Press, 2006.

O'Reilly, Andrea, and Sharon Abbey, eds. *Mothers and Daughters. Connection, Empowerment and Transformation*. Lanham, MD: Rowman & Littlefield Publishers, 2000.

Passerini, Luisa. "Women's personal narratives. Myths, Experiences, and Emotions." In *Interpreting Women's lives. Feminist Theory and Personal Narratives*. Ed. The Personal Narratives Group. Bloomington: Indiana University Press, 1989. 189–97.

Probyn, Elspeth. *Sexing the Self: Gendered Positions on Cultural Studies*. New York: Routledge, 1993.

Reddy, Maureen T., Martha Roth, and Amy Sheldon, eds. *Mother Journeys: Feminists Write about Mothering*. Minneapolis: Spinsters Ink, 1994.

Rich, Adrienne. *Of Woman Born: Motherhood as Experience and Institution*. New York: Norton, 1976.

Ross, Ellen. "New Thoughts on 'the Oldest Vocation': Mothers and Motherhood in Recent Feminist Scholarship." *Signs* (Winter 1995): 397–413.

Ruddick, Sara. "Maternal Thinking." In *Mothering: Essays in Feminist Theory*. Ed. Joyce Trebilcut. Lanham: Rowman & Littlefield, 1984, 213–30.

———. *Maternal Thinking Toward a Politic of Peace*. Boston, MA: Beacon Press, 1995 (1989).

———. "Talking about Mothers." In *Mother Reader. Essential Writings on Motherhood*. Ed. Moyra Davey. Toronto: Seven Stories Press, 2001. 187–98.

———. "Thinking Mothers/Conceiving Birth." In *Representations of Motherhood*. Ed. Donna Bassin, Margaret Honey, and Meryle Mahrer Kaplan. New York, Routledge, 1994. 29–45.

Sawicki, Jana. *Disciplining Foucault: Feminism, Power and the Body*. London: Routledge, 1991.

Smith, Babette. *Mothers and Sons. The Truth about Mother-Son Relationship*. Sydney: Allen & Unwin, 1995.

Smith, Sidonie. *Subjectivity, Identity and the Body. Women's Autobiographical Practices in the Twentieth Century*. Bloomington: Indiana University Press, 1993.

Smith, Sidonie, and Julia Watson. *Women, Autobiography, Theory*. Madison: University of Wisconsin Press, 1998.

Snitow, Ann. "Feminism and Motherhood: an American Reading." *Feminist Review* (Spring 1992): 32–51.

Stanworth, Michelle. *Reproductive Technologies: Gender, Motherhood and Medicine*. Minneapolis: University of Minnesota Press, 1987.

Swigart, J. *The Myth of the Good Mother. The Emotional Realities of Mothering*. New York: Doubleday, 1991.

Swindells, Julia. *The Uses of Autobiography*. London: Taylor & Francis, 1995.

Tharp, Julia, and Susan MacCallum Whitcomb. *This Giving Birth: Pregnancy and Childbirth in American Women's Writing*. Bowling Green, OH: Bowling Green State University Press, 2000.

Thurer, Sharon. *The Myths of Motherhood: How Culture Reinvents the Good Mother*. Boston: Houghton Mifflin Company, 1994.

Tuttle Hansen, Elaine. *Mother Without Child: Contemporary Fiction and the Crisis of Motherhood*. Los Angeles: University of California Press, 1997.

Umanski, Lauri. *Motherhood Reconceived*. New York: New York University Press, 1996.

Wallbank, Julie. Challeng Motherhood(s). Marlow, England: Prentice Hall, 2001.

From the Personal to the Political

I
Maternal Stories:
From Experience to Praxis

Writing as a Practice of Resistance: Motherhood, Identity, and Representation

Silvia Caporale Bizzini

> One of the many ways in which forms of selfhood have been transmitted and appropriated is through the reading of literary selves.
> —Steedman

IN THIS ESSAY, I WILL DEFINE MY THEORETICAL UNDERSTANDING OF the relationship between motherhood, identity and self-representation by discussing concepts and thinkers that have paved my approach to literary studies and hermeneutics.[1] The theoretical framework that has led to the completion of this essay is based on a multilayered study (Probyn 1993) of the contemporary notion of maternal identities as self-representation of the historical, cultural, and epistemological complexity of the present moment, as well as on an autobiographical perception of the issue. My research, together with my teaching practice, adopts a strongly theoretical approach to the exploration of possible ontologies of the self. The autobiographical dimension has shaped the substance of my discourse, as well as an ongoing reflection as to why, how, and to whom I address as a university lecturer; how I locate myself within the other(s)' gaze as an adoptive parent in a multiracial family, and how these two spheres interact in the context of everyday life through a theoretical understanding of myself as a committed social subject.

Feminist criticism has long demonstrated that the dominant cultural construction of motherhood is mainly based on three recurring ideas: the need to define maternal subjectivity *always* and *only* in relation to feminine identity (and eventually to the individual's social class, race, and/or sexual orientation); the ethics of mothering, that is to say, the discursive paradigm about how a *good* mother must act and behave;

and, as a consequence, the need to establish the limits of maternal agency (Bordo, 1995). According to Lisa Ikemoto: "The mother in a wide variety of race and class specific forms . . . has served as a cultural reference point of framework for particular sets of norms. These norms operate on three overlapping levels. At each level, patriarchy . . . white nativism and middle class privilege interlock into a matrix of standards and presumptions that appear to be part of the 'natural order' . . . Motherhood at this level is about mothering. Biological essentialism has shaped those assumptions, expectations and standards" (1999, 160).

Maternal subjectivities represent a powerful focal point of departure to reconsider in more complex terms the necessity to question established boundaries and rewrite the very definiton of mothers as social subjects. In order to critically face and question some of the contemporary debates that would appear to bring us to relocate motherhood and mothering in the private realm—while paradoxically constructing a "new" public image of what a good mother is or is supposed to be (Swigart 1991; Thurer 1994; Douglass and Michael 2004)—we must analyze the discursive practices that are at the origin of this conservative shift. In my theoretical approach, I consider an autobiographical perspective that does not emphasize the inner, emotional, and private narrativization of motherhood. On the contrary, I feel it is necessary to lay stress on a (testimonial) political perception of the historically determined experience(s) of mothering. In other words and as Sawicki puts it: "We must reject an ahistorical appeal to the theoretical category of mothering. It obscures cultural and historical specificity" (1991, 61). Once we apply this historical prism, we become aware of how the discursive representation of motherhood and/or mothering is roughly and mainly constructed first from a standpoint that narrates maternal experiences from the outside (the mother as object of discourse) (Greenfield and Barash 1999; Thurer 1994; Tubert 1996), then through the mother/daughter relationship and psychoanalysis (the rejected mother) (Hirsch 1989; Malin 2002), and finally from an autobiographical perspective that, as a final point, voices the experience of mothering in a wider sense (the mother as subject) (Chase and Rogers 2001; Kenison and Hirsch 1996; Reddy, Roth, and Sheldon 2002).

Since the early 1990s, I have contextualized my understanding of the literary text as cultural production within the Foucauldian interpretation of the construction and questioning of normative identity. At the same time, I opened my field of research to the post-Marxist reading of the historical process[2] and the Gramscian concept of cultural hegemony, to explore—and problematize—the notion of writers as intellectuals and resilient agents within the "cultural capital" (Bourdieu and Passeron 1973). I am conscious that my analysis focuses on literary discourse and that I do not examine these concepts from a perspective related to, let us say, political philosophy or social science. Anyway, I am also fully aware that, as Laclau and Mouffe state: "Any discourse is constituted as an attempt to dominate the field of discursivity, to arrest the flow of differences, to construct a centre" (2001, 112). I am also aware that I carry out my analysis in a cultural context that considers the use of textuality within a society that is heavily reliant on a globalized understanding of the cultural (visual) product, while weakening the meaning of the historical process in the formation of identity.[3] As Scott Wilson reminds us: "History and criticism . . . are in practice processes of reading . . . the past, as an object of fascination, . . . the mirror in which 'recognition' is always also a 'misrecognition'"(1995, 12–13). Wilson's analysis of the possibilities of new historical readings stresses that reinterpreting the historical process that has forged the Real does not eliminate possibilities of change, but produces new tools for understanding the (Western) historical process *differently*.[4] One of the other aspects that needs to be considered when analyzing the notion of (maternal) subject formation is, as Fredric Jameson among others points out, the pressing influence that a globalized and visual representation of society is playing on our understanding of ourselves as social subjects and how these hybrid discursive practices permeate the (self)narrative of (resistant) writers, artists and intellectuals. When writing becomes a site where conflict and /or contestation are represented, we might have a glimpse of the clash between the hegemonic ideological constructions of how maternal identities are projected onto the world and the struggling identities of "real" mothers that fight back to write their own true story. As Cosslett (1994) and Tuttle Hanson (1997) have shown, the discursive representations of motherhood(s) have slowly moved from the sphere of private writings to the sphere of public and political representation. These new forms of historical interpretation emphasize the importance of resistance in the definition of new ontologies of the self and the role that, eventually, writing can play in the process. Literary texts on motherhood range from the need to reappropiate one own's body in socially committed terms, defy the medical apparatus or, more ambiguously, to vindicate the private experience of the act of mothering. Nonetheless, as Tuttle points out, there exists a tendency to disregard the political meaning of mothering and hide behind revisited idealized images of a private perception of motherhood, while ignoring the collective need to rethink the notion: "Feminists and feminist literary critics have in general assumed that if and when mothers could speak and write, in contradiction to their earlier silence, they could tell us a new and different story . . . In an important sense, many recent stories by or about mothers offer a mirror image of old stories" (1997, 14–15). A perusal of most of the (published) contemporary literature on motherhood reveals that on the one hand, the notion of mothering increasingly encompasses the role of grandmothers. Similarly, much has been written about mature (biological) motherhood, single motherhood and lesbian (biological) motherhood, as well as about the need to revise the notion of the homosexual family, the presence of Alzheimer's disease and the consequent reversal of roles between mothers and daughters, and the ethics of care in the era of AIDS. On the other hand, while the issue of abortion appears to have waned, quite the opposite may be said regarding a notion of the maternal role that—dangerously—stresses the instinctive side, as social values become blurred. Since the beginning of the nineties, the common trend vis-à-vis the social meaning and construction of motherhood has been marked by a return to the celebration of the poetry of biological motherhood and to a notion that Douglas and Michael define as "the new momism": "The fulcrum of the new momism is the rise of a really pernicious ideal in the late twentieth century that the sociologist Sharon Hays has perfectly labeled 'intensive mothering' " (2004, 5). Douglas and Michael devote their analysis to the cultural representation of how an idealized new self-image of (famous) mothers and mothering takes shape within the collective imagery and tends to displace other more real and less attractive pictures of "dark" motherhoods. The media, they insist, play a basic role in the definition of these maternal cultural icons: "Paying lip service to a Botox-injected feminism, celebrity momism trivialized the struggle and hopes of real women, and kissed off sisterhood as hopelessly out of style. This kiss was especially lethal when blown toward other mothers not showcased in the glossy magazines, but displayed in mug shots on the nightly news" (2004, 139). Philosophers like Bordo and Debord point out, even though from different starting points, that the cultural shift toward a visual representation of the Real is producing an apparently "new" symbolic order whose ambiguous messages are contained in a trivialized and commoditised representation of the (autonomous) self:

Ours is an "infocommercial" culture in which the desire to sell products and stories continually tries to pass itself off as "helping" and "informing" the public, satisfying their "right to know." We get our deepest philosophies of life from jingles and slogans. The fantasy—governed, pumped-up, individualistic rethoric of commercial advertisements—like "Just Do It!" or "Know no Boundaries," or "I'm Worth It!"—has become the ethics, political ideology, and existential philosophy of our time, constituting what is probably the only set of communally shared ideas we have, providing people with the one coherent (if reprehensible) set of standards they draw on justifying their own behaviour. The ethical code of Nike and Revlon! Talk about puppeteers being in charge of reality! (Bordo 1999, 12)

Wendy Brown, on a similar cultural basis, underlines how disciplinary practices are defining "new" subjectivities in order to update the mechanisms that conform the order of things: "Even as the margins assert themselves as margins, the denaturalizing assault they perform on coherent collective identity in the centre turns back on them to trouble their own identities" (1995, 53). It is at this point that the centrality of the Foucauldian theorisation on power relations—and its applicability within feminist critical theory—fully comes to light. Foucault does not consider power as simply repressive but also as productive because power produces resistance: "Power is exercised only over free subjects, and only insofar as they are "free." By this we mean individual or collective subjects who are faced with a field of possibilities in which several kinds of conduct, several ways of reacting and modes of behaviour are available" (Foucault 1997, 342). This brings me to refer to the strategic centrality of the Gramscian theory of (cultural) hegemony and intellectuals as resistant (in Foucauldian terms), and in my case writing, agents. If Gramsci's perspective considers not only the subject, but her capacity to act through and within society, Foucault adds a deeper and more structured study of the discursive practices that shape identity. On the other hand, the Gramscian perspective can be seen as complementary when we consider the relatively limited agency that the Foucauldian subject has within the dominant discourse. From this theoretical standpoint, the mother's voice is capable of critically bringing to light a (her) "subjugated knowledge" while stressing that mothering is not a homogeneous/unitary phenomenon, as Moraga states: "But when I can imagine I can speak with the voice of others—that others can speak through me—how wide and hopeful the project of writing becomes again" (1997, 47).[5] Up to a point, the Foucauldian idea of the intellectual can modernize Gramsci's notion and help to situate the foci of power more clearly, and, as a consequence, to signal the targets to deconstruct within a determined social structure and its cultural coding; Nakano Glenn points out how mothering is not only historically constructed but that such construction is linked to the individual's capacity to become a social agent (1994, 3). The Foucauldian and feminist perspective enables us to work on the fragmentation of the contemporary social context, a fragmentation that Gramsci had not wholly considered. Within this approach, the proposed analysis explores the need to break boundaries and, at the same time, analyzes how (some) women writers respond to this as resilient agents because, as Cherríe Moraga points out: "That is my sole purpose, arrogant as it may seem, to write those kind of stories, stories to agitate, stories to remind us what has been forgotten" (1997, 46–47).

The theoretical frame sketched above brings me to a research on textuality and representation that focuses mainly on literary voices. My critical analysis of women's autobiographical writing takes shape in-between discourses and refers to Buci-Glucksmann's statement: "Every new historical situation has to create a new culture for itself, which does not necessarily mean making 'individual' and 'original' discoveries" (1982, 113). The autobiographical discourse on mothering points out that the emphasis is on multiplicity and resistance as opposed to a homogeneous and ahistorical reading of motherhood as well as of body and/or sexual politics. Laura Marcus suggests how autobiography as a literary genre can be redefined and related to what she calls "memory work," an ensemble of written and oral life stories of the self (1995, 13);[6] autobiography can be approached not only as a literary genre but "as an integral part of a lifelong process of identity formation" (Eakin 2001, 114) as well as a tool of analysis to measure the impact of reproduction and reproductive rights and social politics, teenage pregnancy, welfare reforms, and social control on women's lives.

In autobiographical and testimonial texts, as Suzette Henke suggests, the writing subject maintains a dual role in the textual process, as she is at the same time the subject and object of analysis. It is this discursive duplicity that reinstates the (fragmented) writing subject's wholeness and agency by giving her the means to voice her life experience; Henke calls it "a discursive drama of self" (1998, xvi). This approach illustrates how women writers (especially in autobiographical writing) defy, for example, Walter Benjamin's thesis on the impossibility of voicing the historical experience of the oppressed. As Carolyn

Barros points out in *Autobiographical Narratives of Transformation*: "The transformation of a self, central to autobiographical discourse in earlier times, changes to a textual transformation—from the self speaking language to language speaking the self" (1998, viii). A crucial example is represented by Margaret Sanger's activist stance against medical and social censorship regarding birth control, as the lines quoted below from her autobiography demonstrate: "How were mothers to be saved? . . . I talked incessantly to everybody who seemed to have social welfare at heart. Progressive women whom I consulted were thoroughly discouraging. 'Wait until we get the vote. Then we'll take care of that.' . . . I tried the Socialists. Here, there and everywhere the replay came, 'Wait until women have more education. Wait until we secure equal distribution of wealth.' Wait for this and wait for that. Wait! Wait! Wait!" (Sanger 1999, 93).

Margaret Sanger also published *Motherhood in Bondage* (1928), a collection of letters she received during the 1920s from women all over the United States. The fragments of the auto/bio/graphical tragic experiences of many women are put together in this moving collection where the fragmentary presence of women's voices, otherwise silenced because of their gender and social class, stresses their differences while at the same time unveiling their common experience: the dark side of pregnancy and motherhood from the viewpoint of poor, uneducated women.[7] The text is divided into seventeen sections which draw the sombre picture of "enforced maternity," as Sanger defined it (quoted by Feldt in Sanger 2000, v). It is not a coincidence, then, that the subtitle of the book is *Voices that gave Rise to the Planned Parenthood Movement* illustrates the link between writing, agency, and political action. Writing becomes a means of discovering not only social and cultural deprivation, but the living experience of trauma; in this case, it represents the dissemination of information and carries out—if not a revolutionary task—the autobiographical experience of voicing a traumatic experience (Probyn 1993, 98). Here are some fragments from the letters: "I am twenty-six years old. I have had five children, four living. (My husband is deaf and I know he is the biggest drunkard in this world) . . . He gives us a little something to eat and that is all . . . I want you to help me. If I was able I wouldn't ask this of you . . . " (In Sanger 2000, 15–16). Or, "Will you please listen to my plea? I am a mother of seven children, four living and three that are dead. My oldest living child is six years old, there are two dead which are older. My baby is six months old and I have been married nine years . . . I have no health now. I have been to doctors and they tell me that I am having children too fast, but they will not tell me how to prevent it" (41). These testimonies are representative of the tension between life and death, between these women's maternal love and the physical and moral impossibility of enduring such a desperate situation. By publishing these letters as pieces of autobiographical writing, Sanger gives voice to the subaltern subject and, at the same time, constructs a community of voices throughout the text.[8] As Jason Tougaw points out when referring to the "narrativization of trauma" (241), the chance to voice one's own suffering transforms the relation between the reading public and the writing subject, insofar the trauma as experience becomes, up to a point, a shared—as well as historically determined—experience within society. Testimonial writings, Tougaw insists, "help create a model of *relational subjectivity*" (241). The mother's voice (understood in a wider sense) may—through such testimonies—add political meaning to her personal life experience, in all its emotional intensity, both good and bad.

In 1994, for example, Maureen T. Reddy, Martha Roth, and Amy Sheldon edited *Mother Journeys: Feminists Write About Mothering*; it is a text that, through the use of the discourses of theory, poetry, prose, or autobiography, puts together multiple kinds of narratives that are representative of different approaches to motherhood and mothering. The different sections of this collection ("Discovering Ourselves"; "Discovering through Our Children," "The Politics of Mothering," and "Continuity with our own Mothers") outline a feminist dialogue between the public and private realms of motherhood, mothering, and the mother-daughter relationship. Such a dialogue gives voice to a discourse on motherhood(s) that does not privilege an intimist approach, but rather, the political perception of the issue in contemporary culture and society. In the introduction to another collection, *The Voice of the Mother. Embedded Maternal Narratives in Twentieth-Century Women's Autobiographies* (2000), Jo Malin, the editor, emphasizes two ideas that I regard as important: the first of these holds that the choice of texts and the critical stance toward them are in themselves autobiographical acts; the second contends that the mother's narrative frequently underpins hybrid forms of autobiographical writing, as may be seen, for example, in *Waiting in the Wings. Portrait of a Queer Motherhood* (1997) by the Chicano dramatist Cherríe Moraga. Moraga's writing is here representative not only of literary hybridity, but of a need to recover and represent an/other way of being a family: "Growing up, the we of my life was always defined by blood relations. We meant family. We were my mother's children, my abuela's grandchildren, my tios' nieces and nephews. To this day, most of my cousins still hold onto a similar understanding of we. Not I. . . . So, the search for a we that could embrace all the parts of myself took me far beyond the confines of heterosexual family ties" (Moraga 1997, 17). Can this simply be considered as a trangressive political claim? Of course not. As Lisa Tatonetti suggests, Moraga's narrative delves into the inner discourses that conform our culture, while using motherhood both as a starting point for her research and as a "radical place of possibility for the future of Chicanas' culture" (2004, 229). But, in *Waiting in the Wings*, Moraga goes beyond the political and subversive potential of queer motherhood, as she analyses, at the same time, the inner mechanisms of the process of her becoming a mother, as well as the new dimension of her family relations and herself as a subject-in-progress.

Waiting in the Wings merges the author's diaries of her pregnancy and her son's early years of life, and a more public perception of the need and will to negotiate her identity as a lesbian Chicana, a writer, a mother, and a daughter. This is what she writes in the introduction: "The pages that follow are my own queer story of pregnancy, birth, and the first years of mothering. It is a story of one small human being's—my son's—struggle for survival/for life in the age of death/the age of AIDS" (1997, 22).

Autobiographical writings make the mother the subject of her own discourse. It is through these texts that subjugated identities (that also exist within feminism) are revealed and discordant voices are heard. The main challenge faced by feminist criticism at the beginning of the twenty-first century is that of recovering the voices of all mothers and questioning their ontological position in a sociocultural panorama that exploits ideological ambiguity in order to advocate obsolete values which hinder both the development of the ethics of care and the role of the public sphere in defending the rights of those who provide and those who require care.

Notes

1. This essay has been mainly inspired by the European Project entitled "Travelling Concepts in Feminist Pedagogy" (Athena2) and the discussions that our research group held between 2004 and 2007 in Trento, Helsinki, London, Thessaloniki, and

Alicante. Part of the research leading to the completion of this essay was made possible by a Research Project (BSO2002-02999) financed by the Spanish *Ministerio de Ciencia y Tecnología*.

2. This is how Laclau and Mouffe broadly define "post-Marxism" in the introduction to the first edition of *Hegemony and Socialist Strategy*: "Only if we renounce any epistemological prerogative based upon the ontologically privileged position of a 'universal class,' will it be possible seriously to discuss the present degree of validity of the Marxist categories. At this point we should state quite plainly that we are now situated in a post-Marxist terrain" (2001, 4). In the preface to the second edition they insist on the idea: "To reread Marxist theory in the light of contemporary problems necessarily involves deconstructing the central categories of that theory. This is what has been called our 'post-Marxism.' We did not invent this label . . . But since it has become generalized in characterizing our work, we can say that we do not oppose it insofar as it is properly understood: as the process of reappropriation of an intellectual tradition, as well as the process of going beyond it" (2001, ix).

3. "Increasingly, we are witnessing a world without memory where, to use Guy Debord's metaphor, mere images of reality flow and merge randomly like reflections on water . . . Rather than concretizing history in narrative and popular memory, culture, in its degraded commodified form, serves to induce amnesia and thwart collective action" (Best 1995, xi–xii).

4. The nodal point in his reinterpretation of the "history of 'history' " (122) is the notion of subjectivity: the history of the "discourse of the master" (122) before the Enlightenment becomes the history of the discourse of knowledge (*a discourse of university*, 122) during the Enlightenment, only to be transformed into the history of *the discourse of the hysteric* (122) within Cultural Materialism: "*hysteria/history* is more than a trivial word game—hysteria is the subject's way of resisting the prevailing, historically specified form of interpellation or symbolic identification" (Žižeck quoted in Wilson 1995, 122).ž

5. If Gramsci works with the idea of "subalternity" in mind, Foucault's steady interest in identity formation manages to introduce the theoretical tools that allow us to recognize, analyze, question and accept difference within the collective (normative or nonnormative) process of identity formation in more contemporary terms. Buci-Glucksmann points out that: "there can be no ahistorical, abstract approach to consensus *in general*: hegemony is differentiated according to classes and historical phases." Here is where, I believe, Gramsci and Foucault seems to converge and enrich our understanding of the construction of dominant discursive practices as well as the appearance of strategies of resistance within the cultural apparatus. I also find interesting points of contact between Gramsci's and Foucault's concepts of intellectuals as specific and/or organic agents of change. Some hints of Gramsci's ideas can be found in Foucault's "specific intellectual" (intellectual that can eventually move on to the political arena or to the public sphere) (Said).

6. She also stresses that "current work in the field of autobiography is pushing towards an interdisciplinary synthesis, turning away from generic history towards a more conceptual approach to the history of culture, marked by recent works on, for example, self-fashioning subjectivities, collective memory, confessions and the social construction of childhood" (1995, 16).

7. Beth Widmaier Capo points out how "until 1936, the Comstock Act criminalized the distribution of 'lewd and lascivious' material through the US postal system, including medical information on birth control, pornography, and fiction that touched on the subject" (111). She also reminds us that: "By 1933, Sanger's American Birth Control League was opening birth control clinics across the nation" (112).

8. Claire M. Roche, in "Reproducing the Working Class: Tillie Olsen, Margaret Sanger, and American Eugenics," gives an altogether different reading of Sanger's activism. Roche problematizes Margaret Sanger's ideological bases of her activism and illustrates how: "Margaret Sanger's *Birth Control Review* . . . presents often troubling and ideologically informed representations of the working class, particularly as they pertain to human reproduction and the American eugenics movement" (2003, 259).

Works Cited

Barros, Carolyn A. *Autobiography. Narrative of Transformation*. Ann Arbor: University of Michigan Press, 1998.

Best, S. *The Politics of Historical Vision*. London and New York: Guilford Press, 1995.

Bordo, Susan. "Are Mothers Persons? Reproductive Rights and the Politics of Subjectivity." In *Unbearable Weight. Feminism, Western Culture and the Body*. Edited by Susan Bordo. Berkeley and Los Angeles: University of California Press, 1995. 71–97.

———. *Twilight Zones. The Hidden Life of Cultural Images from Plato to O.J.* Berkeley: University of California Press, 1999.

Bourdieu, P., and J. C. Passeron. *Los estudiantes y la cultura*. Buenos Aires: Labor, 1973.

Brown, Wendy. *States of Injury*. Princeton: Princeton University Press, 1995.

Buci-Glucksmann, C. "Hegemony and Consent: A Political Strategy." In *Approaches to Gramsci*. Edited by A. Showstack. London: Writers and Readers Publishing Cooperative Society, 1982. 116–26.

Chase, Susan E., and Mary F. Rogers, eds. *Mothers & Children. Feminist Analisis and Personal Narratives*. New Brunswick: Rutgers University Press, 2001.

Cosslet, Tess. *Women Writing Childbirth*. Manchester: Manchester University Press, 1994.

Douglass, S., and Meredith W. Michael. *The Mommy Myth: The Idealization of Motherhood and How It Has Undermined Women*. New York: Free Press, 2004.

Eakin, Paul John. "Breaking Rules: The Consequences of Self-Narration." *Biography: An Interdisciplinary Quarterly* 24, 1 (Winter 2001): 113–27.

Foucault, M. *Essential Works of Foucault 1954–1984, Power*, vol. 3, Edited by J. D. Faubion and P. Rabinow. New York: New Press. 1997.

Greenfield, Susan, and Caroline Barash. *Inventing Maternity. Politics, Science and Literature, 1650–1865*. Lexington: University of Kentucky Press, 1999.

Henke, Suzette. *Shattered Subjects. Trauma and Testimony in Women's Life Writing*. New York: St. Martin's Press, 1998.

Hirsch, Marianne. *The Mother Daughter Plot. Narrative, Psychoanalysis, Feminism*. Bloomington and Indianapolis: Indiana University Press, 1989.

Ikemoto, Lisa C. "Lessons from the *Titanic*." In *Mother Troubles. Rethinking Contemporary Maternal Dilemma*. Edited by Julia Hannisberg and Sara Ruddick. Boston: Beacon Press, 1999. 157–77.

Kenison, Katrina, and Kathleen Hirsch, eds. *Twenty Stories of Contemporary Motherhood*. New York: North Point Press, 1996.

Laclau, Ernesto, and Chantal Mouffe. *Hegemony and Socialist Strategy*. London: Verso, 2001 [1985].

Malin, Jo. *The Voice of the Mother: Embedded Maternal Narratives in Twentieth-Century Women's Autobiographies*. Carbondale: Southern Illinois University Press, 2000.

Marcus, Laura. "The Face of Autobiography." In *The Uses of Autobiography*. Edited by Julia Swindells. London: Taylor & Francis, 1995. 13–23.

Moraga, Cherríe. *Waiting in the Wings. Portrait of a Queer Motherhood*. Ithaca and New York: Firebrand Books, 1997.

Nakano Glenn, Evelyn, Grace Chang, and Linda Rennie Forcey, eds. *Mothering Ideology. Experience and Agency*. London and New York: Routledge, 1994.

Probyn, Elspeth. *Sexing the Self: Gendered Positions in Cultural Studies*. London: Routledge, 1993.

Reddy, Maureen T., Martha Roth, and Amy Sheldon, eds. *Mother Journeys. Feminists Write about Mothering*. Minneapolis: Spinsters Ink, 1994.

Roche, Claire M. "Reproducing the Working Class: Tillie Olsen, Margaret Sanger, and American Eugenics." In *Evolution and Eugenics in American Literature and Culture, 1880–1940: Essays on Ideological Conflict and Complexity*. Edited by Lois A. Cuddy and Claire M. Roche. Lewisburg, PA: Bucknell University Press, 2003. 259–75.

Sanger, Margaret. *An Autobiography*. New York: Cooper Square Press, 1999.

———. *Motherhood in Bondage*. Planned Parenthood of Northern Michigan, 2000 [1928].

Sawicki, Jana. *Disciplining Foucault: Feminism, Power and the Body*. London: Routledge, 1991.

Steedman, Carolyn. "Enforced Narratives, Stories of Another Self" in *Feminism and Auto-biography: Texts, Theories, Methods*. Edited by Tess Cosslett, Celia Lury, Penny Summerfield. London: Routledge 2000. 23–38.

Swigart, Jane. *The Myth of the Good Mother. The Emotional Realities of Mothering*. New York and London: Doubleday, 1991.

Tatonetti, Lisa. " 'A Kind of Queer Balance': Cherríe Moraga's Aztlán." *MELUS* 29, 2 (Summer 2004): 227–47.

Thurer, Sharon. *The Myths of Motherhood. How Culture Reinvents the Good Mother*. Boston and New York: Houghton Mifflin, 1994.

Tougaw, Jason. "Testimony and the Subjects of AIDS Memoirs." *A/B: Auto/Biography Studies* 13, 2 (Fall 1998): 235–56.

Tubert, Silvia. *Figuras de la madre*. Madrid: Cátedra, 1996.

Tuttle Hansen, Elaine. *Mother Without Child. Contemporary Fiction and the Crisis of Motherhood*. Los Angeles: University of California Press, 1997.

Widmaier Capo, Beth. "Inserting the Diaphram In(to) Modern American Fiction: Mary McCarty, Philip Roth, and the Literature of Contraception." *The Journal of American Culture* 26, 1 (March 2003): 111–23.

Wilson, S. *Cultural Materialism: Theory and Practice*. Oxford: Blackwells, 1995.

Narrating the (Lone) Maternal Subject: The Validation Stories of "Ordinary Women in Extraordinary Circumstances"

Lesley Patterson

MOTHERS NEGOTIATE THEIR SUBJECT POSITIONS WITHIN A HIERARCHY OF maternal legitimacy in which not all mothers are equal. With this in mind, this essay describes the concept of "validation stories." This concept was developed through a research project that examined how New Zealand lone mothers made sense of their lives in the late 1990s, a period of intense neoliberal welfare reform. During this time, dominant welfare reform discourses constructed "lone mothers" as "particular types of people," and as a consequence their citizenship rights and obligations became much less stable. Those same discourses, in turn, stabilized a hierarchy of maternal legitimacy that was far from benign, especially for lone mothers. As Haraway poignantly evidentiates:

> The stabilization of identity is a world industry. You can think of the history of capitalism as the stabilization of some identities and not others. Who gets to have a stable identity? Is it a good stable identity or a rather costly one? How many identities does one get to have? Are you forced into your multiplicities or are you invited? Which one, at which times of your life? Which mobilities at what cost? For whom? What kind of identity effects come readily? What kinds are subsidised? What kind of identity effects are practically impossible to avoid? (Haraway, in Bhavnani and Phoenix 1994)

Becoming a lone mother required women to negotiate a contested identity category and narrativize both what happened to them and the type of person they became. In talking of their lives, validation stories enabled lone mothers to position themselves as ordinary women in extraordinary circumstances, in effect repairing the disjuncture between the idealized maternal subject and what actually happens in their lives.

Introduction

In this chapter, I introduce and outline the concept of validation stories developed to theorize the narratives of lone mothers within the context of unprecedented neoliberal welfare reform. Throughout the 1980s and 1990s, successive New Zealand governments undertook radical and intensive programmes of welfare reform, informed by neoliberal discourses that constructed particular types of people (that is, those in receipt of welfare benefits) as "problematic citizens." Lone mothers were strongly positioned and negatively stereotyped through these discourses because of their "weak connection" to the labour market, their overreliance on welfare assistance as family income, and an enduring moral conservatism that linked increasing numbers of lone mothers and their dependence on welfare with negative familial and social change more generally.

In 1999, I interviewed lone mothers who agreed to participate in research about the experience of parenting alone (Patterson, 2004). Some of the research participants were in receipt of welfare assistance; some were not. Nevertheless, although all were lone mothers, over the duration of the research I came to understand that they had not only told me about their experience. They had also told me about who they were, and more importantly, who they were not. This essay is based on that research.

The essay is in two parts. In part one the context for the research is briefly outlined. Here, the neoliberal welfare reforms that restructured the material and discursive character of New Zealand welfarism during the 1990s are outlined. Understanding these reforms is crucial for understanding the ways in which lone mothers came to think of themselves during this period. In part two, I introduce the concept of validation stories, a narrative form that draws from the amalgam of discourses that construct particular types of people to simultaneously ameliorate the oppressive experience of being that type of person.

In theorizing lone mothers' narratives as validation stories, the coercive power of neoliberal discourse in identity formation is highlighted. However, validation stories also, in effect, offer opportunities for meaning-making in ways that both account for what happens in women's lives and validate the type of person those experiences compel. In talking of their lives, validation stories enabled lone mothers to position themselves as ordinary women in extraordinary circumstances. Thus, through theorizing validation stories as a contemporary narrative form, the identity claims open to women who parent alone can be more explicitly located within the context of gendered social relations more generally.

Part One: Neoliberalism and Welfare Reform in New Zealand, 1990–2000

In 1999, a decade of unprecedented neoliberal welfare reforms in New Zealand was drawing to an end (Peters 1997; see also Kelsey 1993). That year, a Labor-led government was elected that favored the more inclusive (rhetorically at least) Social Development model of welfare provision. Over the preceding nine years, successive governments had cut benefit entitlements and rates, reduced socially provided services through targeting and privatization, and in the late 1990s, introduced a welfare-to-work program. As in other similar liberal welfare states, these programs sought to move dependent benefit recipients off welfare and into (paid) work. In New Zealand, those in receipt of the Unemployment or the Domestic Purposes Benefits (DPB) were especially targeted. These benefits had historically been available to working-age adults and crudely reflected the gendered history of New Zealand breadwinner-caregiver welfarism. Breadwinners (typically men) were compensated for the loss of paid work through the Unemployment Benefit, while caregivers (typically women) were compensated for the loss of a breadwinner through the DPB.

The history of welfare provision in New Zealand, and especially the provision of income assistance through benefits, has been the subject of public debate since the first poverty ordinances of the mid-nineteenth century (Tennant, 1989). Arguments over who deserves what have reflected the ways in which the subject positions and agency of both beneficiaries and benefactors has been constructed at particular historical moments. In relation to lone mothers, a shifting hierarchy of maternal legitimacy has not only made up women who parent alone as different types of mothers, but shaped the ways in which lone motherhood has been understood and how the various needs of lone mothers should be addressed (see for example, Tennant 1992). The statutory provision of a benefit for lone mothers did not occur until the 1973, when the Domestic Purposes Benefit was introduced (Nolan 2000). All unsupported single parents (women and men, married and unmarried) were entitled to this modest benefit (if they met the income test)[1] and a new category of administratively constituted person emerged: the sole parent. Most of these parents were mothers, and in part because of the gendered nature of breadwinner-caregiver welfarism, most women who became lone mothers simultaneously became beneficiaries: a dual identity transition common across liberal welfare states.

Some authors have argued that the introduction of the DPB was a response to widespread recognition of the special economic needs of unsupported mothers: needs necessary to meet to enable these women to fulfill their maternal role (Beaglehole 1993, 30). Although the benefit did reflect the breadwinner-caregiver idealization of family life by defining women's citizenship entitlement through their relationship (or lack of a relationship) to men (Saville-Smith 1987), it also gave women some prospect of economic autonomy should they become lone mothers. It is not surprising, then, that the DPB immediately became a controversial benefit. The then minister of Social Welfare, Bert Walker, described DPB recipients as "bludgers" (a term until then used to more typically to refer to work-shy men living off unemployment benefits) while the then prime minister, Robert Muldoon, "speculated that [lone mothers] preferred the overly generous DPB to honourable marriage or honest work" (Janiewski and Morris 2005, 153). In the 1980s, when neoliberal economic restructuring lead to high levels of structural unemployment it was claimed that young women were getting pregnant "to go on the benefit" (Bedggood, 2000). By 1991, when the budget-signalled policy initiatives cut public spending and encourage individual responsibility, the DPB was already becoming a central symbol in welfare reform discourses, and the "solo mum" cultural shorthand for the excesses of welfarism.

The 1991 budget, ironically dubbed the "Mother of All Budgets," cut benefit rates and entitlements, and a range of publicly provided social services (for example, free hospital care) that had especially pernicious effects for lone mothers (Jackman 1992; Dann and Du Plessis 1992). Indeed, families headed by lone mothers were among the poorest families in New Zealand *before* benefits were cut. *After* the cuts successive neoliberal reforms were much more ideological than material in character and underscored by a battle over the legitimacy of particular types of people to make claims on the state as particular types of citizens (Peters 1997). Over the decade, the promulgation of neoliberal ideas (and related policy initiatives) was increasingly managed by public relations experts working in various government departments and agencies who rewrote the institutional language of postwar welfarism.[2] Some of these departments and agencies were renamed. The benefit section of the Department of Social Welfare had been rebranded in the early 1990s as Income Support. In 1998 it was rebranded again as Work and Income New Zealand. Government policy units hosted conferences like "Beyond Dependency" (subtitled "From Welfare to Work") in 1997,[3] which championed the Wisconsin model of welfare reform. Locally made documentaries about welfare abuse[4] were screened on prime time television, as were advertising campaigns exhorting tax payers to "dob in" their neighbour to reduce benefit fraud.[5] Finally, in February 1998 the government mailed to every New Zealand household a *Proposed Code of Social and Family Responsibility* (Department of Social Welfare, 1998),[6] seeking to make "people's responsibilities clearer," especially those "bringing up children or . . . receiving income support" (Department of Social Welfare 1998, 3). Although never overtly named, *she* was the "problem beneficiary." Through a decade of welfare reform discourses, all lone mothers had become *that* particular type of person: the irresponsible, welfare-dependant solo mother.

As in other liberal welfare states, New Zealand's neoliberal welfare reforms saw a fundamental shift from an explicitly gendered breadwinner-caregiver welfarism to a citizen-worker model (Lewis 2001). Under this latter model, the social rights of citizenship became much more closely tied to individual employment status, and participation in paid work became an obligation of all working-age citizens[7] (Patterson and Briar 2005; Copas 2001; Dean 2001). The rise of the citizen-worker model sits alongside wider changes in the political economies of liberal welfare societies in the last decades of the twentieth century (Kingfisher and Goldsmith 2001). The impact of globalization on the labor market changed the nature of paid work and the certainties of lifelong employment in the biographies of the employed. The crisis of welfarism saw the renegotiation of the role of the state in both economic and social matters. The gendered nature of postwar welfarism was destabilized by a vanguard of antidiscriminatory and equality-oriented legislative reform. Women's biographies became less determined by marriage and reproduction (themselves, increasingly untied), and family life was reshaped by a decline in lifelong marriage and a rise in ever more contingent relationships (Lewis 2001; Beck-Gernsheim 2002). As in other similar societies, New Zealand women increasingly delayed childbirth and had fewer children. Their participation in paid work increased, with especially marked increases among mothers of young children (Else and Bishop 2003).

In the context of these changes, the rise of the neoliberal citizen-worker model appeared to reflect the equalizing tendencies of the late twentieth century. As men and women became more equal, the gendered nature of breadwinner-caregiver welfarism appeared increasingly anachronistic, as was New Zealand lone mothers' historic dependence on welfare benefits. The idea that lone mothers in receipt of the DPB were in fact bludgers became dominant in political rhetoric throughout the 1990s: a rhetoric deployed to legitimate cuts in welfare support for lone parents, who despite more equality, were a group that was (and remains) comprised predominantly of comparatively very poor women (Bedggood 2000).

Part Two: Validation Stories
—Making Sense of Experience

Neoliberal discourses of the 1990s succeeded in transforming the welfare bludger from its early-twentieth-century entomological origins (the unemployed man) to the solo mother[8] of the fin de siècle. Throughout the 1990s, I was interested in the ways in which lone mothers (and especially lone mothers entitled to welfare benefits) were made up in welfare reform discourses, and in the ways in which these constructs were tied to the materiality of women's lives. I was particularly struck by the electoral appeal of reforms that further impoverished a group of women already clearly materially disadvantaged. My materially focused interests for some time elided what were for me anyway, quite unexpected findings. That is, that welfare reform discourses were important resources for lone mothers to draw upon in narrating their life stories. Those discourses penetrated the participants' accounts of their experiences as lone mothers and as they worked to position themselves as ordinary mothers, women and citizens, making the most of the extraordinary circumstances of their lives.

In late 1998, I began recruiting lone mothers to talk with me about their experiences parenting alone. In my research proposal, I made it clear that I was interested in adding these women's voices to the partial picture painted through welfare reform discourses. Participants were recruited in two ways: posters in community locations (libraries, parent rooms, etc.) and a press release in free-to-reader community newspapers. One such story resulted in over thirty responses within two days of the paper being published. Many of these women did not want to be interviewed: they simply wanted to tell me that the politicians were wrong; or that they "hate[d] Jenny Shipley" (the then prime minister, a former Minister of Social Welfare, and a strong proponent of workfare), or that their children were "good kids." While the recruitment of participants had given some women an opportunity to speak back to welfare reform discourses, at the time I didn't think much about these opinion-registering calls, except with some private pleasure at such resistance.

Plummer (1983, 116) describes the research as a staged process: "preparing, gathering, storing, analysing and presenting." Of course, doing research is never linear, and doing qualitative research is an inevitably messy business (Kelly, Burton, and Regan 1994, 46). In the process of talking with women about their lives (gathering) and presenting that data, the way in which I made sense of (analyzed) the women's accounts changed. I began with a tentative thematic analysis. But, in my very early attempts at doing this to the transcripts, I realized I was also doing something to the participants. I quite quickly came to see that my analytical approach was reproducing constructions of the participants as if there were *real* differences between them and other types of mothers, cementing into the analysis a taken-for-granted ontological otherness. I realized too, that although the participants had contacted me to tell me about their experiences, what they were also doing was telling me they were not one particular subject. They were lone mothers, but they were not solo mothers. In other words, the participants were negotiating their subjectivities through the *stories* they were telling about their lives. I also began to also see how these stories of their experiences, and the subject positions available to them within these stories, were situated within the context of neoliberal welfare reform discourses that were simultaneously shaping the meanings they and I had available to make sense of their experience.

My turn to narrative was particularly influenced by Plummer's "sociology of stories" (Plummer 1995). A sociological approach to narrative attends not only to the ways we story our lives and our selves as "socially organised biographical objects" (Plummer 1995, 6), but how these stories are told (and heard) within "a stream of power" (Plummer 1995, 26). Women who parent alone do so in the context of powerful, unequal, and contradictory discourses that, in effect, make them up as particular types of people, shaping not only their subjectivities as lone mothers, but also the material realities of their lives. For lone mothers themselves, these discourses are the linguistic resources through which their experience can be narrated and their sense of self produced. In other words, women who parent alone make sense of their experiences though a process of "dynamic nominalism" in which the namer and named are linked discursively, and through which "human beings and human acts come into being hand in hand with the categories labelling them" (Hacking 1986, 236). Given this reorientation, I became more interested in *why* some stories are told, including the "the extent to which official categorisations shape self understanding" (Brubaker and Cooper 2000, 27). If lone mothers were categorically constructed through neoliberal welfare reform discourses as particular types of people, how did this categorisation shape their sense-making as a practical everyday activity, situationally located at that particular historical moment?

Validation Stories as Contingency Narratives

Twenty-one women were interviewed about their experiences parenting alone. However, adopting a narrative approach required me to rethink the status of the interview transcripts, and my analysis (or meaning-making) of them as maternal biographies, focusing on both the stories told and the effects of such telling.[9]

Maternal biographies are not simply a sequential account of life events, signalling real changes and shifts in the participants' social world. Although the lives of women who become mothers (and lone mothers) do change in very material ways, the ways in which these changes are experienced and made sense of are socially situated (Bailey 1999), as are the subject positions available to women in becoming and being lone mothers (Patterson 2004; Gardiner 2000). In this sense, different subject positions across one's life course offer different "conceptual repertoires" and different locations for those inhabiting or taking up various positions comprised of the "rights" discursively accorded to those positions (Davies and Harre 1990, 46). Specifically, maternal biographies illustrate the ways in which, as *homo narrans*, women who parent alone narrativize their lives, transforming a sequence of events into a story with episodes, where the relationship between events is explained, and new or changed social identities are negotiated (Somers and Gibson 1994, 60). As stories, such episodes and identities are constructed from a range of discursive possibilities, and in particular, the "images, metaphors, storylines and concepts . . . are made relevant within the particular discursive practices in which [women who parent alone] are positioned" (Davies and Harre 1990, 46). In moving to a narrative approach, it also became clear that maternal biographies could be grouped according to plot (the sequence of events), as well as the narratively constituted meanings from the tropes and phrases used, and the broader cultural imagery and understandings the participants' stories re/produced.

My overwhelming and lasting impression from meeting and talking with the participants in this research was that they participated because although they recognized the subject I had "hailed" (Althusser, 1971), they wanted to tell me they were not that subject. I related this to the potency of neoliberal welfare reform discourses, and especially the ways in which solo mothers were made up through these discourses. However, neoliberal welfare reform discourses were not totalizing. The participants' stories were also shaped by other discourses constituting idealised femininity, maternity, and citizenship, and the multiple subject positions available through these discourses. Indeed, for the participants, significant changes in the how femininity, motherhood and citizenship are understood (and the material effects of these changes) have occurred within their lifetimes and shaped the ways in which they pieced together their maternal biographies.[10] In this sense, storying their maternal biographies to a researcher interested in the experience of lone mothers enabled the participants to construct social identities that discursively positioned themselves as ordinary "women, mothers and citizens,"[11] making the most of the extraordinary circumstances of their lives. I conceptualized these stories as validation stories: a historically and socially specific narrative form that makes sense of (extraordinary) life events that compel the negotiation of a new, but contested, social identity. Within these maternal biographies, multiple validation stories coexisted. In particular, contingency narratives around becoming a lone mother, and core narratives about what they had become dominated the participants' accounts. In this essay, I focus on participants' narrativizing becoming a lone mother, although as validation stories, contingency, and core narratives were typically intertwined.

Becoming a Lone Mother

As Byrne (2003) notes, when one's biography follows a socially prescribed norm, "there is no story to tell."[12] Within the participants' maternal biographies, narrating becoming a lone mother was an important site for negotiating identity and making sense of the experiences of one's life. By narrativizing their becoming through validation stories, the participants storied not only what happened to them, but why, and the consequences and meanings of those events for the person they became.

Becoming a lone mother within the context of neoliberal welfare reform discourses is not a neutral identity transition, but a transition inscribed with wider meanings around femininity, motherhood, and citizenship. For the participants, becoming a lone mother required narrativization that not only accommodated an identity transformation, but also storied a transition to a contested identity category whose members are constructed as socially flawed because of their membership of that category.[13] To make sense of the events that transformed their lives, both materially and subjectively, participants produced contingency narratives that repaired the disjuncture between the idealized maternal subject and the events that had transformed their lives. These narratives, or validation stories, offer a site for a more critical investigation of how women who parent alone make sense of their experiences in the context of the discursive resources available. As Clegg (1993, 5) argues: "[A]ll stories emerge as a practical activity: as we go about our daily rounds we piece together fragments from the toolkit of culture that ultimately . . . cohere into 'our stories.'"

To analyze the participants becoming stories, I distinguished between plot and narrative, and considered the relationship between these. Plot was conceptualized as the temporal ordering of life events; narrative as the way in which plot is storied. While this separation of plot and narrative was rarely straightforward in the participants becoming accounts, four plots were identified: the He Left plot (a husband or partner ending the relationship); the She Left plot (the participant ending the relationship); the Single Mother plot (becoming a mother and lone mother simultaneously); and the ambiguous plot. In this latter group, it was never clear who did what, or when, and this ambiguity shaped the participants' narratives in particular ways. Similarly, participants who narrativized the Single Mother plot often emploted the end of a relationship (either because he left or she left) sometime prior to the birth of the child, mirroring in many ways the He Left or She Left plots.

Three validation stories operated as contingency narratives in the participants becoming accounts: Stories of No Intent; Stories of Inevitability, and Stories of a Self With Needs (Patterson 2004). Each validation story drew upon different meanings but achieved similar effects as contingency narratives. In this essay I focus upon one of those stories: Stories of No Intent. These illustrate how through narrative, the participants emploted the events of their lives in ways that made sense of what had happened to them while at the same time positioning an acceptable or valid self countering the made-up solo mother at the heart of neoliberalism.

Stories of No Intent were most likely to be told by women whose maternal biographies were shaped by either the He Left or Single Mother plots. Importantly, although these plots infer different types of people occupying very different positions within the context of contemporary hierarchies of maternal legitimacy, Stories of No Intent made possible valid subject positions for women narrativizing either becoming experience.

Participants narrating the He Left plot emphasised the unexpected actions of others through Stories of No Intent. These participants experienced events that transformed their maternal biographies (and necessarily their social identities) over which they had little foreknowledge or control. As such, Stories of No Intent were characterized by the emphasis on the participants' shock at what had happened to them, positioning themselves as blameless for the situation in which they had found themselves. For these participants, the unanticipated actions others were often narrativized at counterpoint to claims of their own beliefs or values, and sometimes attempts to remedy the situation as it occurred. For participants narrating the He Left plot, the "what happened" was very similar—husbands or partners had begun relationships with others, often women known to the participant, then informed the participant that their relationship was over:

> [M]y husband . . . went to a night course at the college, and got involved with a tutor. . . . I was coming home and I saw his car at her place, and I thought, "That's strange, he doesn't need to be there now, what's he doing?" And so I stopped and called in . . . and it came out that night that he rather liked her. That was really the beginning of the end. . . . I thought we might have been able to get back together . . .

[but] in the long run, he went, and two years later he divorced me. I don't believe in divorce, I believe that marriage is forever. . . . I think that there are some cases where you've definitely got to get out, you know, with violence or alcoholism, or things like that, but I think where you've just got sick of each other, that can be resolved. (Denise)

Stories of No Intent narrativizing the He Left plot are characterized by the temporal significance of the moment of "finding out," an important event where the innocence of the narrator is established: "Ken had an affair with someone that I work with and I found out—sort of almost by accident. . . . It was an absolute shock to my little system, and what's worse . . . his new partner, was a really good friend of mine. . . . I just felt so betrayed by both of them . . . she and I were really close friends . . . then to find out they were doing that behind my back was just devastating" (Moira).

Stories of No Intent told in the context of the He Left plot were the most homogenous of the becoming stories in terms of the events that constituted the plot, and the tropes and phrases used. For participants' emploting He Left, narrativizing Stories of No Intent offered access to an acceptable experience of becoming a lone mother: the unintentional consequence of the unexpected actions of others. In this sense, Stories of No Intent draw upon discourses of traditional gender identities and relations where "he is the actor, she is acted upon" (Gergen 1992, 131). In this respect, Stories of No Intent overlap with Victorian melodramas that positioned fallen women and deserted wives as women "more sinned against than sinners" who "loved not wisely but too well" (Kunzel 1993, 19–21).

Stories of No Intent were also told by participants whose becoming stories cohered around the Single Mother plot. These participants were unpartnered women who typically unexpectedly "found out" they were pregnant. More than the other plots, the Single Mother plot mirrors neoliberal welfare discourses that construct lone mothers as particular types of people: young, unmarried "problem girls" deliberately becoming solo mothers to live on welfare. However, the participants who storied the Single Mother plot told Stories of No Intent that positioned themselves as women whose lives were very different to such neoliberal constructions of solo mothers.

Carlene narrativized the Single Mother plot, becoming a lone mother in her late twenties. Like participants who told Stories of No Intent to narrativize the He Left plot, Carlene also narrated the moment of "finding out" as an unexpected event:

We'd just broken up, and I'd been so sick.... I was at work one day and I was having all these tests... I didn't know what was wrong with me. It never crossed my mind, never not once. I can't believe it, I'm not usually so naive, and the nurse rang me from the doctors and she said, "Congratulations, you're pregnant." I didn't even know I'd had a pregnancy test! They must have taken bloods or whatever and sent it all away and tick, tick, tick on the boxes, and of course I just about died of fright. I said, "Positive!" All the girls in the office go, you know what that means. So anyway [the nurse said], "Oh, maybe I've got your results mixed up, you'd better come round and check them." So I had to go around to the doctor's surgery and do another sample.

Similarly, in both Colleen's and Anna's stories, pregnancy was unintended:

I [didn't] plan to have him, but when I found out I was pregnant, I was thirty-two I think when I conceived him, and I thought I was actually getting quite old, and I had this feeling that I might never meet a man that I could live with and that I would never have children, and I think I thought that well, I don't have to miss out on having a baby as well. (Colleen)

I had a two-month relationship with a guy in Australia, and I got pregnant. We didn't stay together for a variety of reasons but when I got pregnant... I decided that I would go ahead and have the child.... I'd been working for fifteen years and I was financially secure, and I thought... "I'm strong enough, I can cope," you know, "this is no problem." (Anna)

In narrativizing the Single Mother plot, participants not only positioned themselves as women something (unexpected) had happened to, they also stressed characteristics about themselves that differentiated them from the solo mother constructed through neoliberal[14] welfare reform discourses. In research with North American women who became single mothers by choice, Bock (2000) found these women narrativized the legitimacy of *their choice* to become single mothers by recourse to four essential personal attributes: age (they were old enough to make a choice, and that time was running out for them to become mothers); responsibility (they saw themselves as responsible, as did others); emotional maturity (they saw themselves as assertive, and possessing a range of valued emotional attributes); and financial independence, above all the most important trait legitimating the participants' choices. As in Bock's research, these attributes were identified by participants' narrativizing the Single Mother plot, simultaneously validating their experiences and differentiating themselves from the solo mother subject.

The exception, Heather, described her first experience of becoming a lone mother at the age of sixteen, more than twenty years ago:

> I was fifteen then, treated like an adult, getting paid like an adult, getting the respect of an adult and sort of thought . . . this is quite good. . . . Before I had left school I had met Penny's father, and had sort of seen him off and on, not in any major capacity. And then when I got my job I thought well, you know, I'm this big sort of woman now so I can do these womanly things and have a relationship. . . . And then basically it was, just got carried away one night, decided to have a few drinks, and boom, there you are.

Even though "what happened" to Heather (and the other participants who narrativized the Single Mother plot) is quite different to what happened to the participants whose maternal biographies followed the He Left plot, there are some important similarities in both the telling of their stories, and what this form of telling achieved. Participants' narrativizing He Left typically positioned themselves as naive in relation to finding out, as does Heather. While in a sense Heather was exactly that mother: a pregnant teenager who after the birth of her daughter went on welfare, she displaces that subject position through narrating a Story of No Intent, simultaneously making sense of her experiences becoming a lone mother in different circumstances across her biography, and positioning herself as very different to wilful young women who, according to welfare reform discourses, *intentionally become* solo mothers.

Although Stories of No Intent position their narrators as women things have happened to, the participants who drew upon this story were not passive. In narrating the events of their becoming into a biographical episode, the participants both made sense of their experiences and positioned themselves as ordinary women in particular circumstances. For these participants, storying becoming a lone mother as an unintentional biographical event distinguishes them from, for example, the deliberate lone mothers that populate neoliberal welfare reform discourses. Stories of No Intent narrativizing He Left and Single Mother plots positioned these participants simultaneously as women who something has happened to, but also as agents making the best of their circumstances for themselves and their children—like other women and mothers. Indeed, for these participants, one's life story did not stop at the moment of becoming. Although becoming a lone mother may have been unintended, it was also an identity transition that offered new possibilities. For example, Geraldine, one of the few participants to use the term "solo mother," narrativized a Story of No Intent, but the events that transformed her maternal biography also provided a platform for Geraldine to assert a new self:

> We moved up here in March of this year . . . [and] my husband turned round and said that he didn't love me anymore. . . . He stayed with us for a few weeks, but we didn't speak. I tried to get us counselling . . . and I tried everything I could to figure out why, knowing that we hadn't had a perfect marriage. . . . [What] I've since found out . . . [is] that he was with another woman who was a friend of ours, and as it turned out he moved in with her. . . . So yeah, I became a solo mum certainly not by choice, but I'm glad I am. . . . I'd like our family back, but I'm doing a really good job and I know it. I just think, "well good on me." This is this new attitude I've developed over about the last month.

Conclusion

Nancy Fraser notes "one is not always a woman to the same degree." Social identities change over time and are drawn together from "the fund of interpretive possibilities available to agents in specific societies" (Fraser 1997, 380). While identities are fluid, plural, and shift over time, they are not just *personal* narratives. The stories we tell about our lives are told and heard within a stream of power; shaping not only what can be told, but what voices are "credible or incredible" at particular historical moments (Plummer 1995, 26–27). Indeed, self-identity, the formation of social groups, and patterns of structural inequality are the outcomes of social processes (Fraser 1997).

In New Zealand, as in similar societies that undertook radical programs of neoliberal welfare reform in the late twentieth century, lone motherhood became a social identity embroidered with new (as well as not-so-new) meanings around maternity, femininity, and citizenship. Neoliberal welfare discourses made up women who parented alone as particular types of people whose rights and obligations became much less stable as those same discourses, in turn, stabilized a hierarchy of maternity legitimacy that was far from benign. Becoming a lone mother required women to negotiate a contested identity category by narrativizing both what happened to them, and the type of person they became. In this sense, under the conditions of neoliberalism, women are never *lone mothers*. Rather, women *become* lone mothers *because* . . .

Despite the call of neoliberalism for rational citizen-workers to enact particular forms of choice, the choices of women in negotiating the (lone) maternal subject are shaped subjectively and materially by the discursive construction of the solo mother as a particular type of person. Indeed, as in other liberal welfare societies, neoliberal welfare reform discourses not only made up solo mothers as particular types of people, but also reified policies and programmes targeting those types of people, transforming them from primarily *independent mothers* in receipt of the welfare benefits that had enabled them to be mothers at home (like other mothers), to become *dependent bludgers* requiring public instruction in the rules of liberal citizenship. In this context, the subjective (and material) effects of parenting alone gave rise to maternal biographies where sense-making was characterized by a particular narrative form: validation stories. As contingency narratives, these stories repaired the disjuncture between the idealized maternal subject and what actually happens in women's lives, and positioned the narrators as ordinary women making the most of the extraordinary circumstances of their lives.

Although the citizen-worker model consolidated during the neoliberal welfare reforms of the 1990s, it remains central in contemporary approaches to welfare provision. New Zealand's third way Social Development approach is based on maximizing labor market participation and making work pay for low-income families through the provision of in-work payments (Ministry of Social Development 2004). Importantly, rather than the citizen-worker model mirroring real changes in the gendered nature of the social world, in practice a one-and-one half-breadwinner household was fast becoming the norm in many family households over the last decades of the twentieth century. More partnered mothers remained in paid work and contributed to household incomes. However, few partnered mothers of young children earned sufficient income to support themselves and their children independently (Else 1997). Indeed, partnered mothers were more likely than their partners to be in part-time paid work, and most were dependent on their partners' contribution to household income (Else and Bishop 2003; Else 1997). The materiality of the emergence and consolidation of one-and-a-half-breadwinner household in reality and the idealization of the citizen-worker model in policy had (and continues to have) particular implications for lone mothers. In effect, contemporary policy initiatives have retained the neoliberal citizen-worker ideal, and assume that all citizens can participate in the labor market in broadly equivalent ways. For low-income lone mothers, the expectation is that they *can* and *should* participate in paid work just like other citizens who *can* and *do*. As a consequence, the economic position of lone mothers in New Zealand is as precarious as ever. Although this essay traverses the discursive terrain, it is important to signal that this work stems from a very materially grounded interest in how gendered inequalities and subjectivities are intertwined.

While the number of lone parents has risen markedly in the last thirty years, the proportion of lone parents who are lone mothers has remained remarkably stable. In all liberal welfare societies, changes in family formation practices have hardly dented the gendered nature of parenting alone. Similarly, changes in both patterns of participation in paid work, and changes in the scope and emphasis of liberal welfarism have done little (if anything) to untie the historic connection between lone motherhood and women's poverty. Indeed, the participants in the research reported in this essay did a lot of narrative work in order to ameliorate the gendered inequalities that continue to characterize liberal welfarism and structure their lives and the lives of other women. In not being the solo mother, the participants' "creative energies ... [were] engaged in coping with old inequalities rather than transforming them" (Jamieson 1999, 491). Indeed, although not that subject—the solo mother—she continued to press upon them discursively with both subjective and material consequences.

Notes

1. The rate of the DPB in August 1973 was the same as the Widows Benefit—$36.50 for a woman with one dependant child. In comparison, minimum weekly wages at this time ranged from $75 for a grocer's assistant and $95 for a carpenter (Beaglehole 1993, 31). Widows remained outside the administratively constituted group of single parents, and continued to receive the separate widows benefit.

2. Carol Harrington generously drew my attention to the ideological nature of this struggle over ideas.

3. An issue of the *Social Policy Journal* in 1997 commemorated the conference. Issue 08, March 1997.

4. *Time Bomb*, a two-part documentary about welfare and the types of people on it, featured on New Zealand's government-owned television channel in prime time in New Zealand in 1997.

5. In late 1997 and 1998.

6. For an interesting range of different perspectives on the code as policy experiment, see Davey (2000).

7. Some exceptions remain. For example, those unable work due to illness or disability.

8. In other countries where liberal welfare states have been transformed by neoliberalism, similar gendered constructions of problem mothers have been deployed. For example, in the USA, President Clinton's abolition of the Aid to Families with Dependent Children (AFDC) program on the grounds of affordability (even though the program accounted for approximately 1 percent of federal spending) was legitimated by ideas about lone mothers as "lazy, unmotivated, of cheating the system or having additional children simply to increase the amount of their benefit check" (Seccombe, James, and Battle Walter 1998, 850).

9. This was because the interviews had focused the participants on their lives as mothers, and particularly as lone mothers. However, my use of the term "maternal biography" was not to exclude the possibility that the participants might position themselves through or have experiences shaped by other social identities. We all construct multiple biographies at different narratives moments, shaped by the social conditions that enable the telling of any particular biographical story. In her research on Australian lone mother subjectivities, Gardiner (2000, 288–89) argues that the subject position of "mother" was principally important in her participants' accounts of their experience, and inseparable from other subject positions they inhabited. As Gardiner notes, "many [participants] could not separate subjectivity in being a mother from subjectivity in being a woman, or a worker, or most other positions they take up in their lives."

10. Many participants were born in the 1960s and 1970s when maternity was much more closely tied with marriage. Some of the participants had been birth mothers (to children subsequently adopted), then married and had children, then become lone mothers. At different moments across their maternal biographies, maternity was imbued with different meanings and materialities. Their narratives effectively drew together these broader historical changes.

11. The research that informs this paper identified three key discursive nodes that lone mothers negotiate and draw upon in storying their lives: femininity (and discourses around being a good woman), motherhood (and discourses around being a good mother), and citizenship (and discourses around being a good citizen) (Patterson 2005).

12. Of course, lone mothers do have stories to tell. In the context of neoliberal welfare reform discourses, lone mothers' biographies necessarily transgress social norms that privilege the idealized nuclear family.

13. Classic approaches to managing stigma (Goffman 1965) were considered as analytical frame, and discounted due to their emphasis on individuated intentionality in performing social actions. Narrative analysis offered opportunities for a more constitutive approach to sense-making as a socially situated process.

Works Cited

Althusser, Louis. *Lenin and Philosophy, and Other Essays*. Trans. Ben Brewster. New York: Monthly Review Press. 1977.

Bailey, Lucy. "Refracted Selves? A Study of Changes in Self-identity in the Transition to Motherhood." *Sociology* 33, 2 (1999): 335–52.

Baker, Maureen, and David Tippin. "'When Flexibility Meets Rigidity': Sole Mothers Experiences in the Transition from Welfare to Work." *Journal of Sociology* 38, 4 (2002): 345–60.

Beaglehole, Ann. *Benefiting Women: Income support for women 1893–1993*. Wellington: Social Policy Agency, 1993.

Beck-Gernsheim, Elisabeth. *Reinventing the Family—In Search of New Lifestyles*. Trans. Patrick Camiller. Cambridge: Polity Press, 2002.

Bedggood, Janet. "Domestic Purposes Beneficiaries and the Community Wage: Her Brilliant Career." *New Zealand Sociology* 15, 1 (2000): 75–100.

Brubaker, Roger, and Frederick Cooper. "Beyond 'identity.'" *Theory and Society* 29, 1 (2000): 1–47.

Byrne, Anne. "Developing a Sociological Model to Research Women's Self and Social Identities." *The European Journal of Women's Studies* 10, 4 (2003): 442–64.

Clegg, Stewart. "Narrative, Power and Social Theory." In *Narrative and Social Control: Critical Perspectives*. Edited by Dennis Mumby. Newbury Park, Calif.: Sage, 1993. 15–45.

Copas, Susan. "(Over)working Women: Gendering Discourses of Market Governance in New Zealand." *New Zealand Sociology* 16, 1 (2001): 202–25.

Dann, Christine, and Rosemary Du Plessis. After the Cuts: Surviving on the Domestic Purposes Benefit (Working Paper 12). Christchurch, N.Z.: University of Canterbury, 1992.

Davey, Judith, ed. *Another New Zealand Experiment: A Code of Social and Family Responsibility*. Wellington: Institute of Policy Studies at Victoria University of Wellington, 2000.

Davies, Bronwyn, and Rom Harre. "Positioning: The Discursive Production of Selves." *Journal for the Theory of Social Behaviour* 20, 1 (1990): 43–63.

Department of Social Welfare. *Towards a Code of Social and Family Responsibility*. Wellington: Department of Social Welfare, 1998.

Else, Anne. "Having It Both Ways? Social Policy and the Positioning of Women in Relation to Men." *Social Policy Journal of New Zealand* 9 (November 1997): 16–26.

Else, Anne, and Barbara Bishop. *Occupational Patterns for Employed New Zealand Women: An Analysis of the 2001 Census Data*. Wellington: Ministry of Women's Affairs, 2003.

Fraser, Nancy. "Structuralism or Pragmatics? On Discourse Theory and Feminist Politics." In *The Second Wave: A Reader in feminist theory*. Edited by Linda Nicholson. London: Routledge, 1997. 379–95.

Gardiner, Janice. *With Three Kids You Can Run a Car: Sole Mothers, Subjectivities and Social Policy*. Unpublished PhD thesis. Bathhurst: Charles Sturt University, 2000.

Gergen, Mary. "Life Stories—Pieces of a Dream." In *Stories Lives—The Cultural Politics of Self Understanding*. Edited by George Rosenwald and Richard Ochberg. New Haven: Yale University Press, 1992 127–44.

Goffman, Erving. *Stigma: Notes on the Management of Spoiled Identity*. Englewood Cliffs, N.J.: Prentice Hall, 1965.

Haraway, Donna. "Shifting the Subject: A Conversation between Kum-Kum Bhavnani and Donna Haraway." In *Shifting Identities, Shifting Racisms: A feminism and psychology reader*. Edited by Kum-Kum Bhavnani and Ann Phoenix. London: Sage, 1994. 19–39.

Jackman, Sally. *Windows on Poverty: A report from the New Zealand Council of Christian Social Services*. Wellington: New Zealand Council of Christian Social Services, 1992.

Janiewski, Dolores, and Paul Morris. *New Rights New Zealand: Myths, Moralities and Markets*. Auckland: Auckland University Press, 2005.

Kingfisher, Catherine, and Mike Goldsmith."Reforming Women in the United States and Aotearoa/New Zealand: A Comparative Ethnography of Welfare Reform in a Global Context." *American Anthropologist* 103, 3 (September 2001): 714–32.

Kelly, Liz, Sheila Burton, and Linda Regan. "Researching Women's Lives or Studying Women's Oppression? Reflections of What Constitutes Feminist Research." In *Researching Women's Lives From a Feminist Perspective*. Edited by Mary Maynard and Jane Purvis. London: Taylor & Francis, 1994. 27–48.

Kelsey, Jane. *Rolling Back the State: Privatisation and power in Aotearoa New Zealand*. Wellington: Bridget Williams Books, 1993.

Kunzel, Regina. *Fallen Women, Problem Girls—Unmarried Mothers and the Professionalization of Social Work 1890–1945*. New Haven: Yale University Press, 1993.

Lewis, Jane. *The End of Marriage? Individualism and Intimate Relations*. Cheltenham: Edward Elgar, 2001.

Ministry of Social Development (2004) *Working for Families Fact Sheet 1: Working for Families*.www.msd.govt.nz/media-information/working-for-families/fact-sheet-1.html.

Nolan, Melanie. *Breadwinning—New Zealand Women and the State*. Christchurch, N.Z.: Canterbury University Press, 2000.

Patterson, Lesley. *Women, Mothers and Citizens: Lone Mothers' Narratives in the Context of New Zealand Welfare Reform*. Unpublished PhD thesis. Victoria University of Wellington, 2004.

Patterson, Lesley, and Celia Briar. "Lone Mothers in Liberal Welfare States: Thirty Years of Change and Continuity." *Hecate* 31, 1 (2005): 46–59.

Peters, Michael. "Neoliberalism, Welfare Dependency and the Moral Construction of Poverty in New Zealand." *New Zealand Sociology* 12, 1 (1997): 1–34.

Plummer, Ken. *Documents of Life*. London: George Allen and Unwin, 1983.

———. *Telling Sexual Stories: Power, Change and Social Worlds*. London: Routledge, 1995.

Saville-Smith, Katherine. "Women and the State." In *Private and Public Worlds: Women in Contemporary New Zealand*. Edited by Shelag Cox. Wellington: Allen & Unwin, 1987. 193–210.

Seccombe, Karen, Delores James, and Kimberley Battle Walter. "'They Don't Think You Aint Much of Nothing'—The Social Construction of the Welfare Mother." *Journal of Marriage and the Family* 60, 4 (1998): 849–65.

Somers, Margaret, and Gloria Gibson. "Reclaiming the Epistemological 'Other': Narrative and the Social Construction of Identity." In *Social Theory and the Politics of Identity*. Edited by Craig Calhoun. Oxford, Blackwell, 1994. 37–99.

Tennant, Margaret. "'Magdalenes and Moral Imbeciles': Women's Homes in Nineteenth-Century New Zealand." In *Women in History* 2. Edited by Barbara Brookes, Charlotte Macdonald, and Margaret Tennant. Wellington: Bridget Williams Books, 1992. 49–75.

———. *Paupers and Providers: Charitable Aid in New Zealand.* Wellington: Allen & Unwin (and) Historical Branch, NZ Department of Internal Affairs, 1989.

White Mothers of Chinese Daughters: Real Mothers of Real Children

Sonya Corbin Dwyer and Lynn Gidluck

How important is the fact that we didn't give birth to our daughters to others' perceptions of us as mothers? The questions and comments we receive on a regular basis demonstrate to us that it is very significant: "Are those children *yours*?," "Are they *real* sisters?," "Do you know anything about her *real* mother?" "Is she *adopted*?" In this essay, we analyze and challenge this discourse. We argue that this language excludes and minimizes our experiences, and we examine the messages inherent in this language about what it means to mother. We interrogate "socially organized illusions" (Brookes 1992, 5) of adoptive motherhood. Through the language of mothering, a hierarchy of motherhood is established, our sexuality/fertility is questioned, and bonds we have with our children are assumed to be weaker than those others have with nonadopted children.

Mothers who are a different race than their children, whether through adoption or not, are a sizable minority. Over the last decade Canadians adopted 21,973 children from abroad (which does not include domestic transracial adoptions, transracial foster families, biracial children, and other family configurations). Well over 60 percent of all international adoptions in Canada in the last decade were from East Asia, Southeast Asia, and South Asia, with China being by far the number one source (Citizen and Immigration Canada [CIC] 2003; Adoption Council of Canada 2005). Our own children make up these statistics as our daughters were all born in China. And we are white, representing the majority of parents who adopt across racial lines (Steinberg and Hall, 2000). As mothers of children who are not of the same race, it appears obvious to others that our children are adopted, prompting strangers to ask questions about our daughters' origins. As Register (2001) points out, people ask personal questions only in situations they perceive as abnormal. This discourse has forced us to reflect on our sense of identity as mothers and the approach we chose to become mothers.

There is a plethora of literature covering what parents may expect regarding the adoption process—their child's health and development and identity issues for the child and family—as well as the mother's role in the development of their children. However, few works have considered the psychological effects on women of being mothers (Barlow and Cairns, 1997), particularly the experiences of mothering a multiracial family or the conceptualizations of maternity, race, and gender that may transpire for adoptive mothers (Moosnick 2004). There are articles written for adoptive mothers in transracial families on how to handle intrusive questions (e.g., van Gulden 2004) but few that explore *why* we are asked intrusive questions.

To achieve this, first we explore the myth that adoption is second best and how this public opinion falls within the larger issue that not all mothers are created equally because some are better than others. This discussion led us to interrogate the definition of womanhood as that of the ability, and activity, of reproduction. We move into an examination of the sociological role of mothers and the issue of race in conceptions of motherhood. This is followed by a description of how the language contributes to our feeling of being on public display. Through the deconstruction of the messages we receive about becoming mothers through adoption, we imagine an inclusive discourse for us.

Adoption as Second Best:
The Hierarchy of Motherhood

"Do you have any children of your own?" "Now that you've adopted, you're sure to get pregnant." Comments and questions like these "perpetuate a socially held myth that adoption is a second-best and less-than alternative for all involved—that in being part of an adoption one has somehow missed out on a 'real' family experience" (Johnston 2004, 3). This myth is an extension of the hierarchy of motherhood that provides status to certain types of mothers.

Mother Imposters

Merriam-Webster (2005) defines "real" as "not artificial, fraudulent, illusory, or apparent." We question why we get asked questions about our daughters' "real" mothers? Are we "artificial" or "fraudulent" mothers? Well, we are not even viewed as "real" mothers by our own Canadian government. When we went to apply for maternity benefits through employment insurance, we were surprised to find out that as adoptive mothers, we are not eligible for such benefits because "maternity benefits are payable to the birth mother or surrogate mother" (Department of Human Resources and Skills Development 2005). Instead, we received parental benefits that "are payable either to the biological or adoptive parents while they are caring for a new-born or an adopted child. . . . Parental benefits can be claimed by one parent or shared between the two partners" (Department of Human Resources and Skills Development 2005). While not outlined in the HRSD guidelines, it has been explained to us that this discrepancy is based on the physical act of giving birth and that this is seen as a recovery period. Therefore, birth mothers receive an additional fifteen weeks of employment insurance benefits, and therefore fifteen weeks at home with their children, more than we do. This policy does not reflect adoptive mothers' needs which may be different from birth mothers' needs, which are often more pronounced the older the child is at the time of adoption: time to bond with their child and for their child to establish a secure attachment, physical and psychological health issues. Plus, birth mothers receive "maternity" benefits while we receive "parental" benefits. When we consider that maternity is defined as "the quality or state of being a mother" (*Merriam-Webster*, 2005), this becomes another way of denying us our maternity, of denying us as mothers, because we are not "maternal."

Qualifiers are often used to refer to our children—"This is Lynn's adopted daughter," "Sonya has a daughter who's adopted from China" —in situations where they would not dream of doing so in a nonadoptive family: "This is Sue's birth-control-failure son," "This is Mary's cesarean-section daughter," "This is Nancy's in-vitro son" (Johnston 2004). We fear what the potential effects of these attitudes, expressed through casual comments, may have on our children. We dread that they may think they are second best. When we are viewed as not normal, by extension our children are viewed as not normal. Like van Gulden and Bartels-Rabb (1993), "as adoptive parents, we feel the need to assert that these are our children: We are not second best or second rate. We are our children's real parents and they are our real children" (3).

All Mothers are Not Created Equal

Many mothers fall outside the club of "good motherhood" as defined by dominant motherhood ideologies (Johnston and Swanson 2003). Teenage mothers, older mothers, single mothers, and lesbian mothers are relegated to the bottom rungs of the hierarchy of motherhood. Racial biases also play major roles in the social construction of good and bad mothers. We acknowledge that as white women, we are in a position of power. Johnston and Swanson provide an example of this privilege for mothers in other circumstances: single mothers of color are often labeled deviant by the dominant culture, whereas white single mothers are considered "troubled" but "redeemable" (22).

The motherhood hierarchy defines the most appropriate mothers as heterosexual, stay-at-home women in first marriage, nuclear families (DiLapi as cited by Ganong and Coleman 1995). Heterosexual privilege is an unearned, often taken-for-granted way of living that is assumed to be superior and also normal (Schick 2004). We acknowledge our place in this category. Heterosexual mothers who are either employed or in nonnuclear families are viewed as marginally appropriate, while lesbians are considered to be inappropriate mothers. Further, women who choose not to mother are often viewed as "deficient as women" (Rogus 2003, 822).

Where does that leave adoptive mothers in the dominant culture's view of the motherhood hierarchy? "Many people who have not experienced adoption personally view us as having 'failed' in an important cultural way. We have failed to create a family that falls within the narrow definition of 'normal'" (Paddock 2002, 2). The hierarchy is further complicated by the fact that adoptive mothers, like single mothers, do not fit into one homogeneous category. We can be married, divorced, widowed, lesbian, of color, or any number of other socially constructed groupings, and our children can be of the same race as us, biracial, transracial, or multiracial. We are aware that being considered "normal" is only possible through the marginalization of other lives. While we are adoptive mothers, we are also white, middle class, and heterosexual with nuclear families, therefore, we are not as marginalized as some other mothers.

A 1997 study indicated that half of the Americans surveyed believed that adopting a child was not quite as good as having "one's own" (Ambert 2003, 6). A quarter of these felt that it may be more difficult to love an adopted child. Since the bond between a mother and a child who is adopted is often seen as weaker than a biological bond, it is no wonder that we get the questions we do!

Bowen's (1992) declaration that "Adoption is an alternative—not a consolation" (15) speaks for us. The assumption that adoption is somehow second best is based on a number of other assumptions, particularly those about our fertility and that we couldn't have children "of our own."

Language and the Conflict Over Female Sexuality

Ambert (2003) writes that "The birth culture constitutes a serious roadblock to the social acceptance of adoption . . . a woman's fertility is still considered an important mark of self-esteem and social recognition despite the liberalization of gender role norms" (2–3). Ambert concludes that biological motherhood is often considered superior to adoptive motherhood even by some feminists.

"When a word acquires a bad connotation by association with something unpleasant or embarrassing, people may search for substitutes that do not have the uncomfortable effect—that is, euphemisms. . . . It is no doubt possible to pick out areas of particular psychological strain or discomfort . . . by pin-pointing items around which a great many euphemisms are clustered" (Lakoff 2004, 51–52). An obvious example are the words for pregnancy—"expecting," "with child," "having a child," and so on. However, we challenge these euphemisms when they exclude us. Is the process of adopting not "expecting" a baby? Since we are raising children through adoption, how can it be said that we couldn't "have" children since we obviously "have" them? Motherhood is an experience as well as an identity, and we will not have our identity as mothers be "dictated and diminished by others" (Rich 1979, 195).

Women describe themselves as deeply embodied because "the essential biological characteristics of women give rise to relations with the world that are different than men's" (Gergen 2001, 22). Therefore, motherhood is a narrative of embodiment. By extension, is giving birth a defining event of femaleness? If so, adoptive mothers may be unsettling for other women because we represent a negation of their identity. We do not fit the traditional symbols of motherhood—the fertile woman with the large belly. Conversely, we are called barren—a term that connotes a shriveled, dried-up uterus or one that is dusty and hollow. We are blamed for not trying to get pregnant earlier, in our twenties, because we were busy putting our careers first (another version of mother blame?). By suggesting that our bodies have failed, we are torn from our embodiment.

Protecting the fundamental rights of women over our bodies continues to be at the core of the struggle for women's equality (Wattleton 2003). Embedded in this debate is an unresolved conflict over female sexuality. We assert that adoption should be viewed in the context of women's reproductive rights—this was the choice we made in how to become parents and raise children. Not only should the choice to be or not to be a mother be available to all women, the choice in how to become a mother is just as important. However, because we have not gone through the experience of pregnancy and birth, we are somehow viewed as *less than female*.

A great deal of attention is focused in the media on biological options for family formation. Millions across the world watched the story of Canadian pop singer Celine Dion's pregnancy through in-vitro fertilization with egg transplantation. Stories about surrogate mothers, donor insemination, women becoming pregnant well into their fifties, frozen embryos, and other pregnancies outside the typical sphere are a regular feature of North American pop culture. As Ambert (2003) notes, all of these methods usually allow at least one of the two parents to be a biological parent. Why, she asks, do so many women subject their bodies to the misery of fertility treatment and its less than certain outcome when adoption is available as an alternative? She suggests that: "The preference given by society to biological over social parenting leads many prospective parents to try everything they can, however painful, before they turn to adoption. Others are led to see adoption as second best and reject it as an alternative. Many are afraid that children they adopt will develop problems because this is an outcome they are often led to expect from the media and even researchers" (7).

Questions such as "Did you try in-vitro fertilization first?" or "Is the problem with you or your husband?" insinuate that there is something wrong with us because we did not give birth and that having a biological connection to a child is the most important, or preferable, choice in motherhood. This assumption of infertility sends the message, "Who would chose adoption if they didn't have to?" This belief also negates the fact that some women, although they are fertile, "would rather forgo the experience of pregnancy and birthing. The idea that all women enjoy being pregnant and reproducing themselves is just that—an idea. It is not a universally applicable fact. Many women actually like the idea of the baby-carrying stork" (Ambert, 9).

Ambert also points out that single adults who adopt are not queried about their infertility because "it would be awkward socially or morally reprehensible [for them] to bear children. Thus, many parents who adopt are not infertile. Some even have . . . or will have birth children" (9). Comments about women's fertility as it relates to adoption lead us to believe that some people are unwilling to acknowledge our mother-daughter relationship as genuine and permanent. It would appear, then, that much of society believes in nature over nurture.

Nature versus Nurture

The sociological role of mothers is the idea that caregiving and child rearing learned cultural experiences are separate from the experience of reproduction (Rogus 2003). However, as we have previously explored, there is strong cultural support for the idea that biology makes motherhood women's destiny. Therefore, the biological and sociological concepts of motherhood have become one and the same (Rogus). This ideology posits that "Perhaps females do not even become women until they experience the physical event of childbirth" (819). As adoptive mothers, we are viewed by some as "unnatural" because we may not even be considered "women," let alone "mothers."

We have been asked, "Does she speak Chinese?" to which we have responded "She's nine months old." The question of "What language will she speak when she starts to talk?" when our Chinese daughters are infants, assumes that nearly everything about their behavior is genetically determined and, thus, the adoptive mother makes either little or no contribution to the child's development (Martin 1998). Some people even comment that our Chinese daughters either look like us or our family members. Is this a way of insinuating that our identities as mothers are somehow tied to the way our children look? It's not.

"Isn't it great she's doing so well!" is a comment that has been said about our children. Why does this appear to be a surprise to others?

Ambert (2003) suggests that comments such as this are stated because many people, even clinical practitioners, do not believe that adoption is as natural as biological parenting. The assumption is that adopted children, and their parents, are at a disadvantage from the outset, which "is the deficit approach to the social construction of adoption" (Wagner, as cited in Ambert, 11).

We are frequently asked about whether we have any information about our children's birth families. In the case of adoptions from China, very little information, if any, is usually known about the birth families. Often, the response is that it's "too bad" that our daughters will never know their medical history, yet "such anxieties are rarely justified because biological inheritance alone accounts for a minute proportion of diseases that can be prevented. For the majority of human beings, the environment is far more influential than genes in the domain of health" (Ambert 2003, 4).

The emphasis on the importance of the first year of life espoused by most parenting books is another aspect that sets our families apart because our children were not adopted as newborns. Added to this is the popular culture of orphanages as being bad places, which either did not or could not provide for our children. Such references to either the months or years our children spent before they became part of our family suggest that adopted children automatically face insurmountable obstacles to leading a "normal," or "well-adjusted," life: "Adoptive families often struggle to feel normal. . . . The cultural beliefs that create this struggle are that the idealized nuclear family's influence on children is paramount, that early difficulties or trauma cannot be undone. . . . These beliefs, however, are often hidden and unspoken. To compensate, strangers smile at our children and tell us how wonderful, special and admirable we are to have adopted (rescued) them" (Paddock 2002, 1).

The Issue of Race in Conceptions of Motherhood

It is important to acknowledge the concept of "white privilege" (Tatum 1997; McIntosh 1988; Frankenberg 1993) because, as many authors point out, many white people have never considered the benefits of being white. Some are unknowingly, as well as others who are knowingly, the beneficiary of racism. "For many Whites, this new awareness of the benefits of a racist system elicits considerable pain, often accompanied by feelings of anger and guilt" (Tatum 1997, 9). Our awareness and conceptualizations of race and motherhood have certainly changed since becoming a multiracial family.

"For children adopted across racial lines, race and adoption often become inextricably connected" (Steinberg and Hall 2000, 11). Therefore, these authors assert that "the best tool you can develop as a parent of a child of another race is a healthy ability to challenge your own assumptions about what you need to do and about what your child faces" (17):

> In truth, if we don't talk about race with young children, it's very possible our kids may attach too much importance to the racial differences they notice between themselves and others. Only we, as parents, can help our kids internalize their absolute worth as we help them process the racial differences they will increasingly notice between themselves and those around them. If, by remaining silent, we (in effect) deny that those differences exist, they are likely to only grow in importance in our children's minds and may even seem more significant than they actually are. (Nakazawa 2003, 9)

As Tatum (1997) points out, the impact of racism begins as early as our preschool years when we are exposed to misinformation about people different from ourselves. There is a great deal of social segregation in our communities as most of neighbors are racially, religiously, and socioeconomically similar to one another. These stereotypes, omissions, and distortions all contribute to the development of racism. By extension, for women who become mothers through transracial adoption, race and motherhood often become inextricably connected. Likewise, we need to talk about our experiences as mothers to challenge the implicit assumptions about what it means to be(come) a mother. If we don't, stereotypes, omissions, and distortions of what it means to be a "real" mother, will continue.

Moosnick (2004) points out that opponents of transracial adoptions focus on how racism affects the child's welfare. However, she goes on to say that "White parents, however, counter that racial distinctions are more than anything else cultural interpretations that have historically ignored gradations of color" and that transracial adoptions can call "attention to public policies that bring transracial adoptees' racial identities into being" (24). She cites literature that suggests that the changing understanding of adoption coincides with changing notions of race, class, and gender. And what about the cultural interpretations of motherhood? We hope it changes with changing notions of reproductive options.

In describing people's responses to multiracial children, Nakazawa (2003) noted these children "often appear quite exotic to others" (21), which is how our families seems to appear to others. Nakazawa goes on to describe what we have already experienced—how our families' "physical appearance is frequently a source of special attention that can lead to jarring incidents as we go about our everyday routines" (21), for example, questions from strangers about where our children are from. These incidents become disturbing when viewed from our children's positions because they are made to feel different—and other—because of race. This is another example of the context in which we, as mothers of children adopted transracially, have to navigate the concepts of race and motherhood. We face the challenge of doing this while being on public display.

Mother and Child as Public Exhibits

Transracial adoption is more complex than same-race adoption because visible differences between mothers and children increase challenges to their social acceptance as a family unit (Steinberg and Hall 2000, 8). However, as Nakazawa (2003) ascertains, race is an artificial distinction that reflects very little genetic difference, "Perhaps one one-hundredth of 1 percent of our DNA" (xiii). She goes on to say that "It is nevertheless true that as long as we live in a world in which race is one of the most salient factors of day-to-day life in determining how we are treated by others, it remains a real fact of life" (xiii). That is why adoptive mothers of children of the same race can avoid uncomfortable questions and comments because they "blend" in with families created by birth, regardless of having different features, such as eye or hair colour.

Transracial adoption means that our family circumstances become public because of the visual differences between us and our children. We are in effect, on display: "If you enjoy being different and standing out from the crowd, as a transracial parent you will get chances every day. On the other hand, if you are shy and like to blend in with others, being out and about with your child is bound to be laborious for you because you will always be noticed. Those of us that are natural hams or easy leaders are likely to find this easier than those who like to be followers or prefer to be one of the crowd" (Steinberg and Hall 2000, 13).

As Hilborn (2004) points out, "In the world at large it's usually not relevant to refer to a child as an 'adopted child'" (19). However, we are constantly amazed by how some people demonstrate that our experiences as mothers—and by extension, the experiences of our children—should be public knowledge when strangers ask very personal questions. Strangers do not ask birth mothers if they gave birth to their child, but we are frequently asked if, and from where, our children are adopted. Strangers do not ask birth mothers how long their labour was or how painful, but we are asked how long we waited and whether it was expensive. We are proud that our daughters were born in China. However, the way that some people make the distinction between a birth child and an adopted child can adversely affect both mothers and children. As Higginbotham (2002) rightly points out, "Our daughter is not a public exhibit. She deserves to be protected from adult questions that subtly invalidate her family's right to exist" (29).

"Where are you from? How can she be your mom if she's white? What happened to your real mom? How come you don't live with her? Is she your real sister?" Why do these questions bother us? Because people ask personal questions in situations that they perceive as not normal, and our children understand these insinuations. It would never occur to us to ask a Caucasian mother with a Caucasian baby, "Did you give birth to that child?" (Register 2001)—or as we are often asked, "Are you the babysitter?"

The Effects of Unintentional Language

> These negative messages are usually, but not always, unintentional. People have an instinct for categorization; when they see situations that don't fit the norm, they comment. Most exchanges are harmless. But the cumulative effect is to undermine the legitimacy of our families. We knew that our decision to adopt transracially would mean kissing our cozy anonymity goodbye. But our daughter never volunteered for this ride. And people often speak to us as if our child is deaf—as if she does not hear and internalize conversations that go on around her (Higginbotham 2002, 29).

As Winant (1994) suggests, "Let's challenge the limits and biases of the categories we use" (115). In adoption this is imperative because, as

Higginbotham points out, "At home, we're telling our children that adoption is a special way of creating a family, and that their birth cultures are something to celebrate" (29). However, individuals' intrusive and insensitive comments can send children a very different message.

It is essential that we address this harmful discourse, particularly now as international adoptions are becoming the choice for more mothers. In 2004, Canadians adopted 1,955 children from abroad. Chinese adoptions represented 51 percent of all international adoptions in Canada. China was by far the preferred country, with the second choice, Haiti, accounting for just 15 percent of Canada's international adoptions (Adoption Council of Canada 2005). We feel that we must educate others about the language of adoption. We try to prepare ourselves for those who use inappropriate language and ask intrusive questions. For example, instead of "real" or "natural" parent, we use "birth parent" or "biological parent." Instead of "abandoned," "gave up," or "put up" for adoption, we use "placed" for adoption, "chose" adoption, or "made an adoption plan."

We also want to set boundaries, so that our children will grow up to feel that they are entitled to boundaries. Questions van Gulden suggests we ask ourselves before responding to intrusive questions include, "Do I want to give this information to anyone?; Do I want to give this information to this person?; Here?; Now (in my child's presence)?; Why is this person asking this question?; What does this person really want to know?; Is it my responsibility to educate this person about adoption?; If so, is this the time and place to do so?; How will my children perceive my interrupting our time together to respond to this question?; and What will they learn about their rights to belonging, and to personal boundaries in public?" (van Gulden, 2004). Van Gulden adds that it is all right for us to not answer others' questions and leave them confused because our children are more important. Although tolerance and politeness do not necessarily lead to social change, we think about the messages that we send our children when we ignore questions about our families. We are not ashamed about how our families were created, and we are proud of their birth culture. Discussing with our children how such questions can be handled empowers and prepares them because they will receive these questions and comments when they are not in our presence.

Melina (1998) puts a positive spin on the "scrutiny," as she calls it, that parents who adopt internationally experience: "I have often wondered if the obvious differences in families with internationally adopted children leads to a greater awareness of the issues and ultimately a greater openness about discussing them, with the result that parents and adoptees address the issues and work through them, rather than ignore them" (231). We now have a greater awareness of the language used to describe mothering and motherhood, and certainly know that we cannot ignore it.

Releasing the Creation and Sustenance of Life into the Realm of the Imagination

> I hope, and believe, that every woman . . . knows that on the subject of motherhood there are no experts. What we need, in any case, as women, is not experts on our lives, but the opportunity and the validation to name and describe the truths of our lives, as we have known them . . . remember that it is your own . . . painfully gathered knowledge of daughterhood and motherhood, which you must above all trust.
> —Adrienne Rich

We wish to thank the editors of this book for providing us with the opportunity to speak the truths of our lives. In doing so, we hope that we contribute to an imagination of the reconstruction of the language around mothering, where motherhood is inclusive of all mothers. Families are created many different ways, not only through pregnancy and adoption, but pregnancy/birth is the predominate discourse that dismisses, excludes, and even invalidates other women's experiences. We hope we have been able to portray that we are mothers—rather than adoptive mothers—first and foremost to our children: "Although [we] came into their lives and they into [ours] through adoption. Adoption is simply the legal mechanism. What [we are] is their 'mother[s]'—legally, functionally, by all the laws and powers of emotional bonds and love. [We] love them fiercely. We Are Their Mother[s]" (Price, n.d., 1).

"To release the creation and sustenance of life into the realm of decision, struggle, surprise, imagination, and conscious intelligence" (Rich 1979, 272) would be to carry us to places of new possibilities of concepts of mothering. We want this not only for ourselves and all mothers, but for our children.

This essay is for our daughters, who give us so much joy—You have loved *us* real.

Works Cited

Abbey, S. (1998). "Mentoring my daughter: Contradictions and possibilities." *Canadian Women Studies* 18(2/3). Accessed June 9, 2005. http://proquest.umi.com/.

Adoption Council of Canada. *International Adoptions up 2,181 in 2003.* www.adoption.ca.

Ambert, A. *The Negative Social Construction of Adoption: Its Effects on Children and Parents.* www.arts.yorku.ca/soci/lambert/writings/adoption.html.

Barlow, C., and K. Cairns. "Mothering as a psychological experience: A grounded theory exploration." *Canadian Journal of Counselling* 31, 3 (1997): 232–47.

Bowen, J. *A Canadian guide to international adoptions: How to find, adopt, and bring home your child.* North Vancouver: Self-Counsel Press, 1992.

Brookes, A. *Feminist pedagogy: An autobiographical approach.* Halifax: Fernwood Publishing, 1992.

Conley, A. [Review of the book *Adopting Maternity: White Women who Adopt Transracially and Transnationally*]. *Journal of Sociology and Social Welfare* (March 2005).

Fancott, H. "Unwanted Adoption Language." *Adoptive Families Association of BC.* http://www.bcadoption.com/articles/aam/lang.htm.

Ganong, Lawrence H., and Marilyn Coleman. "The content of mother stereotypes. *Sex Roles: A Journal of Research.* www.findarticles.com.

Ganong, L., and M. Coleman. "The content of motherhood stereotypes." *Sex Roles: A Journal of Research* (April 1995).

Gergen, M. *Feminist reconstruction in psychology: Narrative, gender, and performance.* Thousand Oaks, Calif.: Sage, 2001.

Higginbotham, J. S. "Is she adopted?" *Adoptive Families* 29 (May/June, 2002).

Hilborn, R. "Teaching the language of adoption." *Family Helper* 45 (2004): 19–20.

Johnson, K. *Wanting a daughter, needing a son: Abandonment, adoption and orphanage care in China.* St. Paul: Yeong & Yeong Book Co., 2004.

Johnston, D., and D. Swanson. "Invisible Mothers: A Content Analysis of Motherhood Ideologies and Myths in Magazines." *Sex Roles* 49 (2003): 21–33.

Johnston, P. *Speaking Positively: Using Respectful Adoption Language.* Indianapolis: Perspectives Press Inc., 2004. www.perspectivespress.com.

Kelly, U. *Schooling desire: Literacy, cultural politics, and pedagogy.* New York: Routledge, 1997.

Lakoff, R. T. *Language and woman's place: Text and commentaries.* Oxford: Oxford University Press, 2004.

Martin, A. *Societal Views of Adoption: An Interview with Claudia Nelson, author of Little Strangers—Portrayals of adoption and Foster Care in America, 1850–1929.* www.comeunity.com/adoption/adopt/interview-nelson.html.

Melina, L. R. *Raising adopted children: Practical, reassuring advice for every adoptive parent.* New York: Quill, 1998.

Nakazawa, D. J. *Does anybody else look like me? A parent's guide to raising multiracial children.* Cambridge: Da Capo Lifelong Books, 2003.

Paddock, D. *Bent, but not broken: Building resilient adoptive families.* 2002. http://www.rainbowkids.com/2002/06/attachment/attachment.chtml. Accessed May 21, 2005.

Price, R. *Real and Natural Mothers' Reflections on Birth—and Adoptive—Mothering.* www.adoption.com. Accessed May 18, 2005.

Register, C. "Answering nosy questions." *Saskatchewan Families with Children from China Newsletter* (Summer 2001). www.AdoptiveFamiliesMagazine.com.

Rich, A. *On lies, secrets, and silence: Selected prose 1966–1978.* New York: W.W. Norton, 1979.

Rogus, Caroline. "Conflating Women's Biological and Sociological Roles: The Ideal of Motherhood, Equal Protection, and the Implications of the Nguyen v. Ins Opinion." *The Journal of Constitutional Law* (May 2003): 803–30.

Steinberg, Gail and Beth Hall. *Inside Transracial Adoption.* Indianapolis: Perspectives Press, 2000.

Van Gulden, H. *Handling intrusive questions: Selected tips.* St. Paul: North American Council on Adoptable Children, 2004.

Van Gulden, H., and L. M. Bartels-Rabb. *Real parents, real children: Parenting the adopted child.* New York: Crossroad, 1993.

Wattleton, F. "Unfinished agenda: Reproductive rights." In *Sisterhood is forever: The women's anthology for a new millennium.* Edited by R. Morgan. Toronto: Washington Square Press, 2003. 17–27.

Williams, M. *The velveteen rabbit.* New York: Avon Books, 1975.

Winant, H. *Racial conditions: Politics, theory and comparisons.* Minneapolis: University of Minnesota Press, 1994.

Wolff, J. "Secret Thoughts of an Adoptive Mother." www.adoptivefamilies.com/articles.

"Your Shopping Cart Is Empty": Social Texts of Single Motherhood and the Discomforts of Discourse

Ann Elizabeth Willey

Two Scenes in the Birth of a Mother

After forty-two hours of labor, from between my shaking legs, I heard the obstetrician muttering about episiotomies and the misguided trend toward birthing plans as he gathered up ragged folds of my hitherto most internal flesh and tried to figure out what to sew to what eighteen times. My birth coach watched intently as the doctor worked, while he, appreciative of the audience, narrated the entire process. "When you're done with the guided tour of my vagina," I said, "I'd like to put my legs down."

"It's a miracle," the "doula" said, beaming, lavender-scented washcloths still strewn about the room as the nurses handed my son back to me.
  It was not a miracle—I had worked too damn hard; miracles just happened. In thinking about my relationship with my son in the act of being born, I wasn't ready to call it a miracle, but I was willing to acknowledge the otherworldliness of the event. It was sublime, I said. My birth coach and I then carefully explained the meaning of "sublime" to the doula, distinguished it from miracles, and agreed it was a much more appropriate word.[1]

Discourses of Maternity: Single and Multiple

Long before I even considered becoming a mother, I had used the word "doula" in theory classes as a way to think through Foucault's theories of discourse, the way discourses are institutionally situated and reified, and the ways that discourses are complicit in maintaining and perpetuating circulations of power. Students (when they knew the word), easily drew out the implications of comparing "doula" and the natural childbirth movement to "obstetrician" and the medical institutions that authorize, legitimate, and regulate the medicalization of pregnancy and childbirth. This contrast in languages used to describe the experiences of pregnancy and childbirth only begins to intimate the ambivalence with which I approached the public renderings of my path to being a mother. I was thirty-seven years old, tenured at a midsize Midwestern university, and unpartnered. Even this cursory description begs the question of my subjectivity in discourse as I considered motherhood. What do I mean when I use the word "unpartnered"? Does unpartnered mean that I lack a state-sanctioned partner in marriage? The only state entity that has ever asked me to define my marital status is the IRS, and according to them, I am "single." Do I mean that I did not have a long-term committed lesbian partner? I am not homosexual. Did I have a boyfriend? I had been dating a mere five months earlier, but I haven't had a "boyfriend" since I was seventeen. Did I lack a "special friend"? This phrase all too unfortunately brings up convents and their strictures against all kinds of intimacy. I could not even claim a POSSLQ, as the census board so ineloquently tried to describe the relationship. None of the above. I lived by myself, in a house, with my dog, and the occasional company of good friends.

Nor is my status now that I am mother much easier to define. According to the IRS, I am still single, but I have new designation: "head of household." My legal and fiscal responsibility for another life has trumped my marital status, making my status as mother much more significant than my non-status as wife. In this alone perhaps the IRS is closer to accurately describing my new subjectivity than most other public discourses available to me. Though it is odd to say, I am glad of the IRS for this: I am not single. I am still unmarried. I have no other adult living in my house. I haven't had a date since before I got pregnant in fall of 2002. But I am decidedly not single. I am multiple and more involved than I have ever been before. For months after my son was born, I consistently used the plural when referring to myself. His presence has so thoroughly soaked my consciousness that I experience myself as more than one.

And yet the language of "singleness" continues to reassert itself despite its felt inadequacies. I am a member of Single Mothers by Choice (SMC), an organization that in its very nomenclature stresses the inadequacy of most current discourses of motherhood even while reinscribing the fact of singleness as, if not antithetical to, then at least uncomfortably paired with, motherhood. By modifying "single" and "mother" with "by choice," the organization unfortunately, if unintentionally, emphasizes the oddity of being both single and a mother. Noting the tension in the organization's name reinforces my sense of my maternal subjectivity as anything but single. I continue unwittingly to use the plural when referring to myself. I find myself not only outside of the socially normative languages that twin mother and wife, but also resisting the discourse of Single Motherhood as something that plays false my newly multiple self.

My plural consciousness aside, SMC provides a tremendous amount of comfort and support to me even while it continually brings home the failures of public discourses of motherhood for women in many different maternal positions. Let me be clear here: it is not that SMC fosters, creates, or perpetuates these aporias. Instead, the anomalous (in normative terms) positions of its members push at the limits of the discourses we use to explore our situations. Even within this community of common interest, there is an ever-present anxiety about the language of maternity. As in any special interest group, there is an elaborate system of jargon and self-identification. In that group, I had been a "thinker" and briefly a "TTC" before becoming SMC to Maxwell (21 months), ADI, 2nd IUI cycle, med.[2] And while most SMC members can slot themselves into this jargon, many feel compelled to identify and/or explain their deviance from the paths the jargon most often identifies. Some are single not by choice but have been left by birth fathers; others explain that they had been married but no longer are; still others remind the listserv and themselves that having children on their own is "plan B."

I mention these examples to indicate that the language of maternity, whether in the classroom or in an online support community of mothers, continues to be a question that shapes my everyday actions as a professor and as a mother. Or even more significantly, as my felt need to distinguish between a miracle and the sublime literally moments after my son was born indicates, I find it hard to separate my subject position as a scholar from my subject position as a mother. And in each case, I find myself struggling for a language that will more adequately reflect my own experiences as a mother who lives and works in a community of academics, most of whom happen to be parents in conventionally constituted heterosexual unions. The ways in which my maternal position came into being constantly pits me against discourses of motherhood/maternity/working mother/subjectivity that I find myself resisting.

Medical Discourses of Fertility

When considering having a child on my own, I found the language available to me in the relatively private and self-centered conversations among friends to be fairly transparent. It wasn't until I started thinking about the mechanics of getting pregnant that language began to fail me. My gynecologist was encouraging, recommending a local university-related fertility clinic for the insemination. I had rarely felt myself intimidated in my interactions with the medical profession until I went to my initial consultation at the fertility clinic. It wasn't until I left my first meeting with the "reproductive endocrinologist" (RE), bewildered and mad, that I realized that a greater part of my frustration with the visit was due to the fact that the doctor kept referring to infertility and the common procedures for treating it. I was clear with him about my marital status and desire to have a child without the intervention of any man whom I knew but that did not change the tone of our conversation. At one point the doctor looked at me and declared that there was no way to know if I was fertile and so he would treat me as if I were not. My argument that there was no reason to assume that I was infertile, that in fact my gynecological history gave every indication that my reproductive system was healthy and functioning normally, seemed not to have any effect. After this meeting I called my gynecologist who remarked, "Well, of course you're not infertile, you just don't have any sperm. And you shouldn't because you're female." My conundrum in a nutshell.

Beyond my personal frustration at being labeled with a term was both unwarranted and unwanted, the language of infertility turned out to have serious ramifications on other levels. For example, it was the language of insurance and billing. My insurance at the time did not cover infertility treatments. It would not pay for any of the procedures I underwent, even the routine medical profiles like blood-typing or testing for common problems like exposure to tuberculosis, that in other contexts would be covered. More importantly, I believe that this language contributed to my uncharacteristic reticence in the face of the medical profession. I did not object to certain procedures that I later understood to be baseless. I let the RE designate the level of medical interference in monitoring my ovulation, for example. Over other things, I was simply told that I had no choice given the standard operating procedures at the fertility clinic. While I would like to think that I did not believe the rhetoric of presumed infertility, in retrospect, I can see how at least part of my silence in the face of unnecessary costly and invasive procedures was due to the threat of infertility raised by the RE and clinic protocol. Unfortunately, I took it out on the billing department, insisting over and over again that they had misfiled my insurance claims by misrepresenting the procedures. Their repeated insistence that infertility was the only "code" available to them for purposes of billing the insurance company led me back to my doctor's coda about being female and single. Is being single the same thing as being infertile? Or more insidiously in the RE's language, is not ever having carried a pregnancy to term sufficient evidence of infertility in a woman of her mid-thirties? The assumption inherent in either of these paradigms left me in a position I did not want to occupy and would not in other contexts submit to.

My strong reaction to being labeled infertile was due in part, I think, to the burden I share with my many of my female colleagues, whether mothers or not, in the face of cultural discourses about motherhood and professionalism. Many others have explored this discourse far more thoroughly than I can hope to in this essay, but it was a factor in my anxiety in the face of the medical establishment's labeling of me. When I was trying to conceive, I was told repeatedly that I was infertile. During my pregnancy, I was constantly told that according to the medical/insurance industries, I was an "older" mother. All this at the age of thirty-seven. From my perspective, shared by many of my friends, this seemed like the most natural time in my life to become a mother. I had finished my degree (six years), worked in a first job for a while (three years), moved on to a more satisfying position at a second job and was awarded tenure (six years). As someone who had moved fairly briskly through a conventional academic career, thirty-six presented itself as the optimal time to consider having a child. I was not an "older" mother, I was finally ready to be a mother precisely because I had established myself in my career. Was I being selfish because I wanted to be a "single" mother or was I selfish because I wanted professional security before I became a mother? The discourses about single motherhood and professional women as mothers worked synergistically with medical discourses of infertility and aging to render me more much more passive than normal in the face of medical intervention.

"Your Shopping Cart Is Currently Empty"

The next arena in which the language of maternity became oddly opaque to me was searching for a donor. I got several references for sperm banks—from the clinic, from friends of a friend who had conceived using anonymous-donor sperm, online—and began the surreal process of choosing a donor to help me in creating a child. I had shopped online in the past for books, CDs, movies, clothes, shoes, motorcycle parts. Genetic material for creating another human life? How do you describe that and how do you market it? For a market it is. Sperm banks compete for buyers through special programs and features like "identity release" donors (who promise that they will be open to contact when any child conceived using their sperm turns eighteen) or advertising special, more expensive, specimens from donors who are guaranteed to have a PhD or equivalent. As any enterprising commercial concern might, the online sperm banks offer their prospective clients a variety of details about the donors that can be priced à la carte or bought by the package. Want childhood photos? Want an audio file of the donor being interviewed? Want a Meyers-Briggs personality test of the donor? Want to buy surplus samples and have them stored for future use? Any and all of these services can be arranged online by clicking in the appropriate boxes and typing in your credit card info. And until you do decide to purchase something, the banner at the top of the site will most helpfully remind you that "your shopping cart is empty."

This line was perhaps most disturbing to me in the process of purchasing what I would need to have a child. It was almost impossible not to read it as a metaphoric reference to my empty womb, and had I a more sentimental nature, I would have found it profoundly depressing. As it was, I found it insensitive at best and a poor choice for graphically interfacing with people who are driven to the use of "reproductive technology" in order to experience what our culture continually asserts is one of the most "natural" parts of a woman's life. Beyond a most unfortunate use of figurative language, this line also brings me back around to shopping for human material online. I am not of the camp that Monty Python so successfully lampoons in their song "Every Sperm Is Sacred." But I do have to admit to some hesitation about literally buying my motherhood online. I felt, as the Clash sang, "all lost in the supermarket / I could not shop happily / on-sale at a special offer / guaranteed personality."

Perhaps I sound flippant in quoting popular songs to think through my profound discomfort with shopping for sperm, but the clash of discourses of maternity and consumerism were particularly unsettling to me and led me down two paths of reflection: 1) to what extent is anyone's experience of motherhood rendered consumerist in our culture? And 2) what are the ramifications of buying and selling human material, especially in the disembodied realm of cyberspace?

The question of the extent to which consumerism shapes our experiences of motherhood persistently occupied my time.[3] Beyond the concrete fiscal limitations of one salary, the expectations of shopping when expecting are almost overwhelming. My friends generously offered to throw a shower for me. To make things easier for them and myself, I registered at Babies R Us. For me, this was a new experience of virtual shopping: wandering through the warehouse-sized store with an infrared wand scanning labels of anything and everything that caught my eye. And the customer service people at the store don't let you off easy: you are "encouraged" to be as specific as possible (one doesn't register for a playpen but instead a Graco John Lennon Animal Sounds Series Portable Playyard with mobile and optional sun guard). And in case you think you don't need certain items—wipe warmers, special hooded towels, baby toiletry kits—the helpful computer handout you receive with the scanner will remind you that you should indeed be registering for them. Virtual spending led to all too real coveting of things I hadn't even been aware of before my trip to the store. Moral failings aside, the insidious message behind many of these products that trumpeted their ability to provide safety, security, intelligence, and comfort to your infant is that not buying them is a sign of bad mothering. I had a chance to buy Nobel laureate sperm, now I was duty-bound to stimulate my child into becoming the Baby Einstein he was destined to be. His safety, happiness, and intelligence were mine to vouchsafe through the products I purchased.

The gift-giving orgy of the baby shower and its enticement to virtual consumerism is apparently resisted in popular discourse in the discursive arena that gives us the language of doulas and natural childbirth. A friend recommended to me a journal called *Mothering*, an alternative to the formula-shilling products distributed freely in my doctor's office. Among other things, *Mothering* advocates attachment parenting, informed resistance to bureaucratized medical care, and the need to protect children from the onslaught of advertising that creeps into their everyday lives from the moment the "hospital photographer" offers to take their portrait for a princely sum. In perhaps an unavoidable irony, *Mothering*'s anticonsumerist message is literally underwritten by ads for products that encourage a more "natural" approach to mothering: cloth diapers, cleverly designed nursing tops for mothers who want to exercise their rights to breastfeed in public, all natural fiber clothes, ergonomic shoes for young walkers, etc. The irony deepens when one takes into account the exoticism that underlies much of the language of "natural mothering." Many of the ads trumpet their products' origins in third world countries where mothers have been mercifully spared the Western alienation of cribs and strollers. For a small sum, you can buy colorful slings woven by third world women in which to carry your baby and experience motherhood as it was meant to be. While I exaggerate a bit here, once again, the implicit message is that the quality of your mothering practices can be gauged by the physical props you buy to enable it. Consumerism, it seems, is an unavoidable part of any experience of motherhood.

Much more difficult for me to negotiate was the question of whether shopping for sperm really so different from shopping for playpens, crib sheets, or baby toys? And though I don't want to admit it, the answer must remain yes. During my attempts to become a mother, I happily avoided thinking about the ramifications of buying human material online. But the ethics of doing so have come back to my notice in a roundabout way. In teaching a graduate seminar in postcolonial literature and theory centered on questions of globalization and diaspora, I read sociological theory about the spread of capitalism and the ideologies of markets. Through this reading, I have stumbled across a term that helps me to think through my own anxiety about buying sperm online: market inalienability. As outlined by Margaret Radin, market inalienability draws on the distinction between a gift and a commodity. A gift, in anthropological theory (working from the theories of Mauss) as adopted by sociology, is something that is "inalienable" from the giver. It creates networks of reciprocity and social status that involve both the giver and the receiver. Hence the gift always carries with it part of the "power" of the giver; it is inseparable/inalienable from the giver. A commodity, on the other hand, is alienable in that it belongs solely to the buyer and carries with it no claims on behalf of the producer or seller. All capitalist markets have rendered limits on the commodification of things, i.e., have declared some things to be off-limits to the market, or "market inalicnablc." Endangered species, the labor power of children, and human organs intended for donation are technically not legally for sale in our current market.

Market inalienability raises the question of to what extent our society is willing to let people sell parts of themselves in the legal marketplace. We have declared illegal the sale of sex and organs, but we have openly allowed the sale of blood and blood by-products as well as sperm and eggs. If indeed we are not legally permitted to sell our kidneys, why is it legal to sell gametes? It cannot simply be a matter of what the human body can replace or sustain the loss of easily (as in the case of blood or sperm and eggs, or a second kidney), because we have long criminalized the sale of sexual acts. The discourse of buying sperm online confuses the matter further by referring to the men involved as donors even as they are paid for their samples. Most of the companies selling sperm and/or eggs refer to themselves as "cryobanks," calling up echoes of monetary exchanges. While mothering is always inflected by the market, motherhood is not, except in these cases where women like (and unlike) myself have resorted to buying the raw material necessary to make it possible. And for many single women, the alienability of the "donor" sperm is precisely what makes it attractive. There were no bonds of reciprocity, no networks of interpersonal exchange or obligation with another adult human, involved in my coming into motherhood. I am solely responsible for my child and I like it like that. While I continue to be troubled by the ethics of buying and selling human material, I revel in the personal freedom of "owning" my child outright, with no other person possibly claiming a legal right to his personhood. Perhaps this is a larger dynamic of consumer capitalism and its necessary conflicts with a social discourse of ethics. Buying sperm online leads me to experience a kind of maternal subjectivity that is obviously mediated by the troubling ethics (or lack thereof) of the marketplace and at the same time the inalienable sense of my connection to my son.

Incest Is Best, Put Your Brother to the Test

Another lacuna in the publicly available languages of maternity tripped me up as I was making the choice of a donor. While some adults describe their search for a companion at least in part as a quest for an ideal reproductive partner, most men and women privilege the romantic aspect of the relationship between two adults. This obviously should not have been a concern for me in choosing between anonymous donors with whom I would most likely never meet, let alone establish a relationship. And yet, as I was looking at the donor profiles, my choice was complicated by the inescapable feeling that I should "like" the donor I ultimately picked. The physical restrictions were fairly easy to identify: no histories of Parkinson's or depression (these already run in my family); no history of cancer preferably. But beyond these basics, I was stumped. What physical attributes should I find attractive? Should I pick a donor with physical attributes echoing the men I tend to be attracted to in everyday life? Dark curly hair. Big shoulders. No cleft chins. I found myself looking at profiles of people who physically reminded me of an on-and-off again romantic interest of ten years and then rejecting those very same donors precisely because of their resemblance to him. Either reaction, I realized, was irrational. I wasn't looking for a romantic partner. Beyond this realization I wasn't sure what I was looking for.

Much of the discussion around single motherhood inevitably raises the question of the father. Books have been published, studies have been done, endless listserv threads have been typed, about how to deal with the absence of fathers in the lives of children conceived by single women via anonymous donor insemination. All the experts (and non-expert participants) have agreed on one thing: openness within the family is the best approach. As with adoption, it is secrecy or flat-out lying that seems to cause emotional problems for adult children conceived through either egg or sperm donation. Part of the freight in choosing a sperm donor, then, lay not only in my irrational desire to imagine being attracted to the donor, but also wanting to be able to share positive feelings about him with the child conceived. In other words, not only did I want to be physically attracted to the donor, but I wanted to like him based on his short essay and even shorter audio interview. I wouldn't sleep with any real man that I knew so little about but I wanted this man to help me have a child. I didn't want a relationship, but I wanted a man with whom I would conceivably want to have a relationship.

This realization, my own confusion over the role of the donor in imagining my own maternal subjectivity, continues to raise questions for me about the implied other in maternity. A donor is a kind of simulacrum of a father, an "unreal imitation." This lack of a concrete other is obscured by the wealth of information that clinics will offer about donors. Most clinics now even offer (for those of us psychically mature enough to grapple with it) the promise of delayed satisfaction in the form of providing mediated contact with the donor when a resulting child of ADI turns eighteen. This possibility notwithstanding, I was left with trying to discern how I should choose the always invisible other that would literally shape my life and the life of my child. The answer became one of insularity or solipsism: I came to the conclusion that I should pick a donor whose physical description sounded the most like a male me as possible. In other words, I wanted to buy sperm from someone who looked like my brothers.

And so the threat of incest became an ironic trope in my choice for a donor. It was not a trope I was comfortable with and yet I found myself returning to it again and again. Just as my experience of consumerism and maternity was the same yet different from the more "common" experiences of maternity I had witnessed, my options for choosing a donor placed my experience of maternity in a realm untrammeled by my friends who were also mothers. The possibility of my maternity was from the very beginning shaped by a kind of narcissism interrupted by a gender difference that erupted as the threat of incest. The other that made my maternity possible was at the same time both unknown (by legal convention) and unknowable (by social and moral convention). I wonder if other mothers think about the other that literally provided the grounds of possibility for their own maternal subjectivities. Every time I think about the genesis of my son and therefore my own maternal self, I am once again in the chiasmus of the stranger that is part of me but forbidden to me, familiar but anonymous.

Cash Transactions, the Mysterious Stranger Syndrome, and Strange Bedfellows

Most of my struggles with the language of maternal subjectivity that I have described so far have been rather private affairs shared between myself and my friends. But in any pregnancy, there comes a time when the maternal "shows." In my case, my colleagues pretended not to notice until the baby shower was announced (though interestingly enough, my students swore they knew much earlier than my colleagues and some of my female students did indeed invite me to verify my pregnancy in private conversations by announcing their own maternities). My pregnancy was treated by both my colleagues and neighbors cautiously: their reactions were often led by my own tone as I announced it. My neighbors tended to address me directly—no surprise as we have pretty much one-to-one relations. Our street is our only common ground. When told, most simply congratulated me, though some did start fishing around for a father. One neighbor in fact looked relieved when I identified my mode of conception, admitting that she had wondered if the father were that gentleman she had seen at my house a few times last winter (which would have made my pregnancy an unbearable sixty-five weeks!).

My colleagues were generally much more circumspect, asking my friends for information. One older colleague approached the hostess of the baby shower and asked directly if I had found a partner. When she replied no, he went to ask if then I was happy about the pregnancy? Was it a good thing? he added. Another colleague, with whom I had spent more social time, asked me, oddly indirect and forthright at the same time, if the pregnancy had been planned.

This question in particular brought me back to traditional discourses of motherhood, particularly motherhood in the professional sphere. As our culture is increasingly consumed by the argument over whether it is indeed possible for women to "have it all," the irony of my own situation became increasingly obvious to me; as plain as the bump on my belly. Planning pregnancies to coincide with professional work opportunities is increasingly prevalent, though my particular situation required that I take into account not just the long-term factors of sabbaticals or promotions but the three-day shipping of frozen specimens and the medically optimal twenty-four-hour window from ovulation to insemination. These concerns required elaborate mapping and strategizing on my part to take into consideration factors such as available time off, immediate professional obligations, long-term professional goals, the viability span of frozen sperm once thawed, and the length of time an egg, once released, stays in the fallopian tubes.

The pregnancy was indeed planned. It was planned, strategized, timed, monitored from the first moment of a menstrual flow to the last possible hour for insemination. It was researched and paid for online, shipped via dry ice, and scheduled for noon after my 10:00 class. To the question asked, I responded "Planned? It was a cash transaction." My colleague looked somewhat startled and then puzzled. I found out later that he, like other colleagues, sought further explanations from a friend.

While I was toying with language at the expense of a friend, my response was true and not true in the same way that I am still single yet no longer single. Again, interestingly enough, my students had a much different reaction to my concealed and then revealed pregnancy. I often use personal anecdotes in class to illustrate various points about interpretation or argumentation, or simply as a way of "warming up" a class to get conversation flowing. I mention family and friends, occasionally dates. I had surely never discussed a husband or a partner. While my current students seem less likely to jump to conclusions based on my limited revelations, the students at my previous institution—a much more rural, conservative institution—quite often assumed I was gay precisely because I never mentioned a husband. (And I have short hair.) But in my position now, my single maternity was accepted by my normally gregarious students with much less interest in the other who made it possible than my colleagues evinced. My students' apparent lack of interest in my child's father may be due to the status difference, though they often asked extremely personal questions. It may also be due to the fact that a significant number of my students live in nontraditional family structures themselves.

Through my interactions with students and colleagues, I was reminded that in some ways I share more with more southern-born, working-class, first-generation college students than I do with my peers. This has complicated my sense of myself as a professional: when I tell stories in class, I find myself worried about not revealing too much, not becoming too "familiar" with my students, not losing too much professional face. I have a new hyperconsciousness of how the stories I tell in class lay bare the connections between my professional self and my private self, a distinction that I maintained fairly easily before motherhood. The psychic spaces I try to delineate everyday between the office and the daycare center take much more work to keep separate. This point was made glaringly obvious recently in a faculty meeting when, as a preface to scolding some colleagues, I announced that I didn't want to sound like anyone's mother, but . . . To a person, my colleagues laughed and reminded me that I am someone's mother. Even when I try to distance my maternal self from my role as a departmental administrator, I am reminded that I am a mother. The two roles cannot be separated, try as I might. "Mother" has become a public role that identifies me both at work and at home in a way that my home life never followed me to work before Maxwell. It makes me more like my students and less "professional" than before.

Conclusion

Whether telling stories about my son in a classroom or negotiating the ethical implications of purchasing motherhood online, I have struggled with the ways in which my unusual path to maternity has shaped my relationship to available discourses. My experiences often do not lead to startlingly idiosyncratic revelations about maternal subjectivity but they have thrown into relief questions of the wider social implications in and of maternity than I had previously associated with the act of becoming a mother. My engagement with the languages of maternity has shaped my perceptions of myself and the experiences of motherhood that I am continually publicly proclaiming and enacting. Whether being coded by a tax filing status, a medical condition, a social role, or a professional discourse, I have found myself uncomfortable with how maternity is described and how it applies to me. I do not think that I am unique in this; I do think that my experiences as a single, academic woman who conceived via anonymous donor insemination has brought pressure on these discourses in ways that my friends' experiences may not have. For this, I am grateful, as I am grateful for their experiences of motherhood, and the many lives and selves with and without children that intersect ours.

Notes

1. These two vignettes are two of my most vivid memories form the birth of my own son (August 17, 2003). I was assisted in a forty-two-hour labor and "natural" childbirth by a labor coach (a very good friend) and a doula. They stand out for me as moments when the involvement of others in this very intimate activity was necessary, even welcome, but also othering in my relation to myself and my body.

2. The informal convention on the SMC listservs often has posters identifying themselves by their status on the path to motherhood as well as the age and method of bringing into their lives any children they might already have. These acronyms often contain a wealth of details including what kind of medication was used, how many cycles it took, etc. A thinker is someone who is considering becoming a mother without a partner. TTC is someone actively trying to conceive. ADI stands for anonymous donor insemination. Maxwell was conceived on my second attempt at intrauterine insemination (IUI) while my cycles were being "stimulated" by medication (med).

3. I have to admit here to a profound blind spot in terms of the intersections of consumerism and motherhood beyond comfortably middle-class professional households. My only points of reference for this discussion are my own experiences and those of my friends, other white-collar professional women.

Works Cited

Clash, The. "Lost in the Supermarket." *London Calling*. Epic Records, 1979.

Mauss, Marcel. *The Gift : The Form and Reason for Exchange in Archaic Societies*. Trans. W. D. Halls. New York: W.W. Norton, 1990 [1924] .

Monty Python. "Every Sperm Is Sacred," from *Monty Python's The Meaning of Life*. Directed by Terry Jones and Terry Gilliam. Universal Studios, 1983.

Radin, Margaret. "Market Inalienability." *Harvard Law Review* 100, 8 (1987): 1849–1938.

The Paradox of Separation and Dependency: A Mother's Story

Jenny Jones

As I compose my thoughts for this paper a gentle breeze is wafting in through the French doors of my office in my home in Brisbane, Australia. It is early November and the heat of summer has not yet struck. The jacarandas are in bloom with a blaze of glorious mauve. Two of my three children are downstairs. I hear their chatter intermittently. Occasionally one or both of them will come and interrupt my thoughts with a request, for a chat, or perhaps seeking a little advice. Sounds idyllic, don't you think? Why then would you want to listen to my story?

Only a few years ago the idyllic scene described above was anything but idyllic. I am the married mother of three children: a son aged twenty-eight, another son, aged twenty-four and a daughter, aged twenty-one. The eldest has followed in his father's footsteps and has become an engineer in his professional life. The younger two are both university students—the older of these two recently returned to study after an interruption. I have watched them develop over the years. However, mixed in with this watching has been an essential tension— the tension of allowing them to grow and develop at their own rate but also tinged with sadness as each step seemed to be a step away from me. This tension remains with me today as I listen to the younger two having a bit of fun together over a game of billiards but knowing that the time of the blooming jacarandas also heralds the time of university exams. So while the introduction seems idyllic a tension still exists as I hear them playing instead of studying! Occasionally still, the scene in our family home is anything but idyllic. Like many other families we have our times of conflict. I would like to tell you about the disruption I, and my family, experienced as our children transitioned to young adulthood.

For some years now I have struggled with my responsibility and also my response-ability to assist our children in creating rich and meaningful lives. My sense of responsibility was closely linked with my felt obligation to carry out my duties for the care and nurturing of our children and was closely bound with my sense of being liable to be blamed if these duties were not carried out appropriately. These duties, I have identified, are consistent with what Sara Ruddick (1989) terms "maternal work"—that of "preservation, growth and social acceptability" (17). My sense of response-ability is bound with the sense of my ability to respond authentically to their needs without fear of reprisal or blame. However, I have also struggled with the responsibility and response-ability to create a rich and meaningful life for myself. Thus, I have found that my construction abilities have undergone a constriction.

The transition of our children to young adults became, for me, a time of confusing and painful change. I felt, during this time, that I was failing to move toward the good in my life, that of loving and caring for the significant others in my life. Hence, I began to experience disorientation through the interactions, and at times constricted interactions, with my family members. It now appears that this constriction is interwoven with the many voices that contribute to the practice of mothering. Through the telling of my story (expressing my voice as a mother, in a family, in a community) I seek to illuminate themes and tensions with and within the dominant narratives which others (mothers, but not only mothers) may, at times, have been exposed to. In telling my story, however, I am not merely telling about myself but also constituting who I was, who I am and who I am becoming as a mother of older children. Furthermore, I am contributing to the myriad conversations of mothers and about mothering.

Dominant Narratives

One of the dominant stories told within my white, Western, middle-class culture is the fairy tale. For generations this story has been told to both girls and boys. Despite feminist criticism, the basic structure of the fairy tale remains the same today as it did when I was a child in the 1950s. There is a damsel, supposedly in distress, in need of rescuing and a "knight in shining armor" who sweeps her off her feet. They receive much advice as they journey through life, particularly if they become parents. There is an expectation in the fairy tale that they will live happily ever after—it is even stated in many of them. However, these stories may constrict and constrain some voices. It was when I found that my voice in the fairy tale had become constricted and constrained that I began to suspect that the fairy tale may have beguiled me.

I sought to educate our children with a social and feminist consciousness. While being a privileged, white, middle-class family we were only too aware of the difficulties experienced by those less fortunate than ourselves. This education came from my own family background, which I openly spoke of with my children. I was born in 1954 into a large, Catholic, Australian family, the eighth child in a family of thirteen. My mother had experienced the death of her third child in the week following his birth and experienced further grief with the death of her eleventh child, a daughter, from an accident in the family home. At the time of this accident I was six years old, and many years later, like other family members, I felt that I had moved on and put the past behind me. I was, after much exploration, able to understand the degree to which grief is embedded in my life history and accept that I have carried this trauma with me like a shadow throughout my life (Davies 1999). Some may say that it was this unresolved grief that left me floundering as my children entered adulthood. I would argue that it was not only my particular grief that left me floundering as a mother but rather the dominant narratives of mother, motherhood, and mothering that have sought to stabilize, universalize and normalize the experience in a constricted way. I also contend that, living in a culture where independence and autonomy is heavily promoted and regarded, I did not understand or appreciate our embeddedness. I particularly did not recognize our sons' embeddedness in a masculine culture. Intimately interwoven with this embeddedness is the stance each of us brought and continues to bring to our interactions with the other.

Patriarchy

The patriarchal narrative appears to be a dominant theme throughout my life story. As a child, our family life was shaped around the home. My father worked in the public sphere and took his responsibilities as a breadwinner seriously even though he suffered severely from asthma.

My mother had been a stenographer before their marriage but gave up her employment upon marriage as was expected of a woman at the time. The view that education for females was not a priority became the dominant view for all their daughters, thus I left school at age sixteen and became a clerical assistant. From here I moved into nursing and became a registered nurse, a role I maintained until the birth of our second child until, like my mother before me, I became the primary carer of our children.

My embeddedness within a patriarchal family greatly influenced the direction my life would take as a mother. Within my married life, our roles as mother and father were learned from our family of origin. My husband is a loving, caring and supportive partner, a wonderful father, and a successful engineer. His role as engineer has proved to be a dominant feature in our lives. His employment has meant being relocated to various parts of the country, but these moves were not without much prior discussion between us. However, the dominant articulation in our culture, of man in the public and woman in the private, greatly influenced our decisions. My primary role was that of wife and mother, which carried with it the major responsibility for the welfare of our children. This role was first learned within my family of origin and further supported by our embeddedness in a patriarchal culture. However, in exploring my narrative it appears that we have incorporated, into our life narratives, a social and cultural construction that was formulated for a particular time frame, for a particular class or culture. In seeking a sense of belonging in white, middle-class, Australian culture it appears that I have reconciled my own life story with the dominant narrative and thus maintained the dominant social order.

Woman as Mother

The fixing of female identity to that of mother not only constricts and constrains her, but also leaves a mother vulnerable, particularly as she ages. The dominant stereotype of woman in the popular narratives is "woman as mother" in which a mother is seen as asexual, self-sacrificing, weak, dependent, and inarticulate in matters other than children. This stereotype, I contend, arises in patriarchal society from the physical, emotional, and mental burdens a mother of young children is expected to carry. The mothering of older children is rarely recognized or acknowledged. When it is, it is from a marginalized position. This marginalization is very well depicted by Sonya Hartnett (1995) in her award-winning Australian novel *Sleeping Dogs*, where the mother is marginalized and silenced by herself, as well as, others. I find that, as a mother of older children, I can no longer leave myself out of the conversation. I need to speak up; I need to bring to light tensions, both with and within the woman-as-mother narrative. A tension, I have found, is that this stereotype is in conflict with the lived reality of many women and mothers: constraining identity to a dominant and constrictive stereotype, restricted to a particular phase in a woman's life, within an oppressive power structure, leaves her unprepared for the future, thus constricting her be-ing and be-coming.

The woman-as-mother narrative, also contained within the patriarchal narrative, has also been incorporated into my own life narrative creating further tensions. My embodiment allowed me to give birth to the children my husband and I created. It was my "natural" nurturing ability that had set in motion my role as carer. Andrea O'Reilly (2004) asserts that the dominant stereotype of mother found within "normative discourse is white, middle class, able-bodied, thirty-something, heterosexual married woman who raises her biological children in a nuclear family, usually as a stay-at-home mother" (20). However, the dominance of the woman-as-mother narrative set me up for confusion when my embodiment no longer conformed to the dominant stereotype due to aging. Furthermore, my children no longer conformed to the dominant stereotype of child who was dependent on a mother for their "intellectual, social and emotional development" (Richardson 1993, 39). Perhaps, there is another tension here—that of dependency for "intellectual, social and emotional development" and "preserving, growing and training" (Porter 2000, 116).

The patriarchal and woman-as-mother narratives, I believe, contributed to my confusion and the disruption our family experienced. Through these narratives I reconciled my responsibilities as a mother with my response-abilities and provided my children with a safe, nurturing environment in which they could grow and orient themselves to the good in their life. While I had followed the standard characterization of mother with the dominant narratives, which designated responsibility for children's well being primarily to the mother, I found that as my children grew, my voice, and with that my authority as a mother, became constricted and constrained. I believe that my embodiment as a woman of short stature and our sons' embodiment as taller men, as well as, the web of interlocutors (Taylor 1989) of patriarchy with whom we dialogued, contributed to the disruption. I became excluded from offering them advice and guidance, thus my orientation to the good in my life—mothering—was constricted and constrained.

"The Expert Narrative"

Sheila Kitzinger (1978) claims that in preindustrial society, knowledge of mothering was "handed down from mother to daughter" but the move to an industrialized, educated society led women to seek this same information from books and the voice of "experts" (31). Catherine Doyle (2004) in her dissertation *The Grieving Self* asserts that with modernity and industrialization "our understandings and experiences began to pivot on distinctly modernist ideologies such as 'universalisation,' 'standardisation,' 'individualisation,' 'medicalisation' and 'commercialisation'" (30). This, I contend, has given birth to what I have termed "the–ization narrative." This narrative is one in which aspects of lived reality have been theorized, universalized, medicalized, pathologized, commercialized and, some would argue, normalized. It appears that the expert narrative is so intimately dependant on the –ization narrative that separation is near impossible. However, one must question the authority of these experts. It appears that much popular fiction in contemporary society is written by nonprofessionals, and those not directly embedded in the field. However, we do engage with popular literature in the form of books, magazines, and movies on an everyday level. Therefore, it must be asked if, in seeking advice, are we, in fact, surrendering authority?

One area where these narratives are found in increasing numbers is in the plethora of child-rearing books currently available. The focus of the majority of these books is on *what one ought to do as a mother* and have given birth to a new narrative in industrialized society—that of the "good" mother narrative. These narratives, according to Sharon Hays (1997), contain three distinct themes: (1) "children are sacred, innocent and pure, their value immeasurable" (288); (2) good child rearing requires "an intensive commitment on the part of the caregiver" (288); and (3) "childcare is primarily the responsibility of the individual mother" (288). These narratives have become hegemonic in our society for the narrative of mothering. However, the dominant narrative of child rearing is focused on the child as infant, thus the dominant recognition of mother in our society is that of mother of young children. Through this stereotype the voice of the mother of older children appears to be silenced. I believe that this may constrict the identity of a mother which, in turn, constricts and constrains her authority as a mother when the process of mothering older children requires change in the relationship. The constricted identity of mother to that of the good mother, determined by the mothering of young children, leaves a mother, her children and any others that are party to the relationship, vulnerable.

The expert narrative is also found in the narratives of developmental theory, in particular personal development books. Surrey (1991) asserts that developmental theory stresses the importance of separation through the developmental phases. However, she further asserts that this concept has arisen from "current assumptions about male (often generalised as human) development" (Surrey 1991, 52) and claims that the developmental process for females is different. She asserts that "for a woman a different—and relational—pathway is primary and continuous" (Surrey 1991, 52). So perhaps the first paradox of separation and dependency becomes evident. It appears that the autonomy narrative is so entwined, embedded, and perhaps, dependent on the patriarchal narrative that separation is, again, near impossible. Perhaps my further exploration will confirm this.

Autonomy

Throughout their lives I sought to guide our children into independent, responsible adulthood. This goal was closely linked, I believe, with the dominant narrative in our lives of autonomy and independence. This narrative appears to have become so entrenched in modern society that it appears to be a natural dimension of the human condition. However, on closer exploration it becomes obvious that it, too, is a social and cultural construction that first appeared in "Aristotle's discussion of 'voluntary action' in the *Nicomachean Ethics*" (Charlesworth 1993, 11). The autonomy narrative is one that proposes that "if I am to act in an ethical or moral way I must choose for myself what I am to do" (Charlesworth 1993, 10). The modern-day concept of autonomy is one which professes the right to self-determination, the right to choose for oneself, and take with it the responsibility for these choices and the right to control one's own life. In traditional societies, the concept of individualism is subordinated and, with that, the concept of choosing what one ought to do with an emphasis on one's obligations to others is acknowledged. In modern societies, this obligation to others appears to have been subordinated by the concept of one's own rights. However, it must be asked, whose rights?

Life appeared to progress blissfully until our children began to reach culturally determined adulthood. While being the primary caregiver I also had a public life. However, as stated earlier, no longer was I able to do my "maternal work" (Ruddick 1989, 17). I, as well as my significant others, was guided by the dominant cultural narratives that determine adulthood by age and that profess a need to cut the ties. Thus, I contend, my work of "preserving, growing and training" was disrupted. And so, chaos entered our lives. Where did it come from? I believe that the autonomy narrative professes a progression to adulthood according to the mainstream, or perhaps, normative pathway. This pathway, I now find, was, for us, in sight from the time our children were very young. We placed on them an expectation that they would progress from a good school education into university and from there into their chosen career and with that autonomy and independence. While we expected a few speed humps, at no time did we expect these humps to be complete roadblocks. These roadblocks were experienced by our children, by me, as their mother, and by their father and left us all directionless. It was only through hard work, both individually and collectively, that these roadblocks have been dismantled. We now find that we are, in fact, all on separate journeys, sometimes parallel, sometimes intertwined.

I also find that my embeddedness within my own mother's life may also have contributed to our vulnerability. While not apportioning blame to my mother, her experience of mothering has contributed to my own experience. This is consistent with Sheila Kitzinger's (1978) assertion that one's knowledge of mothering *is* found in relation to [m]other's knowledge. It is also consistent with Carol Shields's statement "I am my mother's daughter . . . and although it's been twenty years since I left home, her sayings form a perpetual long-playing record on my inner-ear turntable" (in *Mothers: A Loving Celebration*, 1997, 98). My mother was never a "bad" mother and, in fact, always sought to be a good mother. She sought to preserve, grow, and train her children to responsible adulthood. However, the tragic, accidental death of her daughter and its embedded grief, I believe, exposed her to "the gaze [and perhaps judgment] of others" (Ruddick 1989, 111) which, in turn, led her to engage more strongly with the good mother narratives. In turn, she encouraged her daughters "to be good mother[s] . . . giving herself to her children selflessly, providing them with concentrated attention, generous care, a lively mind quick to offer stimulus of an appropriate kind, perfectly balanced and delicious meals, unlimited time, and unstinted love—just as all the magazines and books say" (Kitzinger 1978, 43). However, in trying to live the ideals of good mothering, which, I have argued, are based on the mothering of young children, I was not prepared for the inevitable vulnerabilities in life that come with change.

The Paradox of Separation and Dependency

A common theme within the autonomy narrative, directed particularly to mothers, is the need to cut the cord. Christiane Northrup (2001, 81), for example, asserts that women need to cut the cord in order to return to an autonomous state. This is consistent with the breaking the bonds discourse within contemporary grief literature. However, if one accepts that "we live in relationships and relationships live in us" (Massey 2001, 14), cutting the cord is not as simple, desirable or necessary as cutting the umbilical cord at birth. Arguably, it is this cutting of the cord at birth that begins, for a mother, the paradox of separation and dependency. This paradox, I now find, further challenged my responsibility and response-ability as our children reached culturally determined adulthood and the deemed-as-essential time of separation.

The paradox appears to be a frequent theme in the narratives of women who have given their children up for adoption. Howe, Sawbridge, and Hinings (1992) assert that similar to the "stage theories of grief" the birth mother is encouraged to relinquish her emotional ties with her adopted child and "get on with her life" (74). The feelings the birth mother experiences are interwoven with her past, present, and future, as well as the management of her "spoiled" identity (Howe et al. 1992, 74). A further finding in their research shows that women who were supported by family and friends and allowed to talk of their "lost" child, adjusted better than those whose grief was restricted to an internal dialogue with themselves, a dialogue they found hard to interpret without the external referent point one needs in order to make meaning of their life (Taylor 1989). Thus, through articulation, their suffering was recognized and acknowledged. And so another tension, for me, becomes evident. While acknowledging that my children were not leaving my life completely, to me it felt like they had become the "living dead." The dominant narratives were telling me we needed to separate but my internal dialogue and feelings were that this was impossible and perhaps not the best option for our children. I spoke of feeling a sense of grief in that I felt that I was losing my children but rationally it did not make sense. Others could not understand my confusion and sense of grief and thus could not hear or understand me. As a mother, my life story became for me a "chaos narrative" (Frank, 115). The autonomy narrative, within which the breaking of the bonds and cutting the cord are dominant features, I believe, blinded me to my future relationship with them.

However, in viewing my story within the concept of living in relationships and relationships living in us (Massey 2001), perhaps, it was not only me who was thrown into a chaos narrative but also my family. In ruminating on this point I am unsure which came first—my chaos narrative or my family's chaos narrative. In fact, I am unsure if they can even be separated. I am also unsure when it began. Did it begin with the cutting of the umbilical cord? As stated earlier, this cutting signals the beginning of the paradox of separation and dependency. However, I do not believe that we lived in chaos. Rather, I believed that I, and my significant others, kept the chaos under control by conforming to the dominant narrative. In illuminating the tensions and ambiguities of these narratives, the question now arises—in living a life according to a constrictive narrative, perhaps, we are, in fact, limiting our possibilities of who we are at the present moment and who we might become, thus "leave[ing] us unprepared to cope with the losses that will inevitably occur in our lives" (Parkes 1986, 26). Furthermore, we may be left "unprepared to help others cope with the losses in theirs" (Parkes 1986, 26). Therefore, we may be ignoring the "cost of commitment" (Parkes 1986, 26). In particular, we may be ignoring the cost of commitment as mothers, and fathers.

It is only when I ponder from a distance that I am able to see that, instead of scripting our own life story through the living of our lives, our "life as led" is inseparable to our "life as told" (Bruner 1987, 31). However, in seeking to live our lives according to the dominant, and constrictive, narratives of autonomy and patriarchy, and in particular the good mother narratives, I feel that I have erred in my responsibility to my children. When chaos entered their lives I saw it but was prevented from guiding them through it. No one voice in particular caused this; rather it was the combination of many voices. However, the strongest voice appears to be embedded in the independence/autonomy/patriarchal narrative. Embedded within this voice is the belief that children, as they reach culturally determined adulthood, need to stand on their own two feet and thus cut the ties that bind. Thus, my own voice, and my ability to respond to them, was constricted. I also believe that I, as well as my significant others, erred in not allowing the concept of the chaos narrative to enter into our life narratives. In failing to know or speak it, we, as a family, did not see or hear the chaos enter our lives. Thus, we erred in our responsibility and response-ability to each other.

I have found that the perception of time as linear and sequential is one that is used to support the dominant narratives. Events and lives are seen as ordered, in much the same way as many stories are presented in an ordered form. As a mother, I have found that life is not necessarily ordered and sequential. Events happen that cause us disruptions. Somewhere along the way my voice became constricted and constrained. How it happened appears to be linked with narratives that have been constructed to support the fair and common ground. But is it really a fair and common ground? Is it a ground in which all voices have a space? Is it a ground that has been constructed in which mothers are seen as responsible and hence accountable and, perhaps, culpable for their children deviating from the set path as told?

I do not believe that it is a fair and common ground. I contend that it is a ground in which a monoglossic (Macy 2000) voice dominates. Thus, it was not only my voice that was constricted but also the voices of my significant others. Furthermore, I believe that it is a ground that has been constructed within the strict parameters of "remedy, progress, and professionalism" rather than one in which "vulnerability, futility, and impotence" are present (Frank 1995, 97). The lack of acknowledgment of these aspects of human frailty, I believe, has caused my family and I further suffering. By adhering to the dominant narrative I have suffered through the constriction of my voice within my family and community, not only in the capacity of mother offering advice and guidance but also in my capacity to understand who I was and who I was to become as a mother of older children. My family has suffered by having their need to be mothered constricted. However, it now appears to me that the ties that bind a mother and her child are too great to be simply cut like an umbilical cord. I would contend that this is because, for a mother, the creation of her child within her body becomes part of the ontological dimension of her selfhood and is, therefore, enduring rather than ephemeral.

I have stated that I have struggled to create a rich and meaningful life for myself. This struggle arose, I believe, because a meaningful life is seen as one in which life is seen as a progressive series of events. I contend, however, that a meaningful life is one in which chaos is recognized and valued. It is only then that disruptions such as the transition from one phase of life to another are not seen as something to be conquered through separation. Rather, what is called for is a differentiation of selves as separate individuals, but individuals who live in relationships. I now find that, like many mothers of color, lesbian mothers, stepmothers, and mothers of disabled children my mothering is in the margins. Perhaps it was always this way. Perhaps I just didn't see that the dominant narratives of mothering that are embedded in a "patriarchal, expectations-generating power system" that determine who can mother and how a mother ought to mother marginalize all mothers (Nelson 2001, 136). It is for this reason that I have shared my story with you. Perhaps other mothers of older children have also experienced the paradox of separation and dependency. Perhaps, also, mothers of younger children, also, experience the paradox. By sharing my story I have sought to refuse, repudiate, and contest the dominant narratives (Nelson 2001). I contend that through the recognition of diaological selves (Taylor 1989), as individuals who live in relationships, a mother's ability to flourish would be enriched. Furthermore, others' ability to flourish would also be enhanced. Thus more enchanting stories could be told.

Works Cited

Bruner, J. "Life as Narrative." *Social Research* 54, 1 (1987): 11–32.

Charlesworth, M. *Bioethics in a Liberal Society.* Cambridge: Cambridge University Press, 1993.

Davies, B. *Shadows in the Sun: The Experience of Sibling Bereavement in Childhood.* Philadelphia: Brunner/Mazel (Taylor Francis Group), 1999.

Doyle, C. *The Grieving Self.* Queensland University of Technology, School of Humanities and Human Services. Honors Dissertation, 2004.

Frank, A. *The Wounded Storyteller: Body, Illness and Ethics.* Chicago: University of Chicago Press, 1995.

Hartnett, S. *Sleeping Dogs.* Ringwood, Victoria: Penguin Books, 1995.

Hays, S. "The Ideology of Intensive Mothering: A Cultural Analysis of the Bestselling 'Gurus' of Appropriate Childrearing." In *From Sociology to Cultural Studies: New Perspective.* Edited by E. Long. Malden: Blackwell, 1997. 286–321.

Howe, D., P. Sawbridge, and D. Hinings. *Half a Million Women: Mothers Who Lose Their Children By Adoption*. London: Penguin Books, 1992.

Kitzinger, S. *Women as Mothers*. United Kingdom: Fontana Books, 1978.

Macy, D. *The Penguin Dictionary of Critical Theory*. London: Penguin Books, 2000.

Massey, D. "Identity pragmatics." A paper originally presented at the colloquium *Applied Ethics: Challenges and Explorations*. Carseldine campus, Queensland University of Technology, June 1–2, 2001.

Nelson, H. L. *Damaged Identities: Narrative Repair*. London: Cornell University Press, 2001.

Northrup, C. *The Wisdom of Menopause: The Complete Guide to Creating Physical and Emotional Health and Healing*. London: Paitkus, 2001.

O'Reilly, A. *Mother Matters: Motherhood as Discourse and Practice*. Toronto: Association for Research on Mothering, 2004.

Parkes, C. M. *Bereavement: Studies of Grief in Adult Life*. London: Penguin, 1986.

Porter, M. "A Mother, Two Sons, Then Another." *Journal of the Association for Research on Mothering* 2, 1 (Spring/Summer 2000).

Richardson, D. *Women, Motherhood and Childrearing*. Hampshire: MacMillan, 1993.

Ruddick, S. *Maternal Thinking: Towards a Politics of Peace*. London: Women's Press, 1989.

Shields, C. *Mothers: A Loving Celebration*. Philadelphia: Courage Books, 1997.

Surrey, J. "The Self-in-Relation: A Theory of Women's Development." In *Women's Growth in Connection: Writings from the Stone Center*. Edited by J. Jordan et al. New York: Guilford Press, 1991. 51–66.

Taylor, C. *Sources of the Self: The Making of the Modern Identity*. Cambridge: Cambridge University Press, 1989.

"My Mum's a Dyke":
Maternal Subjectivities in Midlife Transition from a Heterosexual to a Lesbian Identity

Susan Kentlyn

A LESBIAN IS NOT A WOMAN, SAYS MONIQUE WITTIG (1992, 20), either economically, politically, or ideologically, because what makes a woman is a specific social relation to a man. Historically, however, what has defined a woman is the capacity to give birth (Wittig 1992, 10). So the mother who transitions from a heterosexual to a lesbian identity stands on the fault lines of gender and sexuality, a challenge both to the compulsory heterosexuality of the hetero-normative world, and to the identity politics of the homosexual world. She embodies the incoherencies and inconsistencies of sex, gender, and desire, and models for her children, and her networks of family, friends, and colleagues, the dangers and delights inherent in the process of self-formation, the self-conscious demolishing and reconstruction of identity.

Challenging the assumption that most women are innately heterosexual, Adrienne Rich has argued that, for women, heterosexuality may not be a "preference" at all but something that has had to be imposed, managed, organized, propagandized, and maintained by force (2003, 26, 27). In her landmark article, "Compulsory Heterosexuality and Lesbian Existence," Rich documents the "cluster of forces within which women have been convinced that marriage and sexual orientation toward men are inevitable—even if unsatisfying or oppressive—components of their lives" (2003, 20). These forces range from literal physical enslavement to the ideology of heterosexual romance beamed at them from childhood out of fairy tales, television, films, advertising, popular songs, and wedding pageantry (24). For women who have been subjected to this programming all their lives, who have partnered with men and had children, the transition to a lesbian identity in midlife can be likened to a seismic shift of truly epic proportions (Kitzinger and Wilkinson 1995, 100–101).

In their 1995 article, "Transitions from Heterosexuality to Lesbianism: The Discursive Production of Lesbian Identities," Kitzinger and Wilkinson interviewed eighty women with at least ten years prior heterosexual experience who transitioned to a lesbian identity. Noting that most women who self-identify as lesbian do so only after an earlier period in their lives during which they have identified as heterosexual, they were concerned by the prevalence of essentialist models of sexuality, and believed these women's accounts would cogently illustrate a social constructionist understanding of identity development (95, 96). The transition was experienced by all the women as a very dramatic change, and their accounts demonstrated common themes: dislocation from the past, the experience of autobiographical rupture, and an apparent need for total self-reconstruction (100, 101). As I reflected on this process as I experienced it, I found it to be as momentous and life-changing as my earlier experience of an earthquake in the Philippines. Here I will draw on my own experience and the earthquake analogy, as well as published accounts to explore some of the issues involved in midlife transition from heterosexuality to lesbianism for women who are mothers.

Tremors and Cracks

Buildings in an earthquake zone, which is prone to many tremors, are likely to manifest cracks as they encounter continual challenges to their structural integrity. I wonder how many women have suffered cracks to the structural integrity of their heterosexual identity without really addressing the issue? In 2001–2002, an Australian study of health and relationships was conducted (Smith et al. 2003, 139); telephone interviews were completed by a representative sample of over 9,000 women aged sixteen to fifty-nine years from all States and Territories in Australia. Respondents were asked about their sexual identity, but also about their sexual attraction and sexual experience. In terms of identity, 0.8 percent of women saw themselves as lesbians, while 1.4 percent identified as bisexual. However, only 84.9 percent of women indicated they were exclusively heterosexual in terms of both attraction and lifetime experience (140–144). That means 15.1 percent—something like one and a half million Australian women—have felt attracted to women or have had sexual experience with women, or both. Only 31 percent of women who reported both same-sex attraction and same-sex experience identified as lesbian or bisexual. These data suggest that it is possible that a lot of the other women are living in heterosexual relationships, and are papering over the cracks. Whether a woman's heterosexual identity has been gradually eroded over the years, or comes crashing down in a major seismic event, what happens when the time comes when this identity is no longer habitable? Well, first the rubble must be dealt with.

Clearing the Rubble

In an earthquake, heavy earthmoving machinery cannot be used—the rubble must be sifted through by hand, piece by piece, in an effort to preserve life and salvage whatever of value is left. Before constructing a new lesbian identity to inhabit, a mother may have to deal with various kinds of "rubble" from her previous mode of existence—disturbed family relationships, discarded religious beliefs, disrupted ideals of motherhood.

If the woman is a mother, her transition will probably affect the whole of her immediate family—partner and children. Dorothy McRae-McMahon was a Uniting Church minister, pastor of a large Sydney congregation, when she was grappling with this issue:

> So, with a trembling heart and an agony of soul and mind, I acted. In claiming my truth I was going to hurt other people, and they were people I loved who had done nothing to deserve this pain. It was the hardest thing I had ever done. I felt as though I was walking over a cliff and would die at the bottom and carry my loved ones with me. With the loving care of others around us and, I believe, a God who grieved with us, we all survived. I have no doubt that everyone concerned will always carry the wounds of that moment. I also have no doubt that in the awesome and awful complexity of life, if I had my life over again, I would still do the same thing. (1998, 91)

A male partner/spouse can be devastated—he may feel that his inadequacy or failure as a man and a partner may have turned his wife off men completely, or he may be enraged by what he sees as the ultimate betrayal (Kitzinger and Wilkinson 1995, 101). Before I came out, my ex-husband and I had been separated some months, but he has not spoken to me since. When our daughter graduated from high school, he sat at the back of the auditorium, and sent one of her friends over to us with his gift because he didn't want to see my girlfriend and me. I am glad to say that he has since remarried with someone who I am sure makes him far happier than I ever could, but it is an ongoing cause of sadness that I have no contact with the father of my children.

Children also may experience tremendous grief over the loss of the intact family. McRae-McMahon says, "I saw us all lay down a hope of a future with one mother and father at the centre of Christmas gatherings with our children and grandchildren" (92). This may be a delayed reaction. My kids were both incredibly supportive and affirming when the marriage first ended. It was only after about three years, particularly trying to manage the three-way split every Christmas (her partner's family, her dad, and me) that my daughter began to realize the extent of her grief and resentment. Then again, some kids can be extremely hostile to their mother's new sexual orientation from the start.

Divorce and family breakdown are always painful, often bitter, and are longlasting in their effects, even in heterosexual families. However, when a woman transitions from a heterosexual to a lesbian identity, her male partner, children, friends, and the wider society may blame the transition for the breakup of the family, even if it came later, or was not the major factor, with the added load of guilt and resentment that may entail.

The multifarious terrors and triumphs of "coming out" have been documented elsewhere (e.g., Kitzinger and Wilkinson 1995; Rich 2003). Here I offer the briefest of summaries. A woman coming out in midlife must contend with the reactions of family, friends, workplace, schoolteachers, their own children's friends, those children's parents, service providers, sales assistants, government agencies, people in the street—the list goes on and on. However, a mother will not only have to worry about the homophobia she herself may experience, she will also have to worry about what her kids may experience. When a mother comes out, she automatically "outs" her kids. Some will not thank her for that. Other Australian research (Flood and Hamilton 10, 11), conducted in 2005 has shown that schools are the most ferociously homophobic environments in our country, with fourteen-to seventeen-year-old boys being the most homophobic section of the population after men over fifty. Females are generally considerably less homophobic than males; 43 percent of men were found to believe that homosexuality is immoral compared to only 27 percent of women, even less in that fourteen to seventeen age group (10). So girls can be quite supportive. One woman's seventeen-year-old son happily reported that when he tells the girls at school, "My mum's a dyke," they say, "That is *so* cool!" and immediately seem to find him more interesting.

Another piece of rubble that may have to be dealt with is religious faith. The public pronouncements of nearly all the Christian denominations, and a large number of other faith traditions as well, are mostly hostile or at best unsympathetic to homosexuality.[1] This may be a big factor in shaping the attitudes of a woman's children to her new sexuality. If she is a person of faith, this may also have profound implications for an ongoing relationship with her faith community—the woman and her family may be rejected and ostracised, or find themselves in conflict with the group's hierarchies and people. McRae-McMahon's property was vandalized, she received death threats, and she eventually had to resign her ministry (80–81; 98–114). It is not unusual for gay and lesbian Christians to live in agonising fear of being consigned to hell because of their sexuality. In his autobiography, Anthony Venn-Brown (2004), an Assemblies of God evangelist for twenty-two years, reveals the torment and guilt he experienced as he tried to get deliverance from his homosexuality, including very destructive experiences with so-called reparative therapies, and suicide attempts.

However, there is also a quasireligious dimension to motherhood, perhaps best exemplified by the Virgin Mary, but present even in religious traditions that do not venerate Mary directly. This is the image, both of the virgin mother, and of the suffering mother (Daly 1973, 81–84). The virgin mother is asexual. It is commonly accepted that parents have difficulty dealing with their children becoming sexually active, but perhaps children have even greater difficulty in coming to grips with the idea that their parents, especially their mothers, are sexual beings. If there are two kids in the family then mum and dad did it twice, and that was so long ago it can be safely ignored. What are they to make of it when, for example, mum suddenly starts picking up women in gay bars or lesbian dances, brings them home, and has sex with them in the next room?

Mothers in our culture are also meant to be all-giving, all-sacrificing, all-nurturing, and selfless. Rich says, "Institutionalized motherhood demands of women maternal 'instinct' rather than intelligence, selflessness rather than self-realization, relation to others rather than the creation of self" (1986, 42). They are, above all, supposed to put their partners and children ahead of themselves. This creates some very real problems for mothers trying to explore their sexuality. Some will not even contemplate a relationship unless all their children approve of both their sexual orientation and the potential partner or until their children have grown up and left home. It could be argued that the successful integration of the lesbian and maternal subjectivities of any woman may depend largely on how comfortable her kids are with her sexuality.

(Re)constructing Identity/ies

Having cleared the rubble of her collapsed heterosexual identity, the woman then embarks on the process of constructing a new lesbian identity. What does she have to work with?

First, the possibility of a transformed subjectivity, a whole different sense of agency. Rather than being a desired (or not!) object, the woman can be the desiring subject. A gender theory analysis of heterosexuality generally asserts that erotic agency and sexual subject-status are characteristically masculine, while to be normatively feminine is to exhibit erotic passivity and sexual object-status (Wilton 2004, 64). My daughter is a confident, outgoing young woman, but many's the time we waited in agonized fashion to see if some boy she met on Saturday night was going to phone. I love that I can ask a woman for her phone number, ask her out to dinner, send her flowers, seduce her. Wilton's lesbian research participants describe taking scopophilic pleasure in looking at women, their experience of a proactive, agentic desire for and eroticization of women's bodies, and their ability to recognize, acknowledge, and act on their feelings of sexual attraction (68–73). Some women, however, find all this too terrifying for words, and in my own research (Kentlyn 2006) I've heard bittersweet stories of women who've known each other and secretly been in love with each other for years, before one of them got up the courage to say anything. Whether to a greater or lesser degree, however, constructing a lesbian identity will involve a woman engaging with gender and sexuality, and most especially desire, in ways that may be quite different to those of her children. This may be challenging, liberating, disturbing, or even distressing to them.

A woman may also find herself catapulted from mainstream Australia into membership of a whole new community—the GLBTTIQ community (gay, lesbian, bisexual, transgender, transsexual, intersex, queer)—fondly (if ironically) known as the Alphabet Soup. This was brought home to me forcibly one day as I was sitting in a café with a friend. She is a postoperative male-to-female transsexual (M2F) and after telling me all about her fabulous new clitoris, we moved on to a discussion of sexual practices in ancient Greece—one knows, of course, that a male citizen could not be penetrated, only slaves or foreigners could be—and I had a sudden disconcerting vision of the pastor's wife I used to be auditing this conversation with horrified bemusement.

This aspect of a mother's new lesbian identity can be bewildering for her children. Perhaps counterintuitively, a lot of young people are quite sexually conservative, and can find casual discussion of BDSM (bondage discipline sadism masochism) or beats or porn or reconstructive genital surgery somewhat confronting. Furthermore, their mother's membership in this community is something they may feel they cannot share. They may envy her involvement in what seems such a close-knit group, from which they may feel excluded by virtue of *their* sexuality. My daughter was incensed to learn there was a choir she couldn't join because she's straight. There are also alternative forms of family to deal with. A woman I partnered with for a while was interested in having a child, and we asked my son how he would feel about being the sperm donor. This would make me both the child's co-parent, and grandmother, and my son would be its biological father, and step-half-brother. He thought it was a great idea; my daughter could not have been more appalled. Though this may be an extreme example, there are many nontraditional family forms to be found in the GLBTTIQ community, including open relationships, polyamory, co-parenting agreements involving children being conceived from donor sperm, to name just a few. Whilst all of these are to be found in the heterosexual community also, I have encountered more since coming out than I did in all the years before that. Furthermore, in the GLBTTIQ community, there is generally a more self-conscious engagement with the process of relationship formation and choice about its form, than in the straight community where the monogamous couple seems to remain the unchallenged default option.

Which raises the issue of what blueprint a woman will use to construct her new domestic partnerships? Some women may build very much along the same lines as their previous relationship, saving only the gender of their partner. A monogamous relationship, perhaps a commitment ceremony with all the trappings of a wedding, a house in the suburbs, the normal problems faced by any blended family. My first relationship looked a lot like that. The kids loved my partner, whom they fondly called the Evil Stepmother, and my son even said that he thought it was easier for him that I'd partnered with a woman, because he could still be the man of the house. Some lesbian couples may even embrace heterogenderal patterns, known as butch and femme, although this was more common among working class and young lesbians of the 1950s and '60s (Faderman 1991, 167–74). However, my current research on domestic labor in same-sex households (Kentlyn 2006) reveals universal rejection of traditional gender roles, with a strong commitment to egalitarianism and chore selection based on personal preference and efficiency considerations.

In fact, one benefit a later-life transition and the need to construct a lesbian identity does confer is the subversive and liberatory potential to question, deconstruct, and negotiate the way we do gender and sexuality. So to continue the earthquake analogy, instead of constructing a new identity like a building to inhabit in place of the one that has collapsed, a woman could actually make for herself something like a Bedouin tent. This may be minimal or completely luxurious, but the important thing is that it's mobile and flexible. Extra rooms can be added to make space for extra people in her life, or taken off when no longer needed. And any day she can pack the lot up, load it on her camel (figuratively speaking), and take it someplace else.

This is where I see a role for Queer Theory. Arising out of the work of Judith Butler and Teresa de Lauretis in the early 1990s, Queer Theory developed out of a specifically lesbian and gay reworking of the poststructuralist understanding of identity as a constellation of multiple and unstable positions (Jagose 1996, 3, 72–100). It explores the incoherencies in the supposedly stable relations between chromosomal sex, gender, and sexual desire that have traditionally constituted heterosexuality, so that sexuality is seen as always in process and fluid both in direction and content of desire (Jagose 1996, 3; Sheridan 1998, 294). All of this has implications for a person's understanding of their own gender, the gender of the person to whom they feel attracted or with whom they partner sexually, their sexual practices, and the stability or durability of these identities and practices. Wilton posits what she calls the "necessary project of self-fashioning," which requires that every person constitute themselves as sexed and gendered and sexual; however, some individuals are forced to interrogate hegemonic discourses of gender and sexuality in relation to this process of self-fashioning (2004, 58). Mothers making a transition from a heterosexual to a lesbian identity are forced to self-consciously engage with this project, and in fact model this process for their children as well as their networks of family, friends, and colleagues.

Queer Theory provides a mobile and flexible structure within which mothers and their kids can experiment, even play, with their developing understanding of their gendered and sexual identities. Perhaps even more importantly, it can also make room for each other's change and growth. Because Queer Thoery problematizes all forms of the erotic, it forces heterosexuality out of its invisible position of privilege and requires it to give an account of itself (Wilton 2004, 153). This gives children the conceptual tools to interrogate and manipulate their own process of self-fashioning, as well as that of the people around them. Rigid constructions of gender and sexuality are likely to collapse under the seismic challenges of postmodernity, but Queer Theory provides a livable alternative for mothers and their children to inhabit.

I have attempted to show how, in transitioning to a lesbian identity in midlife, women with children may experience something like a seismic shock that renders their heterosexual identity uninhabitable, with all the fear, grief, and pain this entails. Before constructing a new lesbian identity, they may have to sort through the rubble of their old identity, dealing with the damage to their families, and the hazards for their children as well as themselves in coming out. Quasireligious concepts around motherhood may have to be cleared away before the mother can embrace her new sexuality and prioritize her own needs. In facing the challenge of constructing a new identity, the mother and her children may find that Queer Theory, with its understanding that identity is flexible, unstable, and continually negotiated, may provide the kind of structure where all understand that they are continually changing and growing. If mother and children can love and support each other through that process, it can be a unique opportunity that will transform their subjectivities for the rest of their lives.

Notes

1. Religious groups vary markedly in their attitudes toward homosexuality, and official policies may distinguish between a homosexual orientation and homosexual

practice, as well as having differing standards for laypeople and clergy. It is also important to note that people who practice a religion may or may not be in sympathy with its official policy on homosexuality. For an overview of the official policies of Christian groups, see: http://en.wikipedia.org/wik/List_of_Christian_denominational_positions_on_homosexuality. For a wide range of other religious groups, see: http://en.wikipedia.org/wiki/Religion_and_sexual_orientation

Works Cited

Daly, M. *Beyond God the Father: Towards a Philosophy of Women's Liberation.* London: Women's Press, 1973.

Faderman, L. *Odd Girls and Twilight Lovers: A History of Lesbian Life in Twentieth-Century America.* New York: Penguin, 1991.

Flood, M., and C. Hamilton. "Mapping Homophobia in Australia." *http://www.tai.org.au.* (2005): 1–15.

Jagose, A. *Queer Theory.* Melbourne: Melbourne University Press, 1996.

Kentlyn, S. " 'Who gets to clean the toilet?': Domestic Labour in Same-Sex Households." Unpublished thesis in Social Sciences, University of Queensland, Brisbane, 2006.

Kitzinger, C., and S. Wilkinson. "Transitions From Heterosexuality to Lesbianism: The Discursive Production of Lesbian Identities." *Developmental Psychology* 31, 1 (1995): 95–104.

McRae-McMahon, D. *Everyday Passions: A Conversation on Living.* Sydney: ABC Books, 1998.

Rich, A. "Compulsory Heterosexuality and Lesbian Existence (1980)." *Journal of Women's History* 15, 3 (Autumn, 2003): 11–48.

———. *Of Woman Born: Motherhood as Experience and Institution.* New York: W. W. Norton & Co., 1986.

Sheridan, S. "Sexuality and Representation." In *Oxford Australian Feminism: A Companion.* Edited by B. Caine. Melbourne: Oxford University Press, 1998. 286–95.

Smith, A. M. A., C. E. Rissel, J. Richters, A. E. Grulich, and R. O. de Visser. "Sexual Identity, Sexual Attraction and Sexual Experience Among a Representative Sample of Adults." *Australian and New Zealand Journal of Public Health* 27, 2 (2003): 138–45.

Venn-Brown, A. *A Life of Unlearning. Coming Out of the Church: One Man's Struggle.* Sydney: New Holland, 2004.

Wilton, T. *Sexual (Dis) Orientation: Gender, Sex, Desire and Self-Fashioning.* New York: Palgrave Macmillan, 2004.

Wittig, M. "One Is Not Born a Woman." In *The Straight Mind and Other Essays.* Boston: Beacon Press, 1992. 9–20.

The Maternal Autobiography in Performance

Beth Osnes

Introduction

Sitting on a stool facing the audience I start the show with these words.

> I think the mother perspective is a valuable one. And I think it's really different than the dominant perspective in our world today. I feel like a miner. Like I want to dig down deep into the mounds of diapers, wive's tales, errands, dishes, and silence, all that stuff, to discover that thick vein of mother wisdom deep in the earth. I want to carve off a big chunk and carry it up top into the light of day where it can be seen for its extraordinary value. As they say in mining, I want to hit the mother lode.

The name of this one-woman show is *The Mother Load* and a journal-writing form of autobiography is both the content and the structure for the show such that my mother trials and tribulations are the subjects of my own discourse. The script is comprised of eight different stories based on a series of real-life incidents in support of a unifying theme; mothering. This show portrays the personal autobiography played out in public complete with social and political clashes and awakenings. My incentive is to reclaim the portrayal of mothers in performance from a long history of predominantly male playwrights and actors and assert a renegade politicized mother voice that has a sense of humor, struggles with doubt, grows in awareness, and ultimately contributes an alternative view of our world through a mother's eyes.

Contemporary Feminist Theater on Motherhood

Examples of feminist theater directly focused on mothering from the last few decades attest to just how tumultuous the topic of mothering has been on the stage and highlight the differing views within feminism itself. What follows are just a few examples to demonstrate the experience of this type of theater from the perspective of the audience and its creators. In 1987 Martha Boesing, founder of At the Foot of the Mountain in Minneapolis, presented *The Story of a Mother II* at a conference for the Women and Theatre Program in Chicago. The piece was collaboratively produced based on improvisational work centered on the feelings evoked in the actors in response to the idea of motherhood, around which the play was organized (Greeley, 52) After a weaving of stories and narratives, the performance culminated in a final ritual in which the audience was to reenter the body of their mothers. Many in the audience, including feminist scholars Jill Dolan and Sue-Ellen Case, found this expected audience participation to be coercive and to allow for only one acceptable reaction which was to be positive. As Case stated, "I thought that the generalized technique of going into the mother's body overlooked differences between mothers, social class differences, and other differences that might not be positive" (Greeley, 59). This example highlights the differing views of Boesing, who is considered to be a cultural feminist, and Dolan and Case, who are materialist feminists.

When the Magdalena Symposium in 1995 focused a theatrical project on motherhood, they attracted very little interest and few participants. "The pressure on women to 'appear' to be without children is particularly acute—especially for women working in professional theatre in this country (Aston, 178). As Jill Greenhalgh, who is a mother and artistic director of the Magdalena Project, stated, "it almost feels as though we are being treacherous to our work by even giving space to speak about children within an artistic context . . . we felt it seemingly impossible to discuss the difficulties of being a working mother without appearing to join the backlash against feminism" (179). This example pays testimony to the hesitancy of some feminist performers to take on the subject of mothering in performance.

In the arena of performance art, which is often more closely allied with fine art and dance than theater, a healthy dose of humor seemed to propel Bobby Baker along in her performance entitled *Drawing on a Mother's Experience*, created in the U.K. in 1988. In a comically self-deprecating fashion, Baker set out to do a drawing of her last several years of being a mother, which she created on a plastic sheet laid out on the floor. Being careful to be tidy amid the mess her performance created while voicing her concern of being considered artistically sophisticated enough for her audience, she portrayed the private doubts a mother may feel in presenting her experience publicly. The ironic self-presentation and the comedy generated by her seemingly spontaneous commentary all contributed to a vivid demonstration of the public performance of "mother" from her own experience.

Born from a long line of itinerant players in Italy, Franca Rame has been creating politically charged theater for over fifty years with her husband, Nobel laureate Dario Fo. In 1977, Rame and Fo developed a one-woman show for her entitled *Tutta casa, letto e chiesa [All Home, Bed and Church]*, which addressed the contemporary feminist debates on motherhood, birth control, premarital sex and abortion. As an activist and performer, she began deconstructing the Italian idea of "mother" and "woman" to reveal the social constraints and societal expectations that contribute to the oppression of disadvantaged women and mothers. As a performer, she employed her family's style of commedia antics that kept her audiences rolling with laughter—the sugar to help the medicine go down, perhaps.

The general trend in feminist theater on mothering seems to have moved beyond theatrical explorations that tended to idealize a certain aspect of the experience, such as the mother-daughter relationship in *The Daughter's Cycle Trilogy* in 1977–1980, to performances that acknowledge the different ways in which mothering is experienced by different cultures, socioeconomic groups, and by mothers of varying sexual orientation. As Greenhalgh stated, "Thinking about Dolan's critique (of *The Daughter's Cycle Trilogy*) helped to focus on the possibility of the 'mother-daughter relationship' not as 'a device for establishing ... commonality and smoothing over the differences between women,' but for exploring difference and diversity of individual experience within a collective" (179). Though some performances are overtly political, like Rame's, each of these is political in its implications. "According to materialist feminist performance theory, placing a woman in representation—the site for the production of meaning in theater—is always a political act. Female bodies inscribed in the representational frame offered by the proscenium arch, and the frame created simply by the act of gazing through gender and ideology, bear meaning with political implications" (Dolan 1993, 48).

Goal of *The Mother Load* Performance

In my work as cofounder of Mothers Acting Up, a grassroots movement to mobilize the gigantic political strength of mother to advocate for the world's children, I repeatedly witness mothers' trepidation with being public, visible and using their voice in the political arena. I realize how personal these negotiations are and how inner boundaries determine how far into the public domain most mothers dare travel. It has become increasing clear to me that it is not lack of concern for the world's children, or ignorance as to how to be political (as that is easy enough to convey) that keeps many women from being involved, but, rather, an internal hesitation and a reticence deep within that is unsure, afraid, and stubborn. To invite more mothers into the political process, I saw the need to begin by addressing those very personal obstacles. To gain entry in that intimate realm through my performance, I arrived, ultimately vulnerable, with no theatrical affect, tricks, or trappings, exposed my own foibles, doubts, and fears, and beckoned their stories to commingle with mine. My goal in sharing my own stories is to bear witness to the internal struggles many mothers go through when negotiating how to live in relationship with the public world. I want to model bringing these concerns and fears out into the light of day to be shared, admitted, and transformed to begin the process of resolving them. I want to spark a conversation among mothers with my performance. As the last line of the show beckons, "Talk about it!"

The role of mother is one, like gender, that a female learns throughout the course of her entire life through both passive and purposeful cues and modeling. The way in which the role of mother is presented in performance and the media creates expectations against which actual mothers are measured by society and themselves. As Evelyn Nakano Glenn states, "a particular definition of mothering has so dominated popular media representations, academic discourse, and political and legal doctrine that the existence of alternative beliefs and practices among racial, ethnic, and sexual minority communities as well as non-middle-class segments of society has gone unnoticed" (2004, 2). Divergent behavior among even the white middle class is ignored and, thereby, inadvertently discouraged. Any public performance of a mother affects actual mothers significantly, especially mothers who do not conform to the idealized representation congratulated by society. If the mother in performance strays from society's notion of acceptable behavior and suffers because of that, then the status quo is strengthened and all mothers witnessing the performance are duly warned to conform. If the mother in performance strays from society's notion of acceptable behavior and, in doing so, maps out a new terrain for herself in which she can, despite obstacles and hardship, fulfill her role as mother in a manner true to her individuality, then very real possibilities are born and nonconformity is encouraged. When traveling into new behavior possibilities, theatre begins to resemble mapmaking and becomes an actual, viable tool for its audience to find their way through this uncharted territory. Viewers benefit from witnessing another like themselves navigate through difficult territory and obstacles to the desired destination.

Performance can be a powerful tool for normalizing and making familiar different interpretations of the role of mother. In my performance of *The Mother Load*, the audience identifies me as an attractive woman with a generous nature. When I integrate an overtly political agenda, the very notion of a politicized mother is softened by the association and made more acceptable and less threatening or other. I am mindful of this reality and, without apology, use this to further my ultimate goal of engaging mothers in the political process. Indeed, I am combating a very limited, mediatized stereotype of the political woman as angry, overbearing, unattractive, and confrontational. The propagation of this portrayal of the politicized woman is a major obstacle for mothers to engage in political activity.

A Mother-Methodology for Creating Autobiographical Performance

The usual creation of a theatrical performance is steeped in a hierarchical, male-dominated tradition. Traditionally in twentieth-century Western theater there is a director who has ultimate artistic control; the words of a playwright, which are treated as unalterable law; designers who support and bring out the director's vision; and finally, the actors who enact the director's vision through the playwright's words in a space created by the designers. When viewed from this perspective, the structure of our Western theater greatly resembles the larger societal structures that have systematically oppressed women throughout the ages. Therefore, in order to assert a renegade voice through a theatrical performance that is taking this very structure to task, a new methodology, suited to that voice, is advantageous if not necessary. Amid an infinite number of ways to create theater outside the dominant model, I offer one method that I employed when creating *The Mother Load* to demonstrate the contrast needed to ensure the conveyance of the subversive voice. Before my efforts, many brave women have contributed their writing, voices, and physical performances, which have all helped to pave the way. Beyond this model, there is an open expanse of possibilities waiting to be explored by women and mothers from every land, tradition, culture, and faith.

The Script

In the creating of the script, I sought to present an unadulterated, authentic mother voice. For me, journal writing was a natural source from which to draw such material since it is my most uncensoring confidant, one to whom I have turned consistently since I was ten years old. I did not seek outside advice or input on the creation of the script since I wanted to create it in an intimate place of isolation, trusting in my own experience and ability to be effectively expressive. For me, an actor emerging into the performing space as mother, the autobiographical style was the only choice I entertained. Without question, it seemed the only sure footing upon which I could take a first step out into public discourse. Though I have written, directed and performed many of my own solo theater performances previously, I have never done one so overtly autobiographical or theatrically bare. My mother-voice is relatively new and untested. It couldn't risk slipping into a pre-existing notion of what my voice should be or what a performance of that voice should resemble.

As I worked with the writing, the script became eight different stories based around a series of real-life incidents, and though they all dealt with mothering, the pieces were quite diverse. A description of some of the more overtly political pieces gives a glimpse into how they were written. *At the Protest for Charlton Heston (also titled: Ben Hur, Done That)* deals with the issue of gun control and my questioning on how to hand down my beliefs on this issue, among others, to my children. The following passage is spoken after taking my kids to a gun control rally outside a theater where Charlton Heston was speaking.

> So what about this? Are we to be disimpassioned presenters, fairly elucidating each view and position? My God, our children would end up with as much passion as Wonder Bread. So then, do we simply couch everything in "this is what we believe, but not everyone sees it this way." Which works well when talking about Hindus, "Well, kids, we see God as an old guy with a beard but the Hindus see God as a buff destroyer with a trident," but works worse when discussing a pro-gun protestor who is standing four yards away screaming, I mean really

screaming "WE WILL NOT DISARM!" Then I can't help but say, "Look kids, there's a raving lunatic, the last person on earth I would want to entrust with a weapon." It gets personal.

Though the piece *Kids Aren't Cute* comes off as stand-up comedy, it seeks to challenge the notion of motherhood as being cute, and, therefore, not taken seriously. As the script says, "Kids aren't cute, but they are little and little is cute, but it's only the little that's cute, not the kid. Think about it, a six foot newborn would not be cute." Applying this fact to motherhood, it continues: "I want the grit and glory of motherhood revealed through the splendor of their charges, just as liontamers are revered because of the ferocity of lions."

The script goes on to systematically argue for adjectives other than cute when describing kids. Examples are enacted to demonstrate kids' myriad qualities, such as being intense, absurdist, selfish, surrealistic, savvy, and imaginative. This piece simultaneously challenges the long-held assertion that women are not funny. Since the vaudeville days in 1890s till today, women, and now mothers, have had to assert their right to be funny, combating the long-held assumption that comedy was a male domain. For a century the right to be funny for women gained increasing cultural legitimacy and eventually became an item on the emerging feminist agenda (Glenn 41).

The Taming of the Mother Mind takes on an onslaught of societal expectations and repressive forces that creep into a woman's life once she becomes a mother. It begins as follows.

> It happens one day.
> You find a large parcel on your front porch.
> Unknowing, you carry it inside your own home.
> You open it to find the status quo being delivered to you. Yes, the status quo, well, actually, the status quo manual. It's titled, "The Ideal Mother." You flip through the pages, page 16," Giving Up Swearing." Oh, fuck.

It continues on to take on myriad issues facing mothers.

> The status quo wants you to dumb down mother. It will tell you who to trust and who to fear. First of all, make sure you and your children fear strangers, Mother. The status quo actually stores much of its fear concerning children in the ever-looming stranger that barely exists so it doesn't have to look inside its own homes for pain and abuse. The status quo targets the homeless and the mentally ill and the misfit as the stranger, the stranger you should fear, mother.

At its conclusion, it pleads with mothers to think for themselves and own their own views in spite of all that is societally expected: "I say rage, mother. Do not go gently into that good night, rage, RAGE against the dying of your light."

In contrast, *The Good Flirt* is performed in a sparkling black evening gown while I recline in luxurious, recumbent confidence. This piece exposes the sexuality of mothers through a consideration of the harmless flirting that is purely recreational, with no destination in mind. It describes the juiciness of a slightly older, more experienced woman, one who's nobody's virgin and has been around the block. For women, and more specifically mothers, their "sexuality cannot remain private: since one is constructed as 'Woman' through sexuality in relation to male desire, the interrogation of this construction is a political act" (Forte, 259). Its presence in the show challenges the very limiting societal expectations surrounding a mother in terms of sexual behavior and offers a highly sexualized portrayal of motherhood that, among other observations, states: "A good flirt likes a face with a story in it, a smile that knows the difference, a walk that's been somewhere."

The last piece, *Homeless: Us Against "Us Vs. Them"* takes on the subject of homelessness in a literal and a metaphoric sense. By relaying a story about my clash with a mother who spearheaded the opposition to a new and improved homeless shelter in our town, I map out the unlikely path to a place of real acceptance for other people's views. After having both very publicly advocated for opposite sides of the issue, to the extent that she and I were on three different TV news stations expressing opposing views, I relay how I was naturally apprehensive to see her face to face again. As the next excerpt conveys, our first meeting post-conflict wasn't at all the kind of a meeting I was expecting.

> I'm walking towards an intersection on my way to the kids' school, ready to cross when I hear her thunder on up the road riding a motorcycle, brown wavy hair crazy in the wind, no helmet. This vision so dramatically jarred with my previous impression of her. This vision had chutzpa. It had grit. My category for her broke into a thousand pieces just like delicate glass platter you were always so careful not to break but had never really decided to like. She noticed me, waved and gave me a warm smile which I returned. In this moment where she and I hovered, it felt like brand new terrain, some brave new world. Loving your enemy. Now we can get somewhere.

Her fears, her life reasons, and her values are seen as just simply different than my own. I share a glimpse of life lived without judgment that was the gift of that whole experience.

> But that open way of living leaves you largely homeless, for those in communities tend towards an "us-them" dichotomy as a way of defining themselves and once you commit to this way of being, you can't play that game anymore. You may brush against like souls and that will be refreshing. But you'll most likely be tilting at different windmills. As your heart expands you may begin to feel that the whole world is your home, and if enough people could begin to feel this way, then there would be no more of among us who are homeless.

The show ends with my admittedly far-fetched assertion toward a solution for our troubled world.

> In conclusion, I would just like to say that I fully believe that if my mom ruled the earth, she would have fixed all the problems in the Middle East by now. She would have touched the hearts of white supremacists. She would make corporate America clean up its mess. All children would be growing up with health care, enough to eat and with love. We have the means. We lack the will. But if my mother was in charge there would be new world order. Some may doubt she could. I've seen my mother move mountains. She raised ten children, all good people. I've seen my mother endure great sadness and come out on the other end with a pure and thankful heart. I have seen mothers, so many mothers, do amazing things. How did you do that? Talk about it.

In Rehearsal

While my kids were at school, I spent about four hours a day in my backyard studio, a two-car garage with a hardwood floor, skylights, and a full wall of mirrors. I embarked on this endeavor in isolation with a profound inner trust and with a luxurious amount of time. Other than having secured a booking for the premiere of the show six months out, I had no other outside deadlines that are the common fare when collaborating with other artists. In the rehearsal process and in performance, I made it my goal to serve the written material. When creating something out of nothing, you have to ground yourself somewhere. Thus, the script was where I planted my feet as I started to work. This was not an arbitrary choice, but one true to the fact that the written material was the very inspiration for the show and was deemed by me to be the most unadulterated source material from which I would draw out an authentic performance of the mother voice. To keep pure the identity of my original artistic urge, I did not seek outside theatrical direction. I looked to the words themselves to see what they needed to reach an audience.

After a thorough vocal and physical warmup to remove expressive obstacles, I found that if I read through the script again and again while standing in a relaxed and ready stance, the impulse to move and give shape to the words would flow through me. This process demanded faith in the material and in myself as a creative agent capable of expression. When I reached a place in the rehearsal process where I needed feedback or ideas, I would usually just call upon one of my two most trusted, rigorous, and benevolent critics, my friend Juliana or my husband, J.P., who each have an aesthetic sensibility I admire greatly. They both know me so intimately that I trusted them to beckon my true expression out of me and to recognize it when it found its way. It pleases me, in retrospect, that upon examination of this methodology it matches my methods for mothering. Mostly I trust my own direction, but, when in doubt, I turn to my partner in procreation or my closest friends. Mothering is an enterprise largely directed by and starring the woman herself, so why shouldn't a performance of it resemble just that?

Getting my cleverness, my eagerness to please, and my desire to impress out of the way, I tried to make the performance naked in its honesty. Whenever I felt a disingenuous tone creep into my voice, I knew one of those three demons mentioned above was vying for control of the show. I wouldn't stop rehearsing or performing, but, rather, mindful of the obstacle, I would push through it, trying to veer back to a truer course. Achieving honesty in performance can be accomplished by being truly present and in the moment with the material in the task of communicating it to the audience. The rehearsal process resembles the rigorous digging out of a desired, truthful track, such that with all the distractions of performance, the expression of it will still run true to course.

In Performance

I have performed *The Mother Load* now in several different cities and in a variety of different settings, such as at a women's performance festival in Chicago, for a two-week end run as part of an alternative performance season, in a cabaret setting in Denver, an academic conference, for film and even in a church basement. In the coming years, I will be touring it to the many cities where there are Mothers Acting Up communities as a tool to invigorate their activism. In the beginning, I wondered how draining it would be to perform a two-hour one-woman show, something I'd never before attempted. This is where the benefits of rigorous rehearsing paid off. I had built up the endurance over the months preceding and had benefited from the vocal exercises and strength I had gained. What I also found was that the clarity of my commitment to the work fueled my energy. After performing, I felt like a water flask in the desert from which someone had just drunk the last drop, yet, ironically, I felt ridiculously exhilarated. Half of that feeling is relief, I'm sure, and the other half is the human joy of being used up completely to the best of one's ability.

I also wondered how it would be performing such intimate material. What I found was that, given the practical demands of performing, I was left little room for self-consciousness over the material. As for my fear of feeling self-indulgent, I always knew that there was a higher aim, a common experience to all mothers that I was ultimately relaying through my personal stories. My hope is that my effort fits within the confines of the autobiographical performers that Deidre Heddon defends in her article "Performing the Self." "I would suggest that the majority of performers who play themselves display an astute self-consciousness; their representations of themselves are 'knowing.' They are also strategic, and often politically so, using them'selves' as vehicles through which to project particular social perspectives, inflected by positions of race, class, gender and/or sexuality" (2). In this case, the particular perspective is, of course, that of the mother.

It has been extremely gratifying to come to know my creation more intimately over time through sharing it with many audiences. Though I have had some personally profound experiences while rehearsing, they don't compare to what happens in the electrically charged atmosphere of live performance. In rehearsal, I rigorously prepare myself and my performance to withstand the shock of connection that occurs when actually performing. In this exchange, I have to transcend the necessary rigors of the performance and encompass the entire time span between the initial inspiration, the preparation of the material, and this particular moment in performance with all its quirks and needs. I have to be alive and present in that moment with the audience. The alternative is pretending to see and be with them, thereby cutting myself off from any transference of energy and understanding, which, of course, is not satisfying for either party.

Political Ramifications of the Maternal Autobiography in Performance

The notion of mothers performing their autobiographical struggles with being politically active puts into literal practice the pillar feminist belief that the personal is political. It brings out of silence, out of hiding, out of the home, out from the mask of self-sufficiency and the idea of perfection, the mother—stripped bare, still sexy and kickin' for all the wear and tear, ferociously hungry for understanding and connection, passionate for her children and the world they will receive from her, plagued by doubt, ever ashamed she hasn't done more, sacrificed more radically, carried more of her sister's load, and lacking in the full confidence to assert her voice for the woes that ravage her heart for fear she couldn't defend her views with the facts and statistics so expected by the predominantly male discourse of politics. This performance is my execution of all these yearnings made public. Behind it are my negotiations of how to be heard, how to be effective, and how to be radical enough yet not so much so that I'm labeled as such and, thus, easily dismissed in "serious" discourse.

In the performing of autobiographical stories, I do not wish to inadvertently assert that my stories are necessarily superior. I just know that by telling my stories, the only ones I know to be true, I simultaneously convey my belief in the worth of each mother's stories as a source from which she can distill her own insight and wisdom. I believe that hearing stories reminds you of your own and inspires you to share them. It encourages women to claim their voices, to own and operate the portrayal of mothers towards their expression of their own goals and most audacious dreams for the future. I want to validate the mothering perspective through my testimony so that other women feel secure in drawing from that experience to assert their values in public with confidence.

Keeping the stories autobiographical helped to keep me clear of an essentialist portrayal of "mother" that assumes a homogenous identity. My intention was to draw my audience into the conversation without assuming their views or experience necessarily matched my own. Through my activist work, I have become keenly aware that there are divisions between mothers who are feminists, such as "equal rights feminists"—those focused on gaining rights for women in the public sphere—and "maternal feminist" those focused on gaining recognition and support for nurturing children (Wilkinson, 34). In 2003 participants at a conference in New York organized by Enola Aird, founder of the Motherhood Project, created its own manifesto. It claimed that "To get anywhere, the different brands of feminism need to make peace. We seek to build a 21st century motherhood movement that will move us all forward, building on the advances of the women's movement to extend equal right to mothers and put mothers' concerns about children and nurturing at the top of our national agenda" (34–35). Indeed, the more involved one gets with these issues, the more one understands how interwoven the rights of mothers and children are as the viability of the later most often depends on the health and well being of the former. For example, it becomes painfully evident that the mother's access or lack of access to family planning bears heavily on the well being of her already born children, especially internationally in areas where food and resources are least plentiful.

Given that there are many more mothers out there who care about these issues than there are mothers who are actively advocating for them, what intensely interests me is how to effectively invite more mothers to assert their priorities in the political arena. Most particular to the twenty-first century, I have found that, in my experience, the majority of progressive mothers are no longer activated by rage nor do they want their public voice to be angry. In stride with this, at Mothers Acting Up we have evolved an exuberant style of activism that is strong, celebratory and proactive. With yearly MAU Mother's Day Parades held across the USA, we celebrate our commitment and ability to protect the world's children. This doesn't mean we avoid difficult or so-called radical issues, we just take them on from a proactive stance. For example, MAU's soon-to-be trademarked girlcott (opposite of a boycott) is a positive endorsement of a choice made by a corporation that has a positive impact on the world's children. MAU's approach to activism is not being propagated as a superior way to create social change, just as one that suits who we are and seems to be a good fit for many mothers who are often repelled from more confrontational methods. My performance of *The Mother Load* is a three-dimensional, real-time representation of this new style of activism and allows the audience to witness how this approach plays out in public life from one woman's autobiographical experience.

In her book, *Feminist Theatre Practice: A Handbook*, Aston concludes by showing how a mode of autobiographical devising may also serve as a way of discovering and defining feminism (171). This has certainly held true for me within my development as an artist and an activist. Before this process, I had never noticed how much my performance and activism is informed by my being a woman. During the process of creation I came to identify my voice as feminist and to understand my place within the feminist movement. Understanding the feminist theory behind the autobiographical performance of the mother voice has led me to even richer creative ground. As Dolan states, "Theory is not antiaesthetic or anticreative, and *thinking* about theater might actually enhance its value within American culture" (2001, 4). Indeed, through the process of writing this essay, I have changed certain lines in my script that, upon speculation, lended themselves towards an ideal more than a real portrayal of mothers or that depended too heavily upon a notion of the moral authority of mothers.

Given the reactions to some early feminist theater works, I wondered if emotional appeals through my performance were necessarily coercive or manipulative. Of course I realize that in theatre we are in the business of enticing our audience down a certain devised path of feeling, yet when a performance has such an overtly political aim, I question if what is allowable in the realm of emotions changes. Dolan states, "But feminist critiques also need to account for the political effects of emotion that is compelling on the basis of identification. Especially spectators still marginalized by identity categories need the motivation of identification to confirm a drive towards social change" (2001, 87). My intuition tells me that it is the emotions of mothering that most strongly bond mothers who, as a group, have a long way to go towards owning a collective political identity. Furthermore, this emotional bond most easily crosses boundaries of race, socioeconomic status, and sexual orientation. This bond allows for mothers to feel identified as a group capable of banding together in collective action to actually effect social change.

In *Geographies of Learning*, Dolan states, "I proselytize for theatre as an intensely social, still potentially radical site of cultural transformation " (16). The power of the shared experience in the live theatrical setting can be the catalyst that moves a person from concern to action. The freedom to undress any subject in the theater, no matter how private or unspoken, distinguishes the theater as a unique social setting poised to redress some of the most delicate of subjects. It is often a shared experience during which we have felt a deep connection, so rare in our contemporary society, that stands as a beacon in our lives by which we navigate forward. Live theater can be all of that and, thereby, a powerful force for social change. Dolan confirms this sentiment as she goes on to write, "I, too, believe in this particular, local, perhaps even utopian promise of theater, in which temporary communities assemble to look at social relations, to be provoked, moved, enraged, made proud by what human beings can do when they're set in relation to one another. Performance offers us a practice that lets us rehearse new social arrangements, in ways that require visceral investments of bodies, of time, of personal and cultural history" (16).

Because of the actor's powers of persuasion and her capacity to move the hearts and minds of her audience, suffragette Harriot Stanton Blatch declared the vital and strategic importance of the female actor to the cause (Glenn 2000, 135). Over a hundred years later when women, and more specifically mothers, are still not adequately represented in the political process, female performers still have the vital and important opportunity of persuading a more balanced gender leadership and moving hearts toward a style of politics that can chose to nurture rather than control, to cooperate rather than compete, and to plan for our collective children's future rather than steal from it. The power of live performance can deeply penetrate defenses and barriers that defend inaction. My hope is that by exposing my questions, mistakes, and struggles, I map one possible path from ignorance to understanding and from dormant concern to authentic action. Though my way is not a universal fit for all occasions, I hope it is enough to spark a dialogue within regarding the need for travel.

Work Cited

Aston, Elaine. *Feminist Theatre Practice: A Handbook*. New York: Routledge, 1999.

Dolan, Jill. *Geographies of Learning*. Middletown, Conn.: Wesleyan University Press, 2001.

———. *Presence and Desire*. Ann Arbor: University of Michigan Press, 1993.

Forte, Jeanie. "Women's Performance Art: Feminism and Postmodernism." In *Performing Feminism*. Edited by Sue-Ellen Case. Baltimore: Johns Hopkins University Press, 1990. 251–69.

Glenn, Evelyn Nakano. "Social Constructions of Mothering: A Thematic Overview." In *Mothering: Ideology, Experience and Agency*. Edited by Evelyn Nakano Glenn, Grace Chang, and Linda Rennie Forcey. New York: Routledge, 1994. 1–29.

Glenn, Susan. *Female Spectacle: The Theatrical Roots of Modern Feminism*. Cambridge: Harvard University Press, 2000. 1–29.

Greeley, Lynne. "Whatever Happened to the Cultural Feminists? Martha Boesing and At the Foot of the Mountains." *Theatre Survey* 46, 1 (May 2005): 49–65.

Heddon, Deidre. "Performing the Self." *M/C: A Journal of Media and Culture* 5, 5 (2002). http://www.media-culture.org.au/mc/0210/Heddon.html.

Wilkinson, Stephanie. "Say You Want a Revolution?: Why the Mother's Movement Hasn't Happened." *Brain, Child* 6, 4 (Fall 2005): 32–43.

II
Maternal Texts:
From Narrative to Theory

Maternal Fetters:
Motherhood and Slavehood in Harriet Jacobs's *Incidents in the Life of a Slave Girl*

Mary McCartin Wearn

CRITICS HAVE LONG NOTED THE DISTINCTLY DOUBLED NATURE OF Harriet Jacobs's autobiographical roman à clef, *Incidents in the Life of a Slave Girl*. In this abolitionist text, which chronicles the author's slavehood, motherhood, and escape to the free North, Jacobs's narrative voice splits—vacillating, for example, between revelation and concealment, between repentance for her perceived cultural crimes and defiance. The narrative cleft in *Incidents* has been explained, variously, as the reflection of a DuBoisian double-consciousness (Johnson, 23–24) or as the product of Jacobs's melding of sentimental novel and slave narrative genres (Mullen, 244–45). Others see Jacobs's bivocal memoir as typical of African American women's autobiographies, which "seem torn between exhibitionism and secrecy" (Fox-Genovese, 70–71). This study, however, will explore the doubled nature of Jacobs's text, by specifically examining *Incidents* as a maternal narrative with a clear, political agenda. Jacobs's nuanced, multilayered depiction of her own motherhood and slavehood, in fact, both politically exploits *and* critically deconstructs nineteenth-century maternal ideals. At one level, Jacobs's narrative deploys white, middle-class constructions of motherhood to underwrite her antislavery argument. But just as Jacobs hides her true identity behind the pseudonym of Linda Brent in *Incidents*, so too will she hide a more radical maternal subjectivity under the unthreatening veneer of sentimental motherhood. Through legible gaps and elisions in the text and by a discernable if more discreet alternative narrative voice, Jacobs covertly articulates a more subversive, more politically dangerous, maternal subjectivity.

Years after the birth of her children and her escape to the free North, Jacobs was encouraged by the antislavery activist Amy Post to publish her life story. Jacobs, whose children were the product of a consensual relationship with a white man, found herself torn between a deep political commitment to the cause of abolition and her personal reticence to reveal the culturally compromising details of her reproductive life. In the end, Jacobs's sense of social obligation won out, and she declared in a letter to Post that if her life writing "could help save another," from the ravages of slavery "it would be selfish and unchristian . . . to keep it back" (qtd. in Yellin, *Incidents*, 232). Writing specifically on behalf of "the thousands- of . . . Slave Mothers . . . still in bondage" (qtd. in Yellin, *Incidents*, 242), Jacobs thematically and rhetorically constructed *Incidents* upon her maternity and upon her relationship to the mother figures in her life. In one sense, then, Jacobs's autobiographical narrative is a reflection of the author's complex and contradictory experience as a "poor slave mother" (qtd. in Yellin, *Incidents*, 242).

Incidents, however, is something more than a simple reflection of one slave woman's maternal experience. As a political text, Jacobs's story is rhetorically crafted for a specific audience, and the narrative divide that Jacobs created is at least partially strategic. In writing her autobiographical narrative, Jacobs deployed those culturally endorsed elements of her maternal subjectivity that served her abolitionist ends. Specifically writing to arouse the sympathies of white "women of the North" (Jacobs 1), Harriet Jacobs, as Holly Blackford argues, "capitaliz[es] on Victorian culture's sanctification of motherhood," highlighting the maternal ideals she shares with her audience (314). In fact, abolitionists routinely identified the destruction of family bonds as the central evil of slavery, and Jacobs's white predecessors—most notably Harriet Beecher Stowe—made the unjust denial of "natural" maternal rights to the slave a political focal point. Like other abolitionist writers who relied on idealized depictions of slave women, Jacobs tactically presents herself as a heroic slave mother. Wrapping her quest for freedom in the cultural ideal of sacrificial mother-love, she identifies securing her children's freedom and well being as the primary impetus of her own escape.

Jacobs's political employment of culturally endorsed maternal values is, however, not unproblematic, nor is it the whole story. Much like Frederick Douglass, Jacobs learns through her life experiences that it is often the "strong cords of affection"—the emotional ties of family, friends, and domestic life—that most effectively bind African Americans in slavery (Douglass, 142). Because they can be used as a tool of oppression in the slave state, traditional maternal bonds and the cultural values that underwrite them must, at a deeper level, be resisted. As Caroline Levander argues, Jacobs must "strategically reject her motherhood" in order to escape the slave system (35). On the flip side of Jacobs's deployment of Victorian maternal ideals, then, one finds a seditious motherhood and a subversive politics of self.

This study will articulate Jacobs's politically and rhetorically savvy deployment of the Victorian values of motherhood and the dissident maternal subjectivity that deployment partially conceals. Specifically, this doubled maternal narrative will be analyzed by exploring Jacobs's conflicted relationship with her conventionally conservative maternal grandmother, by exploring Jacobs's own troubled and ambivalent motherhood, and by investigating the radical model of motherhood that Jacobs juxtaposes with her grandmother's more traditional example.

Grandmother's Way: Maternity and the Status Quo of Slavery

Throughout *Incidents in the Life of a Slave Girl*, Harriet Jacobs's maternal subjectivity is framed and articulated through her relationship with her grandmother, Molly Horniblow. Accomplishing much through a lifetime of hard work and domestic respectability, Horniblow earned her own manumission, purchased her own home, and gained the respect of both the white and black communities of her hometown, Edenton, North Carolina. When Jacobs's biological mother died, Horniblow served as a mother to "her orphan grandchildren," becoming the dominant maternal figure in young Harriet's life (17). Jacobs's narrative depiction of her relationship with Molly Horniblow contextualizes her own complex subjectivity and exposes how the author both politically deploys and critically deconstructs the Victorian maternal ideals that her grandmother embraced.

As she structures her life story, Jacobs uses the figure of her grandmother to negotiate the cultural divide between herself and her largely white, Northern audience. Re-creating Molly Horniblow in the form of Linda Brent's "Aunt Marthy," Jacobs depicts her grandmother as the very embodiment of nineteenth-century True Womanhood. More specifically, as Krista Walter has noted, Jacobs's grandmother is "steeped in the maternal values of the white ruling class" (202). She espouses the ideals of motherly self-sacrifice, articulating that a true mother must "stand by [her] children, and suffer with them till death" (Jacobs, 91). Jacobs engages her nineteenth-century audience through her own filial devotion, claiming that she had a "great treasure" (5) in Molly Horniblow and that she was "indebted" to her grandmother for all "comforts, spiritual or temporal" (11).

While Jacobs forges bonds with her Victorian audience through praise of her grandmother's traditional maternal values, the author's conspicuous, daughterly devotion is only half of the story. In detailing Molly Horniblow's early motherhood, Jacobs stealthily exposes the hazards of maternity for the slave woman too. In the simplest sense, as Jacobs reveals, motherhood makes slave women the means of production for the antebellum South, as they serve to "increase their owner's stock" (49). But as the details of Horniblow's life reveal, the slave state exploits African American women's maternity in even more insidious ways. Jacobs suggests that having served as a wet nurse both to her master's children and her own, the grandmother had a divided sense of loyalty which was rooted in a genealogy—not of blood—but of mother's milk: "My mother's mistress [Mrs. Norcom] was the daughter of my grandmother's mistress. She was the foster sister of my mother, they were both nourished at my grandmother's breast. In fact, my mother had been weaned at three months old, that the babe of the mistress might obtain sufficient food" (6–7).

Much like the master's rape of his female slaves, shared maternal milk makes black and white children siblings from the wet nurse's perspective, creating conflicting maternal attachments. Indeed, Molly Horniblow's role as "foster mother" to her master's children muddied her allegiances, putting her own children at risk. For as Jacobs reveals, even after Horniblow's white nursling, Mrs. Norcom, grows to be her granddaughter's mistress and mortal enemy, the grandmother will find it impossible to "retain ill will" against the woman "whom she had nourished with her milk as a babe" (89). Emblematically implicating the grandmother in the slave state through the maternal breast, Jacobs also shows that Molly Horniblow's motherly ministrations—even when directed toward her biological children—often served the needs of the slave state. Imbued with the domestic values of nineteenth-century middle-class culture, the grandmother, Jacobs's narrative suggests, privileged family ties over personal freedom and, in so doing, supported the slave state's status quo. Jacobs articulates Horniblow's complicity early in her narrative by documenting her grandmother's response to the escape of her youngest son, Joseph (Benjamin in *Incidents*). While Horniblow was quite willing to pursue the legal avenues of liberty, she refused to endorse the illegal escape of family members. According to Jacobs, her grandmother was filled with "great sorrow" when her youngest son ran away (21). And when Uncle Joseph was briefly brought back into captivity, Molly Horniblow was most concerned with keeping her son nearby and safe, and so she advocated for her son's submission. Fearing that the recaptured, incarcerated Joseph would be sold down the river, Molly Horniblow pled with her son to "Be humble" (22) and to "beg" for his master's pardon (23). As Donald Gibson argues, *Incidents* shows that the grandmother believed it "better to submit to the yoke of slavery than to sever family ties" (165). Jacobs casts oblique judgment on her grandmother's domestic principles and conciliatory temperament by juxtaposing them with the values of her heroic Uncle Joseph, who not only refused to concede to his captors but proved himself quite willing to "part with . . . all kindred" to achieve personal freedom (26). In documenting her Uncle Joseph's ultimately successful escape—a formative event in her young life—Jacobs surreptitiously exposes how her grandmother's conventional maternal values operated as a vehicle of her children's oppression. After becoming a mother, Jacobs would find herself bound by those maternal principles that led her grandmother to privilege family over freedom without exception.

Maternal Fetters: The Links and Ties of Jacobs's Motherhood

The narrative of *Incidents in the Life of a Slave Girl* hinges on the act of reproductive rebellion that made a mother of Harriet Jacobs. Threatened by her sexually aggressive and psychologically abusive master, Dr. James Norcom, the young African American slave girl preempted her owner's advances by taking a white lover of her own choosing. Detailing her "calculations of interest" before beginning an affair with the socially powerful Samuel Tredwell Sawyer, Jacobs suggests that she entered the relationship with the future U.S. congressman—at least in part—for the strategic purpose of becoming a mother (Jacobs, 55). Having yearned for escape from an early age, Jacobs imagined her impending maternity as a source of power and, possibly, freedom. Speculating that when the jealous Norcom became aware of her affair—ostensibly through a noticeable pregnancy—he would "revenge himself" by selling her, Jacobs felt confident that her lover would be willing to buy and free her (55). The slave admits to having embarked on her affair only after "deliberate calculation" on these matters (54). As Eva Cherniavsky has argued, Jacobs's planned pregnancy is an "act of subaltern insurgency" meant to foil her master's plans to make her his concubine (102). Taking a radical leap of faith that would alter the course of her life, Jacobs chose motherhood, gambling that it would offer her new control and might ultimately lead to liberty.

While mothering and freedom were, thus, inextricably linked in Jacobs's imagination, the realities of her life after giving birth would fail painfully to conform to expectations. Dr. Norcom, in fact, refused to sell Jacobs after learning of her pregnancy, and Samuel Sawyer was not proactive in securing the liberty of his lover or his offspring. Realizing that her children would necessarily "follow the condition of the mother" and become Norcom's slaves, Jacobs was deeply ambivalent about her motherhood. In describing her growing attachment to her first child Joseph (Benny in *Incidents*), Jacobs reveals a divided maternal consciousness, as she vacillates between expressions of maternal joy and desolation: "The little vine was taking deep root in my existence, though its clinging fondness excited a mixture of love and pain. When I was most sorely oppressed I found a solace in his smiles. I loved to watch his infant slumbers, but always there was a dark cloud over my enjoyment. I could never forget that he was a slave. Sometimes I wished that he might die in infancy" (62).

Greeting the birth of her daughter Louisa (Ellen in *Incidents*) with even more strained emotions, Jacobs writes, "When they told me my new-born babe was a girl, my heart was heavier than it had been before. Slavery is terrible for men; but it is far more terrible for women" (77). Like other abolitionist writers, Jacobs thus explores slavery's detrimental effects on family life and highlights the emotional ambivalence fostered by a system in which a woman is the vehicle of her own children's bondage.

Jacobs's ambivalent maternity, however, reflects more than just anguish over her children's slavehood or a sense of guilt about her own role in their captivity. For her children not only failed to be the vehicle of freedom that she had hoped for, but they actually served as new impediments to her much-longed-for liberty. Granted the right to care for her own children (a privilege not all slave women could boast), Jacobs found herself further ensnared in slavery's web by the responsibilities, the cultural expectations, and the emotional ties of motherhood. The divided nature of Jacobs's maternal narrative is nowhere more evident than in the context of her escape to freedom after the birth of her children. Carefully balancing her nineteenth-century audience's expectations, her abolitionist agenda, and the realities of her own experience, Jacobs alternatively figures her children as the motivation for and the obstacle to her own freedom.

Writing for a culture that in Ann Douglas's words "seemed bent on establishing a perpetual Mother's Day," Jacobs appeals to her audience by morally underwriting her quest for freedom with motherhood and by figuring her children as the impetus of her unlawful escape (6). Portraying Joseph and Louisa as a source of inspiration, Jacobs explicitly links her desire to run with her burgeoning maternal love: "My drooping hopes came to life again [after the birth of the children]. . . . I was dreaming of freedom again; more for my children's sake than for my own. I planned and planned" (83). Following the model that Harriet Beecher Stowe created with Eliza Harris in *Uncle Tom's Cabin*, Jacobs narratively roots her escape in the ethos of a self-denying, Victorian maternity: "I could have made my escape alone; but it was more for my helpless children than for myself that I longed for freedom. Though the boon would have been precious to me, above all price, I would not have taken it at the expense of leaving them in slavery" (89). In depicting herself as a heroic slave mother, Jacobs, like other abolitionists before her, exploits what Jane Tompkins identifies as American culture's "favorite story about itself"—"the story of salvation through motherly love" (125).

In the shadow of Jacobs's declared motives for escape and her narrative construction of herself as a heroic slave mother, however, lies the more subversive truth. The realities of Jacobs's motherhood underscored the lessons she learned early on through her grandmother's response to Uncle Joseph's escape: the conventional maternal values that bind one to family can actually serve as a force of oppression. And Jacobs would find that her own motherly responsibilities and attachments were in antagonistic relation with her personal desire for freedom. Wary, no doubt, of her nineteenth-century audience's response to her perception of children as an encumbrance, Jacobs sends her maternal ambivalence narratively underground. The florid titles of chapters announcing the birth of Jacobs's children are instructive. Her son Benny is "The New Tie to Life" and her daughter Ellen "Another

Link to Life." While these chapter names overtly acknowledge the life-affirming role of children, their diction is slippery; "ties" and "links," no doubt, carry a shadow meaning for the slave. At the end of the chapter that documents her daughter's birth and christening, the emotional freight of the word "links" is revealed. When a well-meaning white woman clasps a chain around her daughter's neck, Jacobs baulks at the gift: "I wanted no chain to be fastened on my daughter, not even if the links were of gold" (79). Motherhood, in its own way, would hold Harriet Jacobs captive with just such golden links.

The tensions between Jacobs's maternity and her personal desire for freedom are legible through faults in the narrative logic of the text—through contradictions in Jacobs's spoken intentions and her actions. For example, the slave-mother maintains that she wanted freedom for the sake of Joseph and Louisa and claims to reject opportunities to escape without them. Fleeing with small children would be a high-risk proposition, however, and none of the escape plans Jacobs documents in *Incidents* actually include her children. While she hoped to secure their manumission after establishing her own freedom, when Jacobs actually took flight, she left her children behind. As Stephanie Smith argues, Jacobs's "voluntary desertion treads very shaky narrative ground" (146). In fact, Jacobs learned early from her Uncle Joseph that pursuing freedom might mean parting with "all kindred" (26). Despite her Victorian, motherly rhetoric, it is a risk she was willing to take.

Jacobs codes her internal, emotional struggle between the love of her children and her desire for freedom through her external conflict with her grandmother, whose maternal value system barricaded her in slavery. Returning, in memory, to her grandmother's response to her early plans for escape, Jacobs exposes a brutal invocation of filial and maternal obligation and the willful manipulation of her motherly emotions. Arguing for continued captivity, the grandmother rhetorically interrogates Jacobs about her proposed escape, "Do you want to kill your old grandmother? Do you mean to leave your little, helpless children?" (91). Reproaching her granddaughter for a "want of affection," the grandmother holds Jacobs up to her Victorian culture's standards of maternity, arguing that "Nobody respects a mother who forsakes her children" (91). "If you leave them," the grandmother threatens, "you will never have a happy moment" (91).

While Jacobs never directly indicts her grandmother for the value system she wields, she implicitly casts judgment by revealing how the slave state similarly exploits her maternal affections and deploys Victorian codes of motherhood to keep her in captivity. In fact, her actual escape from slavery is precipitated by her mistress Mrs. Norcom's attempts to use the slave's maternal devotion as an instrument of bondage. When Dr. Norcom punished Jacobs by exiling her to an outlying family plantation—away from her grandmother and children—Mrs. Norcom feared that her slave would run. Hoping to prevent such a flight, Jacobs's mistress encouraged her son to bring Brent's children to the plantation, believing that their presence would "fetter [Jacobs] to the spot" (93). While reticent to rebel against her grandmother's values, Jacobs proved quite willing to forgo conventional maternal morality to foil the Norcoms's goals. Learning that Mrs. Norcom was planning on using her children against her, Jacobs's will to flee was solidified. "Now that I was certain my children were to be put in their power, in order to give them a stronger hold on me," Jacobs reports, "I resolved to leave them that night" (95). Jacobs takes flight without her children and refuses to look back—even when the Norcoms temporarily placed her children and several other family members in jail to flush her out of hiding.

Some critics have argued that the mode of Jacobs's subsequent "escape"—the flight to her grandmother's tiny attic crawlspace and her prolonged seven-year stay there—was a proactive and creative way to honor her own maternal values, to stay connected to family, while at the same time, working toward freedom. Stephanie Smith, for example, believes that Jacobs's attic hiding place, provided her with a positive means to "'part with all her kin' without actually departing" (156). But Jacobs own narrative description of her experience undermines such readings. In fact, the slave took no active part in the decision to seek refuge in her grandmother's attic but was brought there by friends without being informed of her destination. And this feminine, domestic "retreat," as Jacobs ironically figures it, is no sanctuary, but a prison—a dark, bug-infested crawlspace that robs her of health and mobility. While Jacobs admits that the sight and sound of her children through the small peephole she creates are "consolations" (116), her hiding place is, ultimately, a "living grave"—a place of physical and emotional torture that is only slightly mitigated by her children's presence (147).

While Jacobs's narration of her seven-year internment in her grandmother's attic is, according to Yellin, historically accurate, at the same time, it is a powerful, metaphoric representation of the untenable role of motherhood for all slave women. For although Jacobs's limbo-like imprisonment was certainly not a common experience, her maternal impotence—her inability to control her own children's destiny from her attic hiding place—would be familiar territory for many slave mothers. From the vantage point of her grandmother's crawlspace, in fact, home becomes a prison and the maternal role that keeps Jacobs bound proves a hollow office. Although pressured by Molly Horniblow to stay in hiding, Jacobs realized she could do no good for herself or for her children while locked inside her domestic prison, futilely holding on to her sham status as mother. "In order to protect my children," Jacobs articulates late in *Incidents*, "it was necessary that I should own myself" (166). Jacobs's narrative paradoxically reveals that, in order to claim her motherhood, the slave woman had to be an agent of her own liberty by freeing herself from slavery—and from the ties that bound her to her children.

An Alternate Maternal Model

Despite Jacobs's untenable living arrangements and her hollow motherhood, Molly Horniblow, according to the narrative, remained the champion of domestic solutions, using her emotional ammunition and Victorian values to keep Jacobs sequestered in her garret prison. As the narrative reaches its climax, however, Jacobs presents an alternate model of motherly devotion through her representation of the slave woman Aunt Sue Bent, "Aggie" in *Incidents*. Illiterate and poor, this bereaved slave mother is the antithesis of her friend Molly Horniblow, and she challenges the middle-class maternal values of Jacobs's nineteenth-century audience. After her grandson's escape to the free North, Molly Horniblow bemoans her loss and complains to Aunt Sue Bent that she won't have any children or grandchildren "left to hand [her] a drink" when she is "dying" (135). In response, Aunt Sue Bent firmly rebukes the grandmother: "Is *dat* what you's crying fur? . . . Git down on your knees and bress de Lord . . . [He's] in free parts; and dat's de right place. Don't murmur at de Lord's doings, but git down on your knees and tank him for his goodness" (135). Jacobs uses dialect sparingly in *Incidents*, and Aunt Sue's language clearly separates her from Molly Horniblow and from Jacobs's middle-class audience. It's a separation, Jacobs stealthily suggests, that is all to Aunt Sue's moral advantage.

From a literary perspective, as Daneen Wardrop argues, Aunt Sue Bent serves as a doppelgänger of sorts for Jacobs's grandmother. The reader learns that just like Molly Horniblow Aunt Sue secretly harbored a fugitive daughter in her own home. But Jacobs will morally delineate between the two old mothers in depicting their dramatically different reaction to the prospect of their children's escape. When Jacobs's chance to leave her attic prison and flee North finally comes, her grandmother reacts with "sob[s], and groan[s]," and she "entreat[s]," Jacobs not to go (151). But when Aunt Sue Bent learns that her daughter is to take Jacobs's place on an escape vessel she "rejoice[s] to hear of such a chance" (151). Aunt Sue, whose social class allows her to escape the narrowness of her culture's maternal mores, proves the more selfless mother in the end. Through her depiction of Aunt Sue or "Aggie," Jacobs provides an alternative model of maternal care—one in which cutting domestic ties and fostering freedom are their own means of nurturance.

In a letter to Amy Post written after the composition of *Incidents*, Harriet Jacobs conceded that there were some things she might "have made plainer" in her life story (qtd. in Yellin, 242). Attributing her narrative indirection to the necessity of gaining her audience's "sympathies," Jacobs identified the "object" of her life-writing as serving the political needs of slave mothers and their children (qtd. in Yellin, 242). In order to garner the moral authority needed to successfully make her abolitionist argument, Jacobs wrote herself into the role of mother-savior and created a sense of shared, maternal values with her white, Northern audience. Despite Jacobs's overt homage to conservative principles of motherhood, however, her covert voice in *Incidents* speaks a more subversive political truth. From her radical planned pregnancy, to the strategic desertion of her children, through her successful escape to freedom, Jacobs narratively argues that resisting the slave state required a rejection of her culture's narrowly defined ideology of motherhood.

While it is debatable how much a nineteenth-century audience would have recognized *Incidents'* political subtext, Jacobs makes clear that she is unwilling to suffer the judgment of the "careless daughters" (title page) to whom she speaks, and she boldly asserts that slave women "ought not" be measured by "the same standards as others" (56). In the end, in fact, Jacobs leaves the final measurement of her success as a woman and a mother to her daughter Louisa, with whom she was reunited after her successful escape North. Despite the culturally compromising facts of her daughter's conception, despite Jacobs's willful abandonment of her children, despite the slave-mother's continued inability to provide a home for her children, Louisa still affirms Jacobs in her maternity and announces to her mother near the end of the narrative, "All my love is for you" (189).

Notes

We are grateful for permission to reprint work here that was originally published by Routledge. Parts of the essay "Maternal Fetters: Motherhood and Slavehood in Harriet Jacobs's *Incidents in the Life of a Slave Girl*" first appeared in a different form in *Negotiating Motherhood in Nineteenth Century American Literature* by Mary Wearn, 2008.

Works Cited

Blackford, Holly. "Figures of Orality: The Master, The Mistress, The Slave Mother in Harriet Jacobs's *Incidents in the Life of a Slave Girl: Written by Herself*." *Papers on Language and Literature* 37, 3 (2001): 314–37.

Cherniavsky, Eva. "That Pale Mother Rising: Sentimental Discourse and the Imitation of Motherhood in 19th-Century America." Bloomington: Indiana University Press, 1995.

Douglas, Ann. *The Feminization of American Culture*. New York: Noonday Press, 1977.

Douglass, Frederick. *Narrative of the Life of Frederick Douglass, an American Slave. 1845.* Edited by Houston A. Baker, Jr. New York: Penguin Books, 1986.

Fox-Genovese, Elizabeth. "My Statue, Myself: Autobiographical Writings of Afro-American Women." In *The Private Self: Theory and Practice of Women's Autobiographical Writings*. Edited by Shari Benstock. Chapel Hill: University of North Carolina Press, 1988.

Jacobs, Harriet. *Incidents in the Life of a Slave Girl*. 1861. Edited by Jean Fagan Yellin. Cambridge: Harvard University Press, 1987.

Johnson, Yvonne. *The Voices of African American Women*. New York: Peter Lang, 1999.

Levander, Caroline. "'Following the Conditions of the Mother': Subversions of Domesticity in Harriet Jacobs's *Incidents in the Life of a Slave Girl*." In *Southern Mothers*. Edited by Nagueyalti Warren and Sally Wolff. Baton Rouge: Louisiana State University Press, 1999. 28–38.

Mullen, Haryette. "Runaway Tongue: Resistant Orality in *Uncle Tom's Cabin, Our Nig, Incidents in the Life of a Slave Girl,* and *Beloved*." In *The Culture of Sentiment: Race, Gender, and Sentimentality in Nineteenth-Century America*. Edited by Shirley Samuels. New York: Oxford University Press, 1992. 244–64.

Smith, Stephanie. *Conceived by Liberty: Maternal Figures and 19th-Century American Literature*. Ithaca: Cornell University Press, 1994.

Tompkins, Jane. *Sensational Designs: The Cultural Work of American Fiction 1790–1860*. Oxford: Oxford University Press, 1985.

Walter, Krista. "Surviving the Garret: Harriet Jacobs and the Critique of Sentiment." *ATQ* 8, 3 (September 1994): 189–210.

Wardrop, Daneen. "'What Tangled Skeins are the Genealogies of Slavery'; Gothic Families in Harriet Jacobs's *Incidents in the Life of a Slave Girl*." Litrany Griot: International Journal of Black Expressive Studies, 14 1 & 2 (2002): 23–43.

Yellin, Jean Fagan. *Harriet Jacobs: A Life*. New York: Basic Civitas Books, 2004.

———, ed. *Incidents in the Life of a Slave Girl*. 1861. By Harriet Jacobs. Cambridge: Harvard University Press, 1987.

The Dialogics of the Sexual-Maternal: Multiple Births in Gilman and Le Sueur

Carolina Núñez Puente

THIS IS A STUDY OF TWO SHORT STORIES, "THE YELLOW WALLPAPER" (1892) and "Annunciation" (1935), written respectively by the American writers Charlotte Perkins Gilman and Meridel Le Sueur. In the title of the essay, the word "dialogics" is obviously connected to Mikhail M. Bakhtin, whose theorizations, together with those by feminist critics, are the critical apparatus of my work.[1] Many of these feminists agree that much of patriarchy is based upon the separation of maternal and sexual qualities, such as in the mother/whore hierarchy. Throughout this paper, I show how Gilman and Le Sueur deconstruct this binary opposition. In so doing, a new concept of the sexual-maternal comes into view, in order to dialogically broaden our understanding of these terms, and to try to represent female experience. The "multiple births" of this essay's title refer to the fact that Gilman's and Le Sueur's female protagonists have had/are about to have children; to the different conceptualizations of certain analytical categories—subject, mother, woman—developed in the stories; and to the multiplicity of endings and of genres—realist and gothic ("Wallpaper"), dialogical and feminine ("Annunciation")—to be found in them.

Bakhtin sees a deep connection between the dialogics of psychological life and the realist novel (e.g., 2000, 338). As for the latter, Bakhtin is referring to the multiplicity of discourses that are welcome by the cannibalistic appetite of the novel. Nevertheless, it is important to emphasize the dialogics existing in other genres, such as the short stories written by women. The gender of these authors and their different dialogized writings are ignored in Bakhtin's analyses. Ironically, he notices that women's symbolic acts are not included as part of culture (Bakhtin 1999, 148). Many are the feminists who have pointed out that gender is Bakhtin's blind spot, starting a new line of research called feminist dialogics.[2] I will now move onto a close reading of the mentioned maternal autobiographical texts.

As Gilman explains in her nominal autobiography, *The Living of Charlotte Perkins Gilman*, it is William Dean Howells who "trie[s] the *Atlantic Monthly* print ["Wallpaper"], but . . . the editor, sen[ds] it back with this brief card: . . . 'I could not forgive myself if I made others as miserable as I have made myself!' " (*Living*, 119). Part of "Wallpaper"'s autobiographical data reveals that Gilman herself had a postpartum depression and was prescribed the nineteenth-century rest cure, which turned out to be even more dangerous than the illness—like her protagonist, Gilman would end up crawling around the room. In her review article, "Why I wrote 'The Yellow Wallpaper,'" Gilman discloses that the story is intended to convince Silas W. Mitchell, the inventor of the popular cure, to change his treatment. Sociologist and fiction writer, Gilman is concerned about the social realities of her time affecting women, such as the lack of efficient treatments for postpartum depression. But women's terrifying everyday needs to be grasped by means of both realism and the gothic. According to Conrad Shumaker, if "Wallpaper" is to be considered realistic in the Howellsian manner, one must read the protagonist as a "type," which would imply "seeing creeping [mothers] everywhere" (91). It seems that the editor of the *Atlantic* reads it realistically, otherwise, why should he be so bothered by it? Gilman wants to make a social critique of her time—for instance, to expose the masculinism of the (medical) institutions—and she succeeds. Another of her purposes, that it appear "dreadful," succeeds too (*Living*, 119). From here we can argue that her short piece is both realist and gothic.

Like Gilman herself, the protagonist of "Wallpaper" is an ill mother and writer whose doctor prescribes her not to "touch pen, brush or pencil" (*Living*, 96). The story time covers three months, from the beginning till the end of the summer. However, the text refers to a time beyond itself too: John hires "a hereditary estate" so that his wife, whose name could be Jane (cf. Veeder), can rest. Ironically the word "hereditary" also points out that her "nervous depression—[with] a hysterical tendency" ("Wallpaper," 25) has been suffered before by other women. Thus, hysteria recognizes a "woman with a [patriarchal] past" (Diamond, 59), which Gilman attacks as the main reason for women's (psychological) problems. According to Elin Diamond, hysteria is precisely what realism tries to suppress (76): a hysteria that is meaningful for some feminists as it disrupts the existing categories and patterns of signification (61). These arguments seem reason enough for Gilman to attack and develop certain patriarchal conventions—such as realism—in order to portray her-story/the voice(s) of gender—by means of the gothic. Continuing with voices, once Jane decides "it [i]s a good time to talk" with her husband about going back home in order to leave that ghostly mansion ("Wallpaper," 33). But John says:

> "*I* cannot possibly leave town now. Of course if you were in any danger, *I* could and would, but you are really better, dear, whether you can see it or not. *I* am a doctor, dear, and *I* know. You are gaining flesh and color, your appetite is better, *I* feel much easier about you . . . Really dear you are better!" . . . "Better in body perhaps—" [Jane] began, and stopped short, for he sat up straight and looked at [her] with such a stern, reproachful look that [she] could not say another word . . . "My darling," said he, "*I* beg of you, *for my* sake and *for our* child's sake, as well as *for your* own, that you will never . . . let that idea enter your mind!" (33–34, emphasis added)

This excerpt cannot be considered as a *real* dialogue between two people, who are able to see each other as both equal—having the same chances to be right—and different—a female and a male (Todorov, 76). The John/Jane hierarchy, conspicuously shown through the use of pronouns, stands for an example of the asymmetry present in many male/female relations.

John "secure[s]" his wife in a house that is "alone," surrounded by "hedges and walls and gates that lock" ("Wallpaper," 24–25). He puts her in what appears to be a "nursery" (26) so that she might become a "little girl" again (33). John's performance of patriarchal law has a very harmful effect on Jane's subjectivity. Patriarchy confers the status of subject on neither girls nor mothers, that is, none of them has an identity neither as a woman nor a lover (Holmund, 290). Since Jane "*cannot be with the* [baby]" ("Wallpaper," 28), he is nursed by a woman called Mary, like the (mother) Virgin. The caretaker's name, pointing out her lack of sexuality, makes her seem a better mother in the eyes of patriarchy. The protagonist's sense of isolation and her craving for relationships are evident in the excessive presence of "and" ("Wallpaper," 26), which might be a gothic feature. Further, the many textual line breaks indicate both her lack of relationships and her wish to consider speakers side by side: his voice–her voice. As a writer, Jane's enforced loneliness is even more unbearable: "It is so discouraging not to have any advice and companionship about my work" (29). In a feminist maternal vein, Gilman denounces patriarchy for forbidding women to enjoy both sexuality (being a woman, a writer, a lover) and motherhood (being a mother).[3] Both the form and content of "Wallpaper" are consistent with Patricia Waugh's argument on women authors. According to this scholar, women authors have decided to represent a relational model of subjectivity, which rejects both the notion of the autonomous "ego" and the nominally "fragmented self," since they are formulated upon a myth of wholeness that women have never been allowed to enjoy (10). Thus, feminist scholars argue for a non "ego" whose first move toward the *other* does not entail the purpose of domination, as in the Hegelian sphere, but that of establishing a relationship. In this new realm, neither is dependence a shame nor does it imply assimilation. For instance, in the Chodorowian scene, differentiation does not imply separateness but connection. For Bakhtin, "I realize myself initially through others" (Bakhtin 1999, 138). Dialogical feminists have linked Bakhtin's and Chodorow's views, arguing for a "new" model of subjectivity that is acquired through a relational self (Pearce, 91). These theorizations can be exemplified with the passage from "Wallpaper" quoted above, where the main character omits both the subject and the verb, "[I am only b]etter in body" ("Wallpaper," 34). Her inability to refer to herself as "I" could stem from the fact that she is not treated as "you" (a subject) by John, who likes to address her in the third person: "Bless her little heart! . . . she shall be as sick as she pleases" (33).

It seems that John is not only bad at conversation but that he might be bad at sex too. William Veeder's comparison to *Gone With the Wind* is appropriate and equally suggestive: " 'And dear John gathered me in his arms, and just carried me upstairs and laid me on the bed, and sat by me and read by me till it tired my head,' [though this] Scarlett O'Hara encounters Book Man" (56). The reading of a bedtime story is another indication of John's paternal(istic) attitude toward her. Instead of the attic bedroom he finally chooses for her, Jane would prefer the one on the first floor that "had roses all over the window" (26). He refuses because "there [i]s . . . no room for two beds, and no near room for him if he took another," making explicit his desire not to sleep with her, although he offers the "cellar" for her (29). That John wants her either up or down, but not at an equal level, as a different subject, reminds us of gender discrimination working in two ways: mother/whore. Moreover, Jane has just given birth to a son ("him," 25), who ensures the male hereditary line, and explains one of the reasons why "the master" does not require her sexual services immediately. In what follows, I will suggest that the yellow wallpaper of Jane's bedroom can be read as a mirror of her sexuality. I also will try to approach the text's ending, which is open to more than one reading, as corresponds to a dialogical short story.

If, as Freud contends, women acquire the phallus only by delivering a son, it seems Jane, a professional writer who already has a pen, is trying to acquire *two*. This entails a too daring breach of the phallocratic order that must be prevented; hence she is prescribed the rest cure. Nevertheless, the fictionalized mother-writer is able to protest against her situation in various symbolic ways. For instance, if her room can be well a symbol of the womb, her supposed final breaking through the wallpaper at the end could be read as a reenactment of her/her child's (re)birth, as if searching for a new, different state of affairs in which mothers' and children's lives would definitively be better. The wallpaper's pattern appears so excessive that Jane feels repelled by it— "a florid arabesque . . . a fungus . . . a toadstool in joints, an interminable string of toadstools, budding and sprouting in endless convolutions" ("Wallpaper," 34). Jane's reaction might be indicative of her repulsion of her own fertility, given patriarchy's lack of dialogic understanding of it.

The imagery used to describe the wallpaper oozes with sexual connotations. Its colour is "lurid" (26), "a smoldering unclean yellow," which makes Jane think only of "old, foul, bad yellow things" (37). Its design, "a kind of 'debased Romanesque' " (31), has a "vicious influence" on her (29) suggestive of an orgasm or "*delirium tremens*" (31). Most critics have noticed its "smooch[es]" (35, 40)—which go "[r]ound and round and round" making Jane "dizzy!" (37)—and some have suggested they refer to masturbation. A subject who masturbates is definitively a *subject* and can be said to rebel against a society that imposes a heterosexual-reproductive regime. Unlike sexual intercourse, masturbation does not entail the risk of (an unwanted) pregnancy. Surprisingly, many medical authorities of the 1920s still associated masturbation with some supposed problematic form (Jeffreys, 170). Then, lesbianism and masturbation are cited as the main cause of frigidity, which is understood as a "dislike or failure to respond to a specific manifestation of sexuality, i.e., sexual intercourse" (171–72). Furthermore, there is a moment when the main character admits that "[i]t is getting to be a great effort to think straight" ("Wallpaper," 32) and the word "queer" appears three times. Some readers have rightly appropriated these elements so as to claim "Wallpaper" as a lesbian text (Allen, White).[4] From this perspective, and rebelliously enough, Gilman's protagonist represents a lesbian mother-writer living in Victorian America. It is clear that John does not consider Jane a *subject* with whom to establish a *true* relationship, for instance a sexual one. This might be one of the reasons why she needs to explore her erotic possibilities by herself. During her consented imprisonment in the yellow room, the protagonist reveals (maybe even discovers) something else about her own sexuality, something beyond John, be it about masturbation, lesbianism, heterosexual nonsatisfaction, etc. Whichever the case, "Wallpaper" manages to show that women's sexual desire and practice continue during motherhood, a continuation that has been denied throughout history, in which could be termed the *sexual-maternal*.

At the end of "Wallpaper," Jane starts to crawl around the room acting like the kind of animal John suggests she is (28). Her hysteric acting can be read as a reclaiming of her *sexual* body. Diane Price-Herndl sustains that Gilman the writer recovers from the rest cure only through a "writing cure." Thus, her main character's final tearing off the wallpaper might very well enact the artist's difficulties and suffering in order to find a voice of her own. Such an artistic ordeal has been summarized by Bakhtin: "[language is] populated—overpopulated—with the intentions of others. Expropriating it, forcing it to submit to one's own intentions and accents, is a difficult and complicated process" even though a *possible* one (2000, 294). In a Derridean vein, Price-Herndl states, "writing is a poison as well as a remedy, because to cure the woman, it must kill the hysteric. Writing takes the place of the hysteric. And leaves the *subject*" (68, emphasis added). Maternal autobiography, then, appears as the Cixousian sortie that confers subjectivity on to mothers-writers. Would Meridel Le Sueur agree with this?

"Annunciation" is dedicated to one of the author's daughters (*Rachel*), which reveals its autobiographical character. As in the preceding section, I evaluate this short story's departure from and re-creation of realism. Le Sueur's feminist proposals are interpreted under the light of both Bakhtinian dialogics and the theory of feminine *écriture*, a mode of writing that can be considered a genre (Cohen). In outline, I claim that "Annunciation" invents the "chronotope of pregnancy."[5] Since the unnamed female protagonist narrates the story, her voice accentuates even more her subjectivity. No doubt, the image of a pregnant woman is profoundly dialogic, as the multiplicity of meanings that will be (re)born: such as a new subject and a socialist-feminist revolution.

As happened to "Wallpaper," the editorial rejection of "Annunciation" might have to do with its capacity to going against the literary-critical current, as the story is both feminine and dialogic. From a feminist Bakhtinian optic, in order that feminine *écriture* can be a variant of realism, it must deal with the critical portrayal of women's realities. Moreover, questions of feminine subject-matter, apart from form, need to be assessed in order to formulate a feminist critique of women's problems in the sociopolitical sphere. In this respect, Le Sueur's "pregnancy chronotope" covers not merely a stylistic function but also an ideological one. Contrary to the well-known detrimental readings of feminine *écriture*, the protagonist-narrator of "Annunciation" is socially and economically situated. She is a very poor pregnant woman living in America during the economic depression. She and her husband, Karl, have worked selling "old fruit" (124) and performing some kind of "show" ("Annunciation," 126, 128).[6] Unlike her husband, who advises abortion (128, 132), the main character is happy about becoming a mother.[7] She is also pregnant with a bursting literary creativity—"Ever since I have known I was going to have a child I have kept writing things down on these little scraps of paper" (124), which contradicts the patriarchal axiom opposing the creative (sexual) to the procreative (maternal). The main purpose of her writing, she continues, is that "[t]here is something [she] want[s] to make clear for [her]self and for others," which ensures her dialogical concern for the listeners, because she has "never heard anything about how a woman feels who is going to have a child . . . [and she] would like to read [about it]" (130). The last statement makes explicit another criticism: literary history has omitted/distorted maternal experience. For about eight years, "Annunciation" is rejected by editorials that consider pregnancy is unacceptable as a literary subject (Coiner, 128). Instead of questioning their ability to read, the male editors of Le Sueur only criticize women's ability to write (130). Nevertheless, Bakhtin celebrates the constant renew of the work of art through the readers' interpretations (Bakhtin 2000, 254). Therefore, future readers will be able to see gendered chronotopes (e.g., of gestation) that are unavailable to its contemporaries. A new feminist dialogical reading can, thus, host a curious dialogue between Le Sueur and Bakhtin as follows.

According to Bakhtin, every "chronotope makes narrative events concrete, makes them take on flesh" (Bakhtin 2000, 250). Le Sueur's dialogic protagonist "feel[s] thick with th[e] child" and is aware that "in [her] . . . are the buds of [her] child" ("Annunciation," 126, 131).

Bakhtin continues that the chronotope "causes blood to flow in [the] veins" (Bakhtin 2000, 250). Also here, "[the] skin shines like crystal with the veins showing beneath blue and distended" ("Annunciation," 130). The Bakhtinian chronotope "materializ[es] time in space" (Bakhtin 2000, 130), and this female character "ha[s]n't any time except the nine months [she i]s counting off" ("Annunciation," 127). It appears that the pregnant body is an actual performance of a gendered chronotope, showing the fusion of time and space in the growing of the woman's belly (and of the fetus). Going doubly against the mainstream, in Le Sueur's text, not only the body but the female body is the chosen site of human experience. David McNally has stressed Bakhtin's insistence that we are *"body-selves"* whose sense of self takes place through embodied relations with others (125). Despite this, McNally criticizes the fact that the Russian thinker does not recognize the mother's subjectivity, who continues to be an object in the child's world.[8] Considering a gendered chronotope of gestation leads both feminist writers and critics to discuss the devaluation of female experience by patriarchal discourses, for instance, by Bakhtin himself.

It is especially French feminists who demand a rewriting of the discourse of pregnancy, arguing that the mother's subjectivity is never taken into account by religious, scientific, and even some artistic discourses on maternity (see Kristeva). For Le Sueur, it is clear that the "mystery" of reproduction is "unknown to scientists" ("Origins," 256), perhaps because it directly correlates with the maternal and sexual imaginaries (Irigaray 1993, 123). It is obvious that the patriarchal imaginary needs to be changed so that woman can be identified as *both* a maternal *and* a sexual subject—Cixous suggests, as "body and sex" (346). Le Sueur's sexual-maternal symbolism rewrites ancient myths on women. Like Demeter, this pregnant protagonist "feel[s] like a pear" ("Annunciation", 129), "like a tree" (131), looks like a "pomegranate" (130): and wants to "[w]alk . . . as a wheat stalk." The character-narrator tells us that she is in her "fourth month" (124). For the Native Americans four is a sacred number (Gelfant, 76) and Changing Woman, such as a pregnant woman, a sacred figure (Le Sueur, *Rites*). "Annunciation" does not only sublimate the maternal à la patriarchal but also observes its sexual-bodily facets—the widening of the female body, the feelings of sickness of the first months ("Annunciation," 126). Continuing with the social body, the sterilization of the poor is a common practice during the American Depression. That is the very reason why this heroine spends the day sitting at the boardinghouse where she and her husband live—"for I do not show that I have you [child]" ("Annunciation," 128)—so as not to be discovered and eventually sterilized. Like other class-conscious writers, Le Sueur "believe[s] it is the privilege and function of the proletarian writer to . . . respon[d] . . . [to] the oppressed, showing not only their suffering but their endurance" ("Preface," unpaginated). In her oeuvre, women who continue with their pregnancies stand for a victory against a society that appears to work against them (see especially *The Girl*).

The gendered chronotope of pregnancy invites us to think of the reproductive process as part of the natural cycle. Thus it tenderly shows that human and other living beings live together in the same community. For instance, when the mother-to-be looks at the mountains, she realizes that their "bony skeleton . . . [is] like the skeleton of the world . . . [and of her] child too" ("Annunciation," 128). A vital character in this story is the pear tree of the porch, whose "leaves twirl and twirl all over the tree . . . Far below . . . runs the trunk; and invisible, spiraling downward and outward . . . lie the roots. I can see it spiraling upward . . . its stem straight, and from it, spiraling the branches . . . and from the spiraling branches . . . the forked stems, and from the stems twirling . . . the tinier stems holding . . . the half-curled pear leaves" (131).

First, if the tree's circling pattern suggests a celebration of female rhythms, it also stands for an alternative to the status quo. As on other occasions, Le Sueur might be reminding us that a self-consciousness of life as circle inevitably leads toward ecology (cf. Schleuning). Second, the pear tree we see comes "from" the roots, the branches "from" the stem, the leaves "from" the branches, and so on. Apart from the pregnant woman, Nature provides us with a model for ethical relations, showing that they are what sustain life. In "Annunciation," pregnancy appears to have an erotic/sexual dimension that reveals vital characteristics of the self.

As suggested above, many feminists reject the notion of the uprooted and atomic ego of Western theory. They remind us that we come from and depend on others since we are born, start to speak, and keep on forming ourselves as persons. Bakhtin also rejects the mere individuality of human beings, therefore questioning the boundaries of a nonsufficient self: "To be means to be for another, and through the other for oneself. A person . . . is always on the boundary; looking inside h[er]self, [s]he looks *into the eyes of another or with the eyes of another*" (Bakhtin 1984, 287). In this sense, Bakhtinian dialogics is connected with the proposals of relational identity and the ethics of care.[9]

As a dialogical feminist, I lament that none of these proposals is practised between the heroine of "Annunciation" and her husband, which conceals the sexual origin of her (coming) maternity. Karl spends the day outside or mistreats his wife verbally and emotionally when he is with her, e.g.: "He took me out and made me walk along the deck . . . and he kept talking to me in a low voice, trying to persuade me [to have an abortion]. It was hard for me to listen" ("Annunciation," 127). By choosing not to be influenced by Karl's authoritarian voice, she matures in her ideological becoming (Bakhtin 2000, 295). Thus, she exultantly confesses: "I stopped talking to him much. Everything I said only made him angry. So writing was a kind of conversation I carried on with myself and with the child!" ("Annunciation," 127). In an *ideal* dialogical situation of this (heterosexual) sort, both mother and father (figures) should be able to share the sexual-maternal aspects of the pregnancy chronotope. With both partners enjoying such a chronotope, one would approach the ideal dialogue described by Bakhtin: "Two voices is the minimum for life, the minimum for existence" (Bakhtin 1984, 252); for the philosophers of feminine writing, "we do not come from *one*: we are engendered by *two*" (Irigaray 1996, 40). Therefore, "Annunciation" fails to show reproduction, love and desire as being intersubjective. Most importantly, dialogical situations are those shared by (speaking) subjects, a title women have not been awarded yet. As happens to Gilman's heroine the dialogic development through writing—as well as through (not) listening and the other relations—turns her into a subject for herself. In this way, she incarnates the hope for a dialogical and *ethical future*.

As expected, Le Sueur wishes to criticize the socioeconomic context of "Annunciation." Thus, the character-narrator lets us know that many people are "out of work. [And that they] are hungry just as [she is] hungry" ("Annunciation," 124). During her enlightened chronotopic state, she comprehends that her pregnancy symbolizes "the kind of spring there should be in the world" and demands "a deep rebellion" (130, 131).[10] She subversively hopes that her child "will come glistening with life power . . . I hope that you will be a warrior and fierce for change, so all can live [like a new Messiah]" (128). Considering all this, "Annunciation" expresses hope for a radical turn in the history of "the dispossessed" (125)—a word that criticizes an unequal class system, which is completely ignored by Gilman's "Wallpaper." One of the most striking differences between both maternal autobiographies lies precisely in the issue of class: while Le Sueur's main character is poor,

Gilman's is upper class. In spite of that, both fictionalized mothers suffer from the incomprehension and mistreatment of those around them, especially of their partners. Moreover, we know nothing about the protagonists' mothers or about other women with whom they could share frustrations and aspirations. On the one hand, Jane's longing for a companion is such that she turns to (perhaps) imagine there is a woman trapped within her bedroom's yellow wallpaper. Susan S. Lanser interprets this "other-other" as an immigrant woman, who appears to be literally more trapped than the mother-writer. On the other, in Le Sueur's fictionalized boardinghouse there is a dying old woman that spent "all her life tending other people's children" ("Annunciation," 125); at the story time, "nobody comes to see" her. The "other" mothers placed in the backgrounds of Gilman's and Le Sueur's autobiographical texts should lead us to reflect upon both social and literary subjects. First, mothers might contribute to the exploitation of other women, who might as well be mothers, such as the lower-class women and women of color who work as so-called nannies for the first world. Second, the autobiographies of the "other" mothers are usually not presented to us in/as literary texts. In a Spivakian manner, Bakhtin urges that we respond dialogically to the other (people), in the sense that we provide them with the means to represent/write themselves. Third, beyond the premises of Euro-Americanism, it is necessary that we dialogically listen to/read texts about the different ways of conceptualizing the maternal by *women* and non-women of different nationalities, ethnicities, sexual orientations and so on. In modest fashion, my paper intends to dialogize the maternal in order to approach the many varied realities of *maternal subjects*.

Notes

1. The concept of dialogics has been attributed to the Russian thinker Mikhail M. Bakhtin. I here concentrate on two of its possible meanings that Bakhtin developed. (1) The dialogics implicit in language use makes words susceptible to change. Besides, any word has different meanings depending on the context within which it is uttered (the speaker, listener, time, place, etc). (2) Dialogics uses dialogue as a form of ethics. Broadly speaking, dialogics promotes having "many" voices/ideas instead of a single "one" and taking into account the *others*, whom we address, and who respond to us.

2. Quoting from Dale M. Bauer's and Jaret McKinstry's introduction to *Feminism, Bakhtin and the Dialogic*, Lynne Pearce summarizes feminist dialogics as "a way of thinking that 'challenges the assumption . . . of a monolithic or universal feminism' . . . a way of living that 'overcomes the public-private split' . . . an epistemology which, like

'standpoint theory,' believes that context and positionality are all . . . a new model of pedagogy which shows 'genders, classes and races in dialogue rather than in opposition' . . . and most importantly, it is the latest . . . form of feminist political resistance" (103).

3. The last denunciation is central in another famous story, "The Giant Wistaria." The maternal is a constant preoccupation in Gilman's oeuvre, a few examples of which are: "An Unnatural Mother," deconstructing maternal instinct; "Turned," where a woman decides to look after her husband's illegitimate baby together with its actual mother; "A Garden of Babies" and *What Diantha Did*, arguing for the modern need of kindergartens; and the *Herland-Ourland* saga, which, among other things, proposes fathers' full involvement in child rearing. The erotic is apparently absent in most of Gilman's work, perhaps due to her conviction that she is a social reformist in the first feminist wave. Exceptionally, "Wallpaper" shows the continuation of women's sensual lives after becoming mothers.

4. Apart from her two marriages, Gilman has been attributed other possible love relationships: one with Martha Luther, another with Adeline Knapp.

5. The "chrono-tope," literally "time-space," is one of Bakhtin's theoretical approaches "for distinguishing generic types" (Morson and Emerson 1997, 250–51). Thus, the chronotope is going to define the relation between the work of art and (social) reality.

6. The narrator says they would "pla[y] in a tent" (128), so it seems possible that they might be actors. Le Sueur herself "studie[s] at the American Academy of Dramatic Art and worked on the New York stage" (Hedges, 3).

7. Le Sueur's writings celebrate the link between mothers (not fathers) and their children, which can be a feature of the second feminist wave. "Spring Story" and "Persephone" rewrite the myth of Demeter and her daughter; *The Dread Road* shows a mother's unspeakable desperation while mourning her child; if "The Horse" narrates and criticizes patriarchal medical interference in labor of birth, *The Girl* narrates and rejoices a natural labor of birth in an all-female community. Closer to the story being discussed, "Sequel to Love" denounces poor women's sterilization, and "Wind" defines pregnancy is as "bliss" (100).

8. The images of pregnancy, the womb, and so forth appear continually in *Rabelais and His World*. However, women and the concreteness of their bodies are absent from the text. With McNally I suspect that Bakhtin's method obeys the patriarchal custom of passing female procreative power onto the male body (146).

9. Theorists of relational identity and the ethics of care encourage the rediscovery of connection, which leads one to realize the intersubjectivity of self and other.

10. The final scene of the text, with the image of the pear tree "falling . . . into the earth" (132), has been read to represent something tragic (Coiner), as if the mother were to be deprived of the child. Nevertheless, the many elements falling (leaves, haze) are the signs of autumn, a season that has positive connotations for Le Sueur (e.g., 130). Dialogically enough, the ending invites more than one reading.

Works Cited

Allen, Paula Smith. *Metamorphosis and the Feminine. A Motif of 'Difference' in Women's Writing*. New York: Peter Lang, 1999.

Bakhtin, Mikhail M. *The Dialogic Imagination. Four Essays.* Trans. Caryl Emerson and Michael Holquist. Austin: University of Texas Press, 2000 (1981).

———. *Speech Genres and other Late Essays.* Trans. Vern W. McGee. Austin: University of Texas Press, 1999 (1986).

———. *Problems of Dostoevsky's Poetics.* Trans. Caryl Emerson. Minneapolis: University of Minnesota Press, 1984 (1929).

Cixous, Hélène. "The Laugh of the Medusa." Trans. Keith Cohen and Paula Cohen. In *Feminisms. An Anthology of Literary Theory and Criticism.* Edited by Robin R. Warhol and Diane Price Herndl. 347–62. New Brunswick, NJ: Rutgers University Press, 1997.

Cohen, Margaret, and Christopher Prendergast, eds. *Spectacles of Realism: Body, Gender, Genre.* Minneapolis: University of Minnesota Press, 1995.

Coiner, Constance. *Better Red: The Writing and Resistance of Tillie Olsen and Meridel Le Sueur.* New York: Oxford University Press, 1995.

Diamond, Elin. "Realism and Hysteria: Toward a Feminist Mimesis." *Discourse* 13, 1 (1990): 59–92.

Gelfant, Blanche H. *Women Writing in America: Voices in Collage.* Hanover and London: University Press of New England, 1985.

Gilman, Charlotte Perkins. *The Living of Charlotte Perkins Gilman. An Autobiography.* Madison: University of Wisconsin Press, 1991 (1935).

———. "Why I Wrote 'The Yellow Wallpaper.'" In *The Captive Imagination. A Case Book on "The Yellow Wallpaper."* Edited by Catherine J. Golden. New York: Feminist Press, 1992. 51–53.

———. "The Yellow Wallpaper." In *The Captive Imagination. A Case Book on "The Yellow Wallpaper."* Edited by Catherine J. Golden. New York: Feminist Press, 1992. 24–42.

Golden, Catherine J., ed. *The Captive Imagination. A Case Book on "The Yellow Wallpaper."* New York: The Feminist Press, 1992.

Holmund, Christine. "The Lesbian, the Mother, the Heterosexual Lover: Irigaray's Recodings of Difference." *Feminist Studies* 17:2 (Summer 1991): 283–304.

Irigaray, Luce. *An Ethics of Sexual Difference.* Translated by Carolyn Burke and Gillian C. Gill. Ithaca, NY: Cornell University Press, 1993.

———. *I Love to You: Sketch for a Felicity within History.* Translated by Alison Martin. New York: Routledge, 1996.

Jeffreys, Sheila. *The Spinster and her Enemies. Feminism and Sexuality, 1880–1930.* London: Pandora, 1985.

Kristeva, Julia. "Motherhood According to Giovanni Bellini." *Desire in Language. A Semiotic Approach to Literature and Art.* Translated by Thomas Gora, Alice Jardine and Leon S. Roudiez. New York: Columbia University Press, (1977) 1980.

Lanser, Susan S. "Feminist Criticism, 'The Yellow Wallpaper,' and the Politics of Color in America." *Feminist Studies* 15 Fall (1989): 415–42.

Le Sueur, Meridel. "Annunciation." Le Sueur 1982.

———. *The Girl.* London: The Women's Press, (1978) 1986.

———. "The Origins of Corn," excerpt. (1976) Le Sueur 1982.

———. "Preface." *Women on the Breadlines*. Albuquerque: West End, (1977) 1984.

———. *Ripening. Selected Work, 1927–1980*. Old Westbury, NY: The Feminist Press, 1982.

———. *Rites of Ancient Ripening*. Minneapolis: Vanilla, 1975.

McNally, David. *Bodies of Meaning. Studies on Language, Labor and Liberation*. Albany, NY: State University of New York Press, 2001.

Morson, Gary Saul, and Caryl Emerson. *Mikhail Bakhtin. Creation of a Prosaics*. Stanford, CA: Stanford University Press, (1990) 1997.

Pearce, Lynne. *Reading Dialogics*. London: Edward Arnold, 1994.

Price-Herndl, Diane. "The Writing Cure: Charlotte Perkins Gilman, Anna O., and 'Hysterical' Writing." *NSWA Journal* 1:1 (1988): 52–74.

Schleuning, Neala. *America: Song We Sang Without Knowing. The Life and Ideas of Meridel Le Sueur*. Monkato, MN: Little Red Hen, 1983.

Shumaker, Conrad. "Realism, Reform, and the Audience: Charlotte Perkins Gilman's Unreadable Paper." *Arizona Quarterly* 47:1 (1991): 81–93.

Todorov, Tzvetan. *The Conquest of America: The Question of the Other*. Trans. Richard Howard. New York: Harper & Row, (1982) 1984.

Veeder, William. "Who is Jane? The Intricate Feminism of Charlotte Perkins Gilman." *Arizona Quarterly* 44:3 (1988): 40–71.

Waugh, Patricia. *Feminine Fictions: Revisiting the Postmodern*. London: Routledge, 1989.

White, Barbara A. Untitled. In *Charlotte Perkins Gilman. A Study of the Short Fiction*. Ed. Denise D. Knight. Albuquerque: University of New Mexico, 1997. 197–209.

The Mother in Mourning as the Subject of Autobiography in Rosamond Lehmann's *The Swan in the Evening: Fragments of an Inner Life*

Nóra Séllei

DEDICATED TO HER ELDEST GRANDDAUGHTER, ROSAMOND LEHMANN'S only autobiographical writing *The Swan in the Evening: Fragments of an Inner Life* (1967) is a "personal statement" (Lehmann, 31), covering a wide range of experiences from (mostly traumatic) early childhood memories through her work of mourning and recovery following the death of her daughter Sally. In this way, Lehmann's text as a narrative is driven by a lack (which is always at the core of both mourning and the process of subject formation) which is specific: the loss of the daughter by the mother, which evokes a pervasive cultural image, the mother in mourning, or *mater dolorosa*. For this reason, in this paper the focus of discussion and analysis will be how a specific maternal autobiographical subject: the mother in mourning creates a space and a subject position from which to speak and to tell a story that our culture renders into unnarratability since the archetypal mother in mourning—*mater dolorosa*—has no story to tell, only tears to shed.

My primary theoretical source will be Julia Kristeva's essay "*Stabat Mater*," which provides a cultural-psychoanalytical interpretation of the mother in mourning. On this theoretical basis, I will provide a close reading of the narrative of *The Swan in the Evening*, and will claim that in this text Lehmann rejects, or at least rewrites, the traditional discourse of the mother in mourning. Instead of repressing and silencing the traumatic event of the death of her daughter, their apparently ultimate separation, the narrator re-creates a cyclical and maternal—even mystical—subjectivity, with generations of daughters involved, in which the autobiographical narrator is both the subject and agent of her narration, but is, at the same time, constructed by her intersubjective—and ethical—relationships.

In this way, my argument will proceed from locating the autobiographical narrator in the story of her birth that implicates her in life and death simultaneously, but also in a specific—and ambiguous—matrilineage through the elucidation of the multiple cultural silencing of the voice of the *mater dolorosa* and Freudian theory on mourning to the structural analysis and close reading of the story. My aim is to point out how this text radically rewrites both the mother in mourning by giving her a voice and a story to tell and the concept of the autobiographical subject by turning it into an ethical subject of intersubjectivity.

Lehmann's text begins with a story that has multiple implications from the perspective of a woman trying to tell the story of her identity, which is loaded with the intermingling of birth and death, of mothers and daughters, of the death of mothers and daughters, of loss and mourning. The story the narrator wants to tell to Miss Davies, one of her teachers—but she is not willing to listen to her—is the story of her birth: that she was born during a thunderstorm in February, a rare phenomenon, which for that reason gained "dramatic force" in "popular imagination," particularly because it was "not long after 1 a.m. of the day of the funeral of Queen Victoria" (9).

The fact that the day of Queen Victoria's funeral coincides with the birth of the narrator may, on the one hand, signify the cultural moment when Victorian decency and codes of femininity are left behind, buried, and put to rest, and in this way, it can be interpreted as a moment when even certain untold stories can be told. On the other hand, however, it may also foretell something of a story in which matrilineage is unnaturally broken; also, it tells us about the permeability of the border between, and about the coexistence, of life and death. Furthermore, perhaps most significantly, this narrative opening recounts a story of the erasure of a female voice, wanting to tell about what she considers the core of her identity, the penultimate experience of her existence: the story of her birth, which uncannily coincides with death.

The erasure of her story (that her teacher is not willing to listen to it), at the same time, points beyond its function in this life story, and calls attention to the question of how a woman can become the subject of an autobiography, how a female voice can make herself heard, how she is listened to, how the female subject is born, how she can be constructed as the agent of a life story—and whether she has a story to tell at all.[1] Much has been written by feminist critics and theoreticians on the silencing of women in Western culture in general (among the earliest ones see e.g., Beauvoir, Kaplan), and on the problem of the female autobiographical subject in particular. As the genre of autobiography evolved in the eighteenth century, and is closely related to the emergence of the autonomous individual subject of liberal humanism, a notion that has been exposed by feminist thinkers as not gender-neutral but gendered as male (cf., e.g., Benjamin, 185–98), women have found it problematic to enter the genre, or to get their writing canonized as autobiography proper in spite of the apparently private—that is, "feminine"—function of the genre.

This general repression of the woman's voice is further enhanced if that voice is supposed to be that of the mother. As Julia Kristeva puts it succinctly, "all of Western culture rests on the murder of the mother" (qtd. in Willett, 13); and can we imagine any more radical silencing than death by murder? Undeniably, in one sense, Lehmann's autobiographical text carries out the ritual murder of the mother, in this case Queen Victoria, yet, in my understanding, this "murder" functions as the willful and dramatic deliverance from a repressive mother, who—to use Virginia Woolf's phrase in her autobiographical writing "A Sketch of the Past"—laid a finger on the lips (*Moments*, 104): imposed a taboo on women who wanted to speak out about their femininity.[2]

The location of the "dark backward of [the narrator's] identity" (Lehmann, 9) in the death of Queen Victoria, thus, is a liberating gesture that is all the more powerful as the thematic focus of Lehmann's text revolves around the question of her own motherhood. The maternal voice—and maternal subjectivity—obviously adds one more element to the problematic position of the possibility of utterance. As Marianne Hirsch claims, "[n]either psychoanalysis nor feminism has comfortably been able to assume a maternal voice. In psychoanalytic theories, the child is the subject of study. The mother exists only in relation to her child; as object of desire or fantasy she may be idealized or disparaged, but she remains distant and mystified. *She cannot be the subject of her own discourse*. Psychoanalytic feminism has added the female child to the male but *has not been able to adopt or to inscribe the perspective of the adult woman, especially that of the mother*" (252, emphases added).

In addition, Hirsch criticizes feminist psychoanalytic theory "for its account of subject formation [which] continues, disturbingly, to represent the mother as the ground against which the female subject develops." She also makes a comment on Kristeva's idea of the prelinguistic maternal voice, which she acknowledges as potentially subversive and dissident, but criticizes its locatedness outside the boundaries of language and the symbolic (253).

What needs to be claimed, found and/or created, thus, is the maternal voice within language—both in theory and in practice. In my view, Lehmann's autobiographical text provides a model—in practice—for the maternal voice and for maternal subjectivity, what is more, for the mother in mourning to speak out. As the central topic of *The Swan in the Evening* is the autobiographical narrator mourning the loss of her daughter, I am also claiming that Lehmann's text fundamentally revises a central motif of Western culture: the Christian icon of the Virgin Mother in mourning, who has neither a story to tell nor words at her disposal to tell that story—only milk and tears, which, as Kristeva points out, are "the signs *par excellence* of the *Mater dolorosa*"; milk and tears, however, are "both . . . metaphors of non-language, of a 'semiotic' that does not coincide with linguistic communication" ("*Stabat,*" 109).

This idea of the semiotic and nonlinguistic communication as *out of the bounds of the Symbolic*—that is, *the cultural*—uncannily coincides with how Sigmund Freud seems to conceptualise the process of mourning (and melancholia). Undeniably, his formulation of mourning allows "grave departures from the normal attitude to life"—that is, from what is generally accepted as culture—but this departure is not considered pathological as long as it is "overcome after a certain lapse of time" (Freud, 252), and if "the ego becomes free and uninhibited again" when the work of mourning is completed (253). If, however, the work of mourning takes an "unnaturally" long time, or includes other elements of object-loss, it is defined as melancholia, as "pathological mourning" (260) that, in turn, "behaves like an open wound" (262). This wound needs to be covered, bandaged, buried—in the same way as death, let alone "the most unnatural of all human bereavements" (Lehmann, 29): the death of a child. Both death and "unnatural" mourning (but who is to tell what length of time is natural for mourning?) are still a taboo, a "forbidden subject" (Lehmann, 88) in our culture, and as such is rendered into invisibility.

It is this multiple unnarratability (*mater dolorosa* as narrator narrating the perhaps "unnaturally long" process of mourning the most unnatural death, the death of a child) that Lehmann's autobiographical text makes an attempt at narrating. The text is self-reflexively aware of its own problematic—and perhaps radical—cultural position: its subtitle claims the text is *Fragments of an Inner Life*, and the narrator calls it both "sub-autobiographical" (65) and a "personal statement" (31, 146). All these expressions function as rhetorical devices that aim to remove and distance the text from the genre of "proper" (relatively coherent, unified, teleological) autobiography. Ironically, though, the implications of the subtitle also resonate with the origins of the genre since autobiography goes back to "the tradition of self-examination of Christian asceticism . . . , to this new spiritual orientation" (Gusdorf, 33).

Yet, the title is most honest about the text: it allows fragmentation, incoherence, instead of promising an all-inclusive and unified life story—instead of the most archetypal metaphor of "life-writing": going down the road, taking one's own way, in a linear chronology, and following a unified teleology. In this sense, one could state that Lehmann's text exemplifies what Estelle C. Jelinek considers the typical textual model of female autobiography, whose basic features she defines as diffuse, mostly nonchronological and nonteleological, reflecting the multiple dimensions—or, from another perspective: fragmentation—of women's lives (17, 19).[3]

That the beginning of an autobiography is fragmentary can almost be considered "natural" inasmuch the beginning is supposed to be the earliest memories—thus incoherent. *The Swan in the Evening*, however, carries on with this fragmentariness till the end—and not only because of the different subject positions of the narrator (she poses as an autobiographical narrator, as a letter writer to her granddaughter, Anna, and as an epilogue writer). Not only the earliest memories are sketchy, incoherent, and fragmented, but so are the later ones as well: with decades missing as "gaps" from this life-writing—this is why the narrator calls it "sub-autobiographical":

> What I have put down so far might almost be called *sub-autobiographical*. It has been like a descent into a vault or cave or crypt, where all is darkness when you first penetrate. Then a torch flares, light is thrown here on a painted fresco, there on a carving or bas-relief: figures in a landscape, real and recognized, yet each with the mystifying impact of a symbol-in-itself, pure of interpretation and interpreter; and able to be caught only just on the outward side of verbal or pictorial existence. Any attempt to treat the findings, or to expose them to more air and light might cause them to vanish altogether. *In between this subterranean record and what is still to come lies, I suppose, all the material for an autobiography proper; but it will never be written.*" (65, emphases added)

Practically, not a word is written about her life beyond the age of (if one can make a guess, but it is never stated) eight or ten; in the second part what we have is some memories of Sally's childhood, very selected ones, without ever mentioning any marriage, husband, father to the child, any familial circumstances, or any "life"—only certain memories of the mother-daughter relationship. The selected memories, nevertheless, both from *her* childhood and from Sally's do coalesce, or at least indicate a very clear thematic focus: primarily *death*, and, to a smaller extent, writing, creation, the power of words—two aspects where this book originates in: the trauma of death as a source of writing—and, as a result, as a means of creating one's self, the autobiographical subject, or the subject of this autobiography.

The childhood memories abound in memories of death: birth, love, death, and identity are irrevocably intermingled. They coexist not only in the time of birth of the narrator as explicated above, but the sense of identity of the narrator is uncannily interfused with death all through the text. The same coexistence and cyclicity of life and death, also of mother and daughter is created again at the end of the text, when the narrator expects Sally to pull her through to what is called "afterlife" or "hereafter," in this way this theme provides a thematic frame to the text.

The fact, however, that the governess obliterates the "dark backward" of the narrator's identity—that she was born on the night of a funeral—indicates our culture's relation not only to the female voice (as pointed out above), but also to death, to death as a taboo, which, at the same time, is an all-pervasive presence—culture's other, relegated to marginality, or, in Kristeva's phrase, to the status of the *abject* (Kristeva, *Powers*). This is how it appears in Lehmann's text: "As for subjects such as births, death, physical and sexual functions, these were taboo, and invested with an aura of murk, shame, guilt, suggestiveness and secrecy" (20). In other words, they are created by, contained within, and, at the same time, excluded by culture, and comprise "a revealed and yet invisible abjection" (Kristeva, *Powers*, 84).

The coexistence of life, death, and sexuality, and their concomitants like love and loss of love as a theme are present not only in their uncanny coincidence in the framework of the text: almost all the childhood memories are traumatic, associated with death, almost-death, unexpected death and loss of love. A few examples may illustrate how this theme permeates the text: a favorite teacher of the narrator, Miss Davies is leaving the school as she is getting married to a Mr. Tinkler, which gives cause enough for the feeling of loss: the children lose their teacher, the teacher will lose her name, and will be turned into Mrs. Tinkler—a name that is recognized as funny *and* sad by the children. This ambiguity is enhanced by the fact that even the teacher is crying on leaving, suggesting loss and mourning, which is confirmed by a scene much later in life when the narrator sees her again as a widow, and compares her two states as *allegra* and as *dolorosa*.

A memorable—and most untimely—death, that of little Wilma, the child of the stableman, the archetype of all children, who used to represent the ideal child for the narrator's father (thus, an always inaccessible alter ego for her), who is taken away by diphtheria at the age of six, provokes a grief in her father from which he is never able to recover, and the disintegration of his personality lingers in the background of the narrator's childhood memories. Love and death are also explicitly linked in the case of the narrator's favorite sweetshop owner, a dashing young woman who one day disappears from the shop, and she turns out to have been killed by her "*True Love*" (51).

The unaccountability of death is signalled by the fact that as a child, the narrator inadvertently causes two accidents of her younger brother, both of which she thinks fatal at first. In one case, the brother falls, starts seriously bleeding, and the narrator-sister irrationally takes the blame on herself. As a symbolic act of self-punishment, she "entombs" herself under the bed while trying to hide from the adults, and does not come out even when they leave for the Henley Regatta—a genuine annual treat. In another instance she holds a bottle of perfume for the brother to smell, which he drinks at a gulp. The nurse, on taking him away, unthinkingly makes the comment: "You've been the death of him" (18), a remark that, although finally no harm is done, imposes guilt and self-retribution on her, in the very way Freud explains as part of the symptom of melancholia. She hides again, and falls into what Freud describes as "painful dejection, cessation of interest in the outside world, loss of capacity to love, inhibition of all activity, and a lowering of self-regarding feelings to a degree that finds utterance in self-reproaches and self-revilings [which] culminates in a delusional expectation of punishment" (252).

It is this melancholia/mourning that organizes the text thematically, but the very process of mourning and melancholia imposes a fragmentary structure upon the text. In this way, the central theme imposes an organizational structure upon the text that makes it both coherent—thematically it is teleological—and fragmentary at the same time. As a result, the text seems to be informed by two kinds of rhetorical moves: on the one hand, it allows—what is more, consciously admits—fragmentation, on the other hand, it has quite a clear teleology and thematic focus: from the traumatic childhood experiences it proceeds in the direction of Sally's unexpected, sudden death at the age of twenty-three, through the work of mourning (*Trauerarbeit*) to the ultimate state of the speaking subject who can tell this hardly narratable story.

This is not to say, however, that the text wants to suggest and create the impression of an undivided, coherent, unified autobiographical subject. Apart from the usual triple division of the autobiographical "I" that one can observe in all autobiographical writings (i.e., the author/writer, the narrating "I" and the narrated "I") the text very consciously, even self-reflexively—perhaps in a postmodern way—gives up the attempt (before making *any* attempt) at creating either a coherent narrating position, or narrated I. As far as the narrator is concerned, the text is divided into five parts, four of which appeared in this first publication in 1967, whereas the fifth section was attached to it on its republication. In this way, one is inclined to think that the first four belong to the text proper, whereas the fifth one is just a supplement, a paratextual device, thus an addition, not an integral part, which does not seem to be the case, as we will see.

The first part is about the childhood experiences of the narrator, the second one is a very short recollection of certain memories of Sally's childhood, the part concluding in hearing the news of her death; the third one covers the work of mourning and the emotional/spiritual healing (for many, perhaps the most disturbing part of the book); the fourth one is a "Letter to Anna," to the granddaughter to whom the book is dedicated, whereas the fifth one is the "Epilogue," written in 1981 (when Lehmann was eighty years old), and can be read as a response to the responses of the readers of the text. This section, at the same time, explicitly defines itself as a last testament, but it can also be considered as a rounding-off of the whole text in more than one way. This is why I claim it is not just a simple "author's note," a simple paratextual device. Perhaps the whole text is best to be unfolded from this end—the ending—if one wants to define how the narrator figures—or self-fashions herself—in the text:

> This is my last testament. What else is left that I might say? I am in my eighty-first year, so it seems more than likely that this particular stage

of my journey is drawing to a close. Once the thought of living on through time without Sally was too huge, too hopeless a burden to be borne. But nowadays I seem to live partly out of time: so that that lacerating illusion we create by having to deal life out in packets of days, months, years, has largely disappeared. Time past, time present, time future are beginning to coalesce. I know that eternity is not to come: that we are in it here and now. . . . No matter how far ahead of me Sally has gone—and I know she has—she will be waiting, as she promised. She will pull me through the door. (167–68)

These are the closing lines of the text, partly playing around, and playing with, central notions of life-writing and autobiography: the metaphor of the journey of life, stages of the journey, and the central notion of linearity, existence in time, measuring out life in days, months, years, positing the rejection of these notions as if this rejection characterized only *this* stage, old age, the stage of awaiting death, being "pulled through" by Sally. Yet, as I see the text, not only the end, but also its totality rejects the notion of time and chronology, let alone the notion of the coherent and unified (autobiographical) subject.

In my view, apart from an almost obsessive concern with life and death, the text articulates the problem of responsibility—or an intersubjective ethics. The childhood incidents of thinking to cause the death of her brother and the consecutive guilt foreshadow the central concern of the text: how can a mother cope with the trauma of losing her child/daughter, for whom by definition she is supposed to be responsible. This theme is emphatically brought to the foreground in the second part, where some memories of Sally as a child are recalled. Two of the most telling ones are the following: the child Sally asking her mother how she will live if the mother dies, and the mother promising she will never die; the other one is a recollection of a boat trip in which they almost went down, but Sally as a baby had an undisturbed, beaming, trusting, baby-look on her all through, and the narrator ponders if she would have had the courage to pull Sally through, to death, without causing pain—the thing she supposes of her daughter in the last words of the text.

These two instances are significant not only because they exemplify the mother's responsibility for the child (and as such, the most traditional duty, care, responsibility, and anxiety related to the child), but also because they foreshadow their joint, or parallel, life stories: the mother surviving the daughter, and the daughter returning the gesture of the mother when giving birth to her, which implies crossing the boundary of life. In this way, the latter experience could be read as a relatively simple reversal of dependence, furthermore, as a mystical experience or foreclosure of a mother who, not able to cope with her very trauma, projects this image of wish-fulfillment upon her dead daughter.

Instead of this mutual dependence, or rather, reversal of dependence, however, a more interesting and intriguing process takes place, not devoid of elements of the subject formation of the narrator. What Lehmann's text performs is a double move: what we hear is a transgressive female voice, speaking of death. What we hear is a transgressive maternal voice—the mother speaking, which, in psychoanalytical terms, is almost impossible: a mother trying to find words for the articulation of her motherhood but also reformulating that concept of maternity that is the par excellence definition of femininity in our culture—as Kristeva puts it: "femininity . . . is confined within the limits of the *Maternal*" ("*Stabat*," 99–100). In the "sophisticated symbolic construct" of Christian maternity (Kristeva, "*Stabat*," 99), however, the mother cannot be figured as a person, in her personhood, only as—in Hélène Cixous's poem—a "dumping-ground" ("Sorties") against which, by way of a background, the identity of the child can be figured, but she cannot be a figure herself.

In this text, the narrator assumes an emphatically maternal voice (which, as Hirsch claims, is an impossibility in current psychoanalytical terms as the mother is erased from representation [252–53]—let me add: let alone from self-representation). What we can hear is the transgressive voice not only of the maternal voice, but also the voice of the *mater dolorosa*. This time, however, she is not just frozen into her semiotic body language (milk and tears), but she actually assumes the Mother's blue gown: while healing, she is surrounded by blue light. As a result of her healing, she metaphorically radiates the light of spiritual healing, but not only for others as the Holy Mother does, but also for herself: by inserting herself into representation, into the self-representation of the maternal voice. Thus, while representing it, at the same time she rejects, subverts and surpasses the iconography of the *mater dolorosa*.

As a result, she can disentangle herself from the position of nonfigure and nonsubject, from the dyadic mother-daughter plot in which the mother has no subjectivity. Also, she can disentangle herself from the exclusive cathexis to the lost object that, in Freudian terms, may result in the loss of the ego. Here, the narrator completes the process of mourning in Freud's terms: "the work of mourning is completed, the ego becomes free and uninhibited again" (253).

The process, nevertheless, is not a return to "normalcy," but concludes in a reformulation of maternity: by dedicating the text to the granddaughter, Anna, and by, at the same time, maintaining her connectedness to Sally, the narrator formulates a subjectivity defined by intersubjective relationships in which, however, libidinal energies—or love—is far from being unambiguous or one-directional. Love implies death, writing, laughter and pain:

> It seems fitting that this record, or testament, should write itself to an end in Sally's little house on the island. I lay down my pen and look out through the same long window to the spot where, nearly nine years ago, I saw the blackbird lying dead. Anna, to whom I dedicate this book, sits opposite me. For two days she has had her nose buried in a book, a Penguin, which has caused her recurrent lapses into quiet laughter. Now she has finished it and lays it down. "A very sad book," is all she says. It is called *The Pursuit of Love*. (137)

What we see again here is the merging of life and death, love and loss, reading and writing, laughter and pain. What, however, does not merge in this autobiographical text are the ego boundaries of mother and daughter, mother and granddaughter. They always stand apart but close, always in relation to each other, always in a mental and spiritual proximity, but as presented by the text, never threatening each other's subjectivity. In this way, this textual representation of female and, in particular, maternal subjectivity rewrites—or rather, writes herself out of—the patriarchal inscription of the maternal: there is no fusion between the mother and the child; as is the self-sacrificial element of mothering missing from the text. What we have instead is an element "fundamental to intersubjectivity: an awareness of the face of the other person," which is a key idea in Cynthia Willett formulation of maternal ethics (27). This awareness of the other's face, in Willett's opinion, does *not* function "in terms of power over objects . . . but rather in terms of social-relatedness" (29). It is only in this way, by recognizing the subjectivity of the other—be it mother or child—that an ethical stance between mother and daughter can be taken, that the mother's autobiographical voice can be heard, and that the mother in mourning *as* the subject of autobiography can be constructed. In this way, Lehmann's sub/autobiographical narrator not only lays claim to a voice for herself, but by turning the loss of the daughter into a gain: into a story told to generations of daughters, the text creates an autobiographical subject that evolves in relationships, in a crossgenerational intersubjectivity, and thus establishes and gives cultural and textual recognition to a maternal genealogy which is modelled upon both self-recognition and upon the mutual recognition of, and responsibility for the other.

NOTES

1. Georges Gusdorf, one of the earliest theoreticians of the genre claims in his "Conditions and Limits of Autobiography" (1956) that autobiography "expresses a concern peculiar to Western man, a concern that has been of good use to his systematic conquest of the universe" (29). Never in his article does he refer to the subject of autobiography in any other way but as gendered masculine, even though he is unaware of his own gendered discourse, and all his expresssions describing the textual representations of a life story resonate with the liberal humanist notion of the unified and coherent identity (e.g., 29, 35, 37).

2. In this respect, we have to consider the rather paradoxical situation that Queen Victoria, empress of the British Empire, and thus the ruler of a world power, definitely opposed the Cause, women's intention to gain suffrage, which can also be read as their wish to make their (political) voice heard.

3. I am fully aware of the potential essentialism of Jelinek's model, but in my view, as it can be read as response to, and an empowering revision of, Gusdorf's concept of autobiography, it opens up the genre for textual models other than the ones already canonized.

WORKS CITED

Beauvoir, Simone de. *The Second Sex*. Trans. and ed. H. M. Parshley. Harmondsworth: Penguin, 1983.

Benjamin, Jessica. "Gender and Domination." In *The Bonds of Love—Psychoanalysis, Feminism, and the Problem of Domination*. New York: Pantheon Books, 1988. 183–224.

Freud, Sigmund. "Mourning and Melancholia." In *On Metapsychology: The Theory of Psychoanalysis*, vol. II. Harmondsworth: Penguin Freud Library, 1984. 251–68.

Gusdorf, Georges. "Conditions and Limits of Autobiography." In *Autobiography: Essays Theoretical and Critical*. Edited by James Olney. Princeton, N.J.: Princeton University Press, 1980. 28–48.

Hirsch, Marianne. "Maternal Voice." In *Feminism and Psychoanalysis: A Critical Dictionary*. Edited by Elizabeth Wright. Oxford: Blackwell, 1992. 252–54.

Jelinek, Estelle C., ed. and intro. *Women's Autobiography: Essays in Criticism*. Bloomington: Indiana University Press, 1980.

Kaplan, Cora. "Language and Gender." In *The Feminist Critique of Language: A Reader*. Edited by Deborah Cameron. London: Routledge, 1990. 57–69.

Kristeva, Julia. *Powers of Horror: An Essay on Abjection*. Trans. Leon S. Roudiez. New York: Columbia University Press, 1982.

———. "*Stabat Mater*." Trans. Arthur Goldhammer. In *The Female Body in Western Culture: Contemporary Perspectives*. Edited by Susan Rubin Suleiman. Cambridge: Harvard University Press, 1985. 99–118.

Lehmann, Rosamond. *The Swan in the Evening: Fragments of an Inner Life*. Revised and with a new epilogue by the author. London: Virago, 1985 (1967).

Whitford, Margaret. "Mother-Daughter Relationship." In *Feminism and Psychoanalysis: A Critical Dictionary*. Edited by Elizabeth Wright. Oxford: Blackwell, 1992. 262–66.

Willett, Cynthia. *Maternal Ethics and Other Slave Moralities*. New York: Routledge, 1995.

Woolf, Virginia. *Moments of Being*. Ed. and intro. Jeanne Schulkind. London: Grafton Books, 1976.

Wright, Elizabeth, ed. *Feminism and Psychoanalysis: A Critical Dictionary*. Oxford: Blackwell, 1992.

Implicated in a Color Change: Darkening the Picture of Jane Lazarre's Maternal Transracial Memoir

Martha Satz

OVER A DECADE AGO, ARRIVING IN CHARLESTON, SOUTH CAROLINA, for an academic conference with my then six-year-old daughter, I immediately sank into a morass of depression and rage. So many friends had praised the beauty of the city with its natural landscape and antebellum homes that I had anticipated my visit with pleasure. But upon arriving, I marveled simultaneously at my friends' lack of political consciousness and my own naïveté. The whole city, it seemed, celebrated the Old South, proudly flying Confederate flags and advertising plantation tours. When I ventured on one of these excursions, my African American daughter in tow, the patter of the tour guide emphasized his, and presumably our, identification with the historic owners of the plantation. For example, he joked about "the whistle walk," the path from the kitchen to the dining room, so named because the owner required the slave to whistle as he walked from the kitchen to the dining room thereby guaranteeing that the slave did not "pilfer" some food. Desperate and claustrophobic in this environment, I located an Afrocentric tour of Charleston. A bit self-consciously, I set out on the tour, the only White member, hoping that my daughter's presence would mitigate my status as intruder.

When we had arrived in Charleston, I had given my daughter a quick age-appropriate tutorial on the history of slavery, so that she could bring some understanding to the situation. She reacted with apprehension, collapsing the present into the distant past, remarking "I'll stay close to you in case they want to take me as a slave." In spite of all my explanations, she still clung. When on the tour, the guide related the details of a planned slave rebellion, the intention of which was to kill all the whites in the vicinity, she clung to me anew. In Charleston, and especially during that time in the tour van, an exquisite complexity of race consciousness bore down upon my daughter and me. To be a White person among Blacks, aware of what one's skin color conveys both historically and presently, intensifies one's sense of racial positioning. But if one is also alienated from most Whites and linked to Blackness by the strongest of loves then one becomes ensnared in a convoluted consciousness. This state is both the analogue and converse of the double-consciousness that W. E. B. DuBois describes. He articulates the experience as "this sense of always looking at one's self through the eyes of others, of measuring one's soul by the tape of a world that looks on in amused contempt and pity" (16–17). But in contrast, as a white person, one may measure oneself by the discord between the approval of the world and the reality of one's soul. And the resultant anguish resonates with the feelings chronicled by DuBois and links me to Jane Lazarre, another white mother of African American children. Ostensibly, she is writing her memoir, but more vitally, she is writing out of a sharply focused political purpose, to communicate and bring other whites to the racial understanding that her unique position in the racial nexus has afforded her. But she engages in a hazardous enterprise. As a white woman whose life experience has shifted her ever closer to the African American experience but whose commonality with her readers may garner her more credence than Blacks, she risks that her very success will implicate her in the racism about which she testifies, a phenomenon of which she herself is acutely aware ("Anything said by a white person, still living the legacy of it all so intensely, seems gratuitous and presumptuous" [9]).

Jane Lazarre begins *Beyond the Whiteness of White*, significantly subtitled *Memoir of a White Mother of Black Sons*, with an acutely complex scene of racial self-consciousness. Attending the African American Studies Department ceremony honoring her son's graduation at Brown University, she calls her readers' attention to her minority status within a minority group, an inverse reflection of her son's usual position, "Here, most of the people . . . are Black, although there are a few other whites besides myself. . . . We stand out as our children stand out in the wider campus of Brown University, scattered faces "of color" in a vast sea of whiteness, the usual tiny minority of diverse Americans on campuses where racial balance has supposedly been achieved" (xiii–xiv). Thus, amid the privileged and elite white environment constituted by Brown, Lazarre portrays a discerning, resistant minority, the African

American Studies Department, and within that group, Lazarre places herself. Emphasizing her whiteness in this setting, she consciously works not to replicate the ideology of the larger environment but to ally herself with its Black audience while candidly admitting the gap separating her from it. However, her text implicitly forges another alliance as well. With her narrative mental musing, she makes evident that she has white people in mind. As she recalls the message of the African American faculty to the graduates ("You are wonderful, yes. But you must always be better than white people, you must be exceptional to succeed in this society" [xiv]), she invokes an absent group: "I can imagine the shock that would be felt by most white people were they sitting in this audience as I am" (xv). However, she contrasts her own response to these other imagined whites, "I no longer experience shock when listening to stories of the pervasive reality of American racism, but only the familiarity of recognition, of truth" (xv). Lazarre thus places herself in an elite position with respect to most Whites, more knowledgeable than they regarding racism. Invoking the tradition of the slave narrative, she declares that she is at the end of a journey that has carried her not from slavery to freedom, but from conceptual ignorance to racial consciousness. Her former ideal of color blindness has been transformed into the recognition of the "obvious and subtle racism in the immediate world around me every single day" (xx).

Like the authors of the slave narratives to which she alludes, Lazarre writes not only to tell of her journey but to lure her readers to accompany her empathetically in order to reach a more realistic understanding of the institutions of the society in which they live. And also like her literary foremothers, she foregrounds a commonality between herself and her readers so that those readers may arrive willingly at the place she has reached, in this case, epistemic. Jane Lazarre is explicit about the tradition in which she writes, "I have tried, in a way, to use memoir to transcend itself; not only to recall and describe experience but to understand its significance beyond the self . . . the link between an individual life story and the collective story which gives context to that life is a defining formal and thematic aspect of African American autobiography" (xviii). She is a white woman who chooses to place herself in the tradition of the African American autobiography. However, her racial positioning complicates her project, rendering it at one and the same time powerful and vulnerable.

If, for example, we compare Lazarre's narrative to Harriet Jacobs's *Incidents in the Life of a Slave Girl*, then we recollect how Jacobs creates sympathy and affinity in her white readers on the basis of their common womanhood and maternity and thus awakens her readers to the brutality of slavery.[1] In contrast, Lazarre has an initial presumptive commonality with her white readers but diverges from them by vicariously undergoing the experience of Blackness through her children. Thus, she offers her readers an account of the Black experience from a white perspective in a mode many of her readers will readily understand, undergoing suffering through one's child. She offers herself as an example of a white woman who once was naive about racism (like her presumed readers), holding color blindness as an ideal and has now become enlightened through the experience of her Black children's lives. Yet, ironically, if she succeeds in converting her readers to her new, more realistic perspective, she may have done so as a result of her racial privilege, in some ways implicitly validating her own point. As in other venues, white voices carry authority. Because Lazarre is white, her testimony regarding racism may be believed.

In her writing, Lazarre oscillates between, on the one hand, a complete identification with and, on the other, a regretful acknowledgment of her separation from Blackness. Perhaps thereby she offers herself as a model of an empathetic white person in a racist society. In the first chapter of her book, for example, Lazarre describes a transformative experience at a traveling museum of slavery. The photographs and the artifacts in the exhibit create within her a profound, emotional knowledge of slavery, more immediate and anguishing than her former intellectual understanding. As she observes an elderly Black man weeping at a photograph, she surrenders to her own feelings, "beyond embarrassment, I stop fighting my knees, I let them buckle, and, crouching on the floor, I weep too" (18). In this scene, crossing racial lines, Lazarre identifies and forms an improvised community with the other person mourning this history of suffering. And in the same chapter, she yields to another identification with Blacks more intimately connected with her. Hearing a laudatory historical portrait of Robert E. Lee on the radio, she weaves her lifelong Jewish identity together with her more recent maternal one, "Listening to the profile on the news, for a moment I became my sons, Black Americans listening to the story of an American hero, Robert E. Lee"(5). She brings to consciousness the contrasting ways Americans regard Nazis and slaveholders, observing that Americans do not ever describe Nazi generals respectfully, but do honor those like Lee who enslaved others and fought for slavery's continuance. As she acknowledges with pain, her moments of melding with Blackness can be only transitory. As she emerges from the slave exhibit, inspired by its content, she concedes her limitations, "I will somehow find the words to teach the narrative history to Black students among whom I shall have to tread with utmost care, proving and reproving what I do understand, acknowledging as respectfully as I can what I do not" (18). But her pain becomes amplified in the most excruciating passage in the book, which occurs in a moment of intimacy between her and her son, Khary: "'I am Black,' Khary explains to me.... ' I have a Jewish mother, but I am not biracial.' He goes on to explain his beliefs and feelings in detail and when I say, 'I understand,' he tells me carefully, gently, 'I don't think you do, Mom. You can't understand this completely because you're white'" (24). Lazarre is anguished beyond words at her son's insistence that race separates them: "I can not find words to express my feelings, or my feelings are too threatening to find easy language. They are mine fields lining opposite sides of the road of my motherhood of this beloved son. What is this whiteness that threatens to separate me from my own child? Why haven't I seen it lurking, hunkering down, encircling me in some irresistible fog? ... I want to cry out, don't leave me as he cried to me when I walked out of day-care centers.... And always, this double truth: she is me/not me; he is mine/not mine" (24–25).

This scene between Lazarre and her son lies at the conceptual heart of the book, at the core of her enterprise. For, throughout her memoir, Lazarre employs her experience of motherhood to change her epistemological position to that of "a person of a color with no precise name" who approaches knowledge of what is virtually unknowable for whites —what it is like to be Black—and to bring that knowledge through her writing to other whites and to move them to "see the world more truthfully" (69). However, her epistemological venture must also acknowledge the non-vanishing gap between Black and White. And such recognition also constitutes part of her point. She writes at the interstices between the races. Lazarre quotes bell hooks in *Black Looks:* "[W]e talk about the way white people who shift locations ... begin the see the world differently. Understanding how racism works, [they can see] the way in which whiteness acts to terrorize without seeing [themselves] as bad, or all white people as bad, and all Black people as good" (Lazarre, 1). It is clear that having undergone that shift in locations, Lazarre is endeavoring to dislodge other whites from their position. Her book is an attempt, as she says, "to do her share" (xvii) from the position she occupies.

Certain theoretical views regarding maternity and epistemology underlie Lazarre's project. She notes that although she was married to a Black man for a number of years, it took the birth of her sons to begin to change her racial stance. Lazarre refers to Sara Ruddick's view that motherhood is a discipline culminating in the virtue of "attentive love," seeing the world from the perspective of the child, without the mediation and intervention of maternal desires. Lazarre remarks about her own motherhood, "Perhaps even more than most mothers, I have identified with my children" (24). And she characterizes her relationship to her sons as "the dangerous loss of self and creative transcendence of self" (22). Ruddick, interpolating the thought of Iris Murdoch, writes, "The difficulty is to keep the attention fixed on the real situation or as I would say, on the real children. Attention to real children, children seen by the 'patient eye of love . . . teaches us how real things [real children] can be looked at and loved without being seized and used, without being appropriated into the greedy organism of the self'" (117). For Lazarre, Chinua Achebe's similar concept of "imaginative identification" provides inspiration, expressed as "human connectedness at its most intimate" (xx). Clearly, these notions function as an ideal. As Ruddick admits, "Of course, many mothers fail much of the time in attentive love and loving attention" (118). Yet, Ruddick argues that maternal practice is a particularly fertile venue for attentive love to appear because its very purpose is for children to flourish. Eva Kittay makes a similar argument about what she terms dependency work, the work of caring for a person with disabilities: "The demands of dependency work favor a self accommodating to the wants of another; that is, a self that defers or brackets its own needs in order to provide for another's" (51). She uses the term *transparent self,* "a self through whom the needs of another are discerned" (51). In the cases of both Ruddick and Kittay, the authors argue not that mothers or caretakers are especially virtuous, but that the practices in which they are enmeshed themselves foster this virtue.

Lazarre details her own experiences as a mother undergoing racism the first time a son, at four, is called "nigger" or the first time a son, at eleven, is followed in a store. She talks of incidents such as this: "'Oh, who would bother you on the street,' some well-intentioned white friend will say. 'A big, strapping (Black) guy like you.' Stated or unstated, the adjective in parentheses is there" (10). And in an offhand way, she indirectly educates her white reader in how to respond to racism: "My sons feel most comfortable with white members of their extended family who take an open interest in race and acknowledge the reality, as well as their own ignorance, of the stress of every single day for Black people in this country . . . 'I understand you' is often less authentic, and therefore less comforting, than 'What are you going through?'"(10).

As a result, then, of her cumulative experiences, with imaginative identification and with attentive love she understands her conversation with her son in his teenage years, "'I am so happy to be in a place where I can be friends mostly with Black kids,' Khary says to me on the phone after his first weeks at college. 'We have so much in common'" (10).

A philosophical thread underlies Lazarre's implicit claims. Vrinda Dalmiya in her article "Why Should a Knower Care?" explicitly argues that a caring relationship produces new knowledge of others' experiences, that it is a valid epistemic tool. She argues the caring relationship yields greater knowledge of others than that in the traditional relationships analyzed by philosophers and cognitive psychologists. When philosophers explain our knowledge of others as a species of reasoning by analogy, they give us knowledge about those who are similar. Simulation, a theory suggested by such cognitive psychologists as Alvin Goldman, proposes that we obtain knowledge of others by projecting ourselves into their situation, their difference incorporated into the imaginative process. Thus, we imagine ourselves, to use Goldman's example in the situation of Anita Hill, suffering the harassments and indignities that she allegedly did and we allow ourselves to experience in a surrogate way the feelings that such actions would produce, thereby in the optimal case, understanding her action. This emotional identification, according to Goldman, produces additional knowledge about Anita Hill. However, knowledge produced in this way may still be subject to egocentricity and gender or cultural bias. As Goldman comments, "it seems to be a general fact, congruent with the simulation theory, that when an agent's life experience is very different from our own, we have a harder time predicting or explaining their behavior" (190). For example, in this method, a man might imagine sexual harassment from a woman's perspective but might do so with a masculine set of assumptions about the relation between the genders. A white person imagines being the object of racism but with inherent hierarchical assumptions.

As a step toward overcoming this potential bias, Dalmiya adds to the analysis of the caring relationship an element of feedback from the one cared about as a check against potential unwarranted assumptions.

In Lazarre's memoir, a clearly articulated feedback occurs when Lazarre's son corrects her and tells her that she cannot completely understand his feelings because she is white.

It is not part of Dalmiya's discussion but nonetheless significant that knowledge of the cared for is characteristically rich. In a caring relation, the carer knows the other intimately, has observed her attentively over time, has acquired a nuanced and subtle view of her with the depth that time and love can provide. In other words, to use the Goldman model, a great deal of information infuses the imaginary projection. Additionally, parental knowledge is typically longitudinal. The mother sees the baby in the ten-year-old, the two-year-old in the teenager, and when she views the adult child, sees him within the context of a panoply of images of his former self. As Lazarre thinks about male violence, she recalls her son's past; she hears "Adam's child voice; he is about ten years old and I am trying to persuade him to walk away from fights with other boys in school: 'He called me a nigger, Mom. You want me not to hit him back?'" (80). Thus, if we compare the knowledge that Goldman imagines a man can achieve by simulation about a woman's position with, say, the knowledge a mother acquires about being male when she watches her son grow, we understand the advantages of a maternal caring relationship. In like manner, Lazarre's memoir implicitly argues that she as a white woman acquires an intimate knowledge of racism as she mothers her Black sons because she attentively and lovingly observes her children over time, over a lifetime of experiences with racism. She thinks, for example, about her sons' sense of their bodies and the way it is enmeshed with historical racism. "The already difficult-to-negotiate terrain of male sexuality is entangled even further by the double bind: you are a sexual trophy and a certain rapist" (81).

However, Lazarre's memoir advances beyond Ruddick's and Kittay's position. They suggest that it is desirable on an epistemological and metaphysical level to bracket the self. But one cannot gain epistemologically or morally if one simply adopts the other's position. It would seem that the extraordinary opportunity for growth occurs when one simultaneously inhabits one's own position and the other's. It seems trivial to state that one cannot fully appreciate the situation of the other and wrest oneself from one's own interpretive framework. But perhaps it is more fully human and fruitful to intermix self and other. Lazarre's sense of self clearly arises in situations when her sons wrestle with racism. She wonders, "Do my children think of me as white before or after they think 'my mother'?"(10).

Arguably, Maria Lugones' work on "world"-traveling derives its power by proposing just such an intermingling. She subtly sketches the notion of "world," as the framework in which subjects are constructed, most notably in which minority subjects are constructed by the dominant and arrogant gaze. Then, in a move parallel to but more elaborate and open than that of Goldman's simulation, she advocates that we travel to each others' "worlds," to understand each others' realities—but, significantly, in a playful manner, an attitude that involves "openness to surprise, openness to being a fool, openness to self-construction or reconstruction" (288). Once we have approached understanding of the other in this manner, by inhabiting her "world," we can come to love her fully. But by traveling to her world, "we run the risk" (as it would be phrased in the dominant ideology) or "enjoy the pleasure" (as Lugones' playful attitude would indicate) of ourselves changing. Thus, the difference between simulation and traveling is that travel involves a dialectic between other and self, so that because one retains a sense of self even as one enters the realm of the other, one may undergo alteration. Thus, Lazarre carries her altered consciousness with her, even when she is without her sons, "I went to a matinee in New York City recently, a delightful musical, accompanied by a good friend. I saw immediately that there was not one single brown face in the audience or in the play. . . . After the play, my friend and I went for a drink at a nearby hotel. Again, I traveled in a white world, comfortably invisible in a way I would never be if I were with my family" (11). She notes of her altered self-conscious self, "When I walk through the white world, I am a white woman who generally blends in, who is not looked at with suspicion or fear or even hatred when I walk down a beautiful ocean beach in New England or northern California, where my children's brown bodies instantly stand out differently than does mine. . . . I am an ordinary American woman protected by this whiteness . . . into a precious invisibility of apparent belonging, and I am weighted down with the transforming shame this knowledge brings (17–18). One is reminded of the late-twentieth-century Black woman who travels back to the antebellum South in Octavia Butler's novel *Kindred*, who as a mark of her transformation returns to her time period missing an arm. I myself am so transformed. Having once entered a small Arkansas café with my daughter, stopping all conversation, drawing the fixed hostile glances of everyone there upon us, I can never walk into such an establishment alone without the heavy bodily burden of that recollection.

Lazarre painfully learns over and over again that her sons will be regarded as potentially violent. When her son undergoes minor surgery, because he struggles frightenedly as he is recovering, he is put under anesthesia repeatedly, his fearful reaction misinterpreted as hostile struggle. When my own son in high school imitated my lifelong practice of an unbridled maternal attitude toward the world and told a toddler on the street to go home, his bicycle was immediately surrounded by police cars. In these ways, we learn how society constructs our children as Others. And so in discussions of racism with her sons, Lazarre feels masked and disguised by her white skin (78).

But in the end, the memoir yields a paradox. To what extent has Lazarre absorbed the realities of racism? To what extent has she learned the hardest lesson for all us mothers, but especially those who mother transracially, to fully absorb—there are some things we cannot do for our sons, for our children. As Lazarre realizes, "I could follow Khary to school when he was in the second grade, making certain he crossed at the green, or that no insane kidnapper snatched him along his vulnerable way. But I could hardly follow a twenty-year-old man to the video store, watching for teenagers with guns with one eye, racist cops with the other" (67). She reports the responses of two friends to these observations. A white friend, with a sudden rush of insight, said, "It's the common story of motherhood, but with this terrible added dimension" (67). A Black friend, according to Lazarre, raises her eyebrows and tolerantly but with real gentleness smiles.

The response of Lazarre's friends enacts the doubleness of her book. Her white friend, fulfilling the narrative intention of Lazarre's work as a whole, sees commonality between Lazarre's maternity and her own. She grasps the contours and torment of racism as an extension of her own experience. However, more chillingly, in this shortly described exchange, the Black friend seizes enormous narrative and moral power, standing in for the Black community at large. Her tolerance is, I imagine, for the white woman newly discovering what for the Black woman is an overly familiar truth. She tolerates the white woman who with her declarations of "revelations" seems to be doing what white people have always done, believe and proclaim only what they know from their personal experience.

Early on in her narrative, Lazarre places herself in the tradition of African American autobiography. But we recall with shame and sadness that Harriet Jacobs could publish her autobiography only under the auspices of the white abolitionist, Lydia Maria Child, who wrote to Jacobs, "Under the circumstances *your* name could not be used you know" (Jacobs 246). This, of course, is not the aspect of African American literary tradition within which Lazarre is placing herself, but nevertheless ironically she may fall there. She may also be subject to Ann duCille's critique that Black culture becomes valorized only when taken up by white intellectuals.

During one hectic moment of Lazarre's narration, when the extended family experiences frustration at the hospital, during the critical illness of a son of Lazarre's mother-in-law, Lazarre is asked to speak for her brother-in-law, "Go tell them we've been here for hours. They'll believe you cause you're white" (106). This request speaks, perhaps, to the limitless love of a mother for her son, in this case that of Lazarre's mother-in-law, Lois, for her son. Lois Meadows-White is willing to yield to racism, to subordinate herself to its power, in the interest of her child. Arguably, Jane Lazarre in her memoir reenacts both parts of this mother-in-law, daughter-in-law exchange. She writes her account perhaps unconsciously knowing "They'll believe you cause you're white" and she writes it, accepting she must thereby yield to the power of racism for the love of her sons. Yet, as Khary, her son remarks upon hearing a draft of one of the chapters, "You are still using the perspective of a white person, Mom" (56). Lazarre includes his comment, includes the forbearing gentle smile of her Black friend listening to Lazarre's frustrations at racism, includes her mother-in-law's momentary concessions to the way the world is, to convey perhaps to her readers her own awareness that she is still in racism's thrall and the book they read manifests that racism. However, implicit also in the work is that if it brings her readers closer to a visceral knowledge of racism, then a transitory yielding to its power is justified. Clearly, she wishes her book to provoke the same effect on its white readers as the slave exhibit caused in her, so that for a moment, however transitory, a community can be forged between Black and white. However, because her book mediates Black experience through white maternity, even such a fragile community bears a lingering mark of inequity.

Notes

1. Elizabeth V. Spelman explicates how complex this process may be, showing how Jacobs simultaneously demonstrates the commonality between white women and slaves and their resistant difference. Additionally, Spelman details how Jacobs instructs her white readership to appreciate slaves as moral agents (59–88).

Works Cited

Butler, Octavia. *Kindred*. Boston: Beacon Press, 1988

Dalmiya, Vrinda. "Why Should a Knower Care?" *Hypatia* 17, 1 (2002): 34–51.

DuBois, W. E. B. *The Souls of Black Folk*. New York: Fawcett Publications, 1953.

duCille, Ann. "The Occult of True Black Womanhood: Critical Demeanor and Black Feminist Studies." In *Female Subjects in Black and White*. Edited by Elizabeth Abel et al. Berkeley and Los Angeles: University of California Press, 1997.

Goldman, Alvin. "Empathy, mind, and morals." In *Mental Simulation*. Edited by Martin Davies and Tony Stone. London: Blackwell, 1995.

Jacobs, Harriet. *Incidents in the Life of a Slave Girl, Written by Herself*. Edited by Jean Fagan Yellin. Cambridge: Harvard University Press, 1987 (1861).

Kittay, Eva. *Love's Labor: Essays on Women, Equality, and Dependency*. New York and London: Routledge, 1999.

Lazarre, Jane. *Beyond the Whiteness of White: Memoir of a White Mother of Black Sons*. Durham, N.C: Duke University Press, 1996.

Lugones, Maria. "Playfulness, 'World'-Traveling, and Loving Perception." In *Women, Knowledge, and Reality: Exploration in Feminist Philosophy*. Edited by Ann Gary and Marilyn Pearsall. Boston: Unwin Hyman, 1989.

Ruddick, Sara. "Maternal Thinking." In *Woman and Value*. Edited by Marilyn Pearsall. Belmont, CA: Wadsworth Publishing Co., 1999.

Spelman, Elizabeth V. *Fruits of Sorrow: Framing Our Attention to Suffering*. Boston: Beacon Press, 1997.

Coalescence in Evolution: Queer Familia in Cherríe Moraga's *Waiting in the Wings*

R. Joyce Z. L. Garay

Cherríe Moraga's *Waiting in the Wings: Portrait of Queer Motherhood* is an intimate rendering of her pregnancy, the premature birth of her son, Rafael Angel, and the ensuing formation and negotiation of her subjectivity as Chicana, lesbian, mother, and writer. Refusing to deny any part of her self in constructing queer Chicana maternal subjectivity, Moraga continually interrogates and redefines "family." She melds queer consciousness with a definition of family grounded in her Mexican cultural heritage and history, theorizing and actualizing the uncharted territory of constructing and nurturing queer familia.

Resonant with the spiritual and emotional rawness of her first autobiographical text, *Loving in the War Years: lo que nunca pasó por sus labios*, *Waiting in the Wings* is a text that Moraga qualifies as a "personal 'fiction' "of memory and interpretation.[1] *Waiting* is composed of journal entries (visually identified through italic script) and prose meditations and is divided into five sections, three central chapters enclosed by a prologue and an epilogue. As Moraga chronologically traces her journey into maternal subjectivity, she integrates Spanish fluidly, having made the conscious choice not to translate for non-Spanish-speaking readers and not to distinguish Spanish from English through italicization.[2] She explains this decision, as well as her decision to refer to her lover as Ella, the generic "she/her" in Spanish, within a concise note that precedes her prologue. Even as throughout *Waiting*, Moraga unifies thematic threads and ideological differences through the tropes of death/life cycle and travel and other formal mechanisms,[3] ultimately, the text foregrounds the distinct facets of her maternal subjectivity—Chicana-mother/blood-mother, butch-mother, lover-mother, writer-mother—she fights to bring together in radical coalescence.

Chicana-Mother/Blood-Mother

For Moraga, a sense of belonging within a strong, multigenerational Mexican family foundationally defines family. "Growing up, the *we* of my life was always defined by blood relations. *We* meant family. We were my mother's children, my abuela's grandchildren, my tíos' nieces and nephews" (17). She asserts that this sense of family is pervasive in her life and her life's work.

As Lisa Tatonetti argues in her examination of the continuum of Moraga's autobiographical texts from *Loving* to *The Last Generation* and, finally, to *Waiting in the Wings*, Moraga "queers the structure" of traditional Mexican family, placing queer familia as a "radical place of possibility for the future of Chicana/o culture" (229). Particularly in relation to Moraga's decision to become mother and in the deliberation of selecting Pablo, a "dark beauty" of a Mexican male, Tatonetti comments that Moraga "extends her cultural heritage *through* queerness, rather than in spite of it" (243). At the foundation of Moraga's queer familia is Mexican identity, Mexican family.

Within this Mexican cultural context, maternity is mythic to Moraga. She writes about Medea's Chicana parallel La Llorona, as she nourishes Rafael within and as infant. She makes the purposeful decision that Rafael will be Mexican, a living branch of her Moraga family tree, and, more broadly, a child of *la raza* with its legacy of cultural richness and complexity. She writes: "Nation. Nationality. I am to be the mother of a Mexican baby. I am the worst and best of those macho Chicano nationalists. I picked a man for his brains and dark beauty. And the race continues" (39). Her connection is to myth, to race, to cosmos at once, all weaving together in her sense of herself as mother. Her faith is in destiny, in the timelessness of maternity. Having given birth to Rafael, she connects her plight—the threat of losing a child—to the Virgen de Guadalupe, to the Aztec moon goddess Coyolxauhqui, to the symbolic feminine realm of the ocean (58).

Coming out as a lesbian not only exiles Moraga as cultural betrayer, a Malinche,[4] who chooses her own desire instead of nationalistic alignment and union with the Mexican male, it also shifts her sense of family, taking her literally beyond the arms of her blood familia and ideologically beyond their rigid perceptions of family. She, however, maintains both her claim to empowering mythology and embraces the concept, the heart and spirit, of familia. Her rejection of the lesbian/gay replication of heterosexual marriage or partnerships in the political and personal realms is measure of her insistence upon the creation of family that is "something Mexican and familial without all the cultural constraints" (18). In fact, Moraga argues for a reconstruction of family with these parameters, "familia resurrected and repaired," for other queer Latinas, and sets this kind of familia as the objective of every single one of her lesbian relationships.

Significantly, as Moraga concludes her first chapter, the worlds of her Chicana self and her queer self align in the city of her childhood. Moraga gives birth to Rafael, 'without division,' among those she loves: "In a way, the most natural thing in the world was to give birth here in Los Angeles, among my blood familia. I knew as I held my lover's and my sister's hands in the grip of labor that this was what I understood as hogar, sustenance; that this how a woman should always give birth, surrounded by women. And how lucky I was to be a lesbian, to have it all—mother, sister, lover—that family of women to see me into motherhood" (54).

If terrifyingly premature, Rafael Angel nevertheless enters the world with Ella, and both Moraga's mother and sister welcoming him; these individuals together represent the families by which he will be nurtured and in which he will develop as an individual. Surely, on a crucial level, this is the achievement of familia Moraga advocates.

Yet, the inclusiveness of such construction of family is not without tension. Made emotional by the inscription in a book of photography, a gift for Rafa from his biological father, Pablo, Moraga is reminded of the conflict in her construction of family that, ultimately, she cannot consistently and flawlessly reconcile: As much as Ella is mother in partnership with Moraga, as a white woman, she is *not* familia, *not* of blood nor culture. Moraga includes the Spanish inscription Pablo has written in a line not translated for readers—"*Para su primer día de Lupita, que nuestra bellez, lucha y cultura siempre te llene*"[5]—to emphasize the importance of Rafael's Mexican heritage and identity. Moraga hesitates, then, in realizing anew this commitment to familia, to consider Ella as the parent to whom Rafael should belong should Moraga herself die. "*There is no denying that I had this baby that he might be a Mexi-*

can, for him to know and learn of mexicanismo, for him to feel that fuego, that llama, that riqueza I call lo mexicano" (91). Moraga even reveals the yearning for a confluence of the threads of queer and familia in form of a lover not Ella: "*And for a moment, I miss that Mexican loving in my life*" (91). In this moment, Moraga's priority is to be blood-mother, to contribute to racialized familia, to a perpetuation of Moraga lineage and legacy.

Butch-Mother

In her article, "Feminist Sublimations, Queer Disidentifications: Losing Touch of Maternal Sexuality," Susan Driver discusses the "theoretical impasse" between queer theorists (exemplified by Judith Butler, Diana Fuss, and Biddy Martin) and feminist psychoanalytic theorists (exemplified by Jessica Benjamin and Julia Kristeva) in analyses of the intersections between sexuality and maternal subjects/subjectivity. Driver argues that while through the feminist lens, mothers are "historically situated speaking subjects," they are nevertheless divorced from all but reproductive sexuality and relegated to heteronormality (26–27). Conversely, while queer theorists undo semiotic and psycho-social gender binaries, "maternal subjectivity continues to be thought in terms of corporeal and symbolic inertia against which queer sexual mobility and defiance are celebrated" (30). Framed as a call to attend to "impasse," Driver's article concludes with the potential embedded in examining motherhood and sexuality as enmeshed in subjectivity rather than as oppositional (36).

Waiting articulates the potential to which Driver alludes, as Moraga organically threads the theoretical through her autobiographical rendering of her achievement of butch-mother-subjectivity. For example, in the initial passages of her prologue, Moraga explains how she reached her early forties before recognizing her desire to bear a biological child. She declares how closely connected her identity as woman is with her potential for maternity, and how her lesbian identity prevented recognition of this fact for so many years. She writes: "I had maintained the rigid conviction that lesbians (that is, those of us on the more masculine side of the spectrum) weren't really women. We were women-lovers, a kind of third sex, and most definitely not men. Having babies was something 'real' women did—not butches, not girls who knew they were queer since grade school. We were *de-*

fenders[6] of women and children, children we could never fully call our own" (20).

Relying upon butch/femme divisions, Moraga conveys the difficulty of imagining herself as mother. Moraga, thus, exemplifies both the heteronormative thinking that equates womanhood with maternal subjectivity, as well as the notion that queer sexuality, especially butch sexuality, is somehow exclusive of maternity. Physically unable to create a child through sexual relations with her lovers and restrained by butch subjectivity, Moraga had, through her twenties and thirties, resigned herself to childlessness.

Interestingly, once pregnant, the way her appearance changes does not disrupt Moraga's claim to butch lesbian identity. She is able still to see herself as sexual being, as queer sexual being, bridging Driver's "theoretical impasse" within her embodied and psychological experience: *"Ella tells me daily how much more feminine I look. I see it, too—my hair longer than it's been in fifteen years, my hips and thighs and breasts rounding from this pregnancy, the softening taking place throughout my body, the tears. I like it and yet in bed feel a strong urge to reassert my butchness, my self as love-maker"* (45). Butch identity is not subsumed by maternity. Within the realm of sexuality, of desire, Moraga asserts this core facet of self, and embodies subversion of what Driver elsewhere calls "prudish parameters of maternal representation" ("Can," 32).

Yet, despite her self-identification on the "masculine side of the spectrum," Moraga is significantly uneasy when she learns Rafael's sex. Both she and Ella had somehow more clearly imagined, expected, desired, a girl child. For days following the revelation, Moraga's journal entries reverberate with anxieties about bearing and raising a son. On 18 marzo, Moraga writes, "There is meaning in the fact that my fetus has formed itself into a male . . . I understood the female, the daughter. The son holds a message I will learn to decipher with my heart" (32). And on 19 marzo, wracked with a virus, she continues, "I feared there was no place for my reckoning with his maleness. I spoke with him all night last night. I spoke with him for understanding. . . . It is not mere feminist rhetoric that makes a woman stop dumbfounded in the face of a life of raising a son. It is the living woman-wound that we spend our lives trying to heal" (33). As a lover of women, as lesbian and as feminist, she wonders at destiny's relegation of son to her womb, to her life. Attending a Native American ceremony, she again prays for strength and wisdom in the challenge of raising a son: "I prayed that I would learn how to raise a male child well, that the wounds men have inflicted on me, even in their absence, will not poison me against my son" (41). Even as she grapples, Moraga accepts the destiny, the challenge, the rightness of her portending role of mothering a son.

Mielle Chandler, in "Queering Maternity," sheds light on Moraga and Ella's difficulty in absorbing the revelation of Rafael's sex. Chandler articulates within discussion of Nancy Chodorow's germinal text, *Reproduction of Motherhood* (1978), the underlay for Moraga's anxiety as the belief that the "gendering of sons as masculine requires a repudiation, within the self, of all that is associated with femininity" (182). It is with this potential, embedded within gendering of her future son, that Moraga struggles.

Indeed, one way Moraga reconciles herself to raising a son is to imagine their relationship as an exchange. Before his birth, Rafael is cosmic gift, a male child destined to come into her life with purpose. And, especially after his birth (and nearness to death), she endows Rafael with spiritual wisdom he is meant to share with her: "*Maybe Rafaelito will bring to me a more profound way of believing . . . Maybe he is my teacher*" (59). What cannot be easily accepted logically can be integrated spiritually.

Once Rafael is born, Moraga is no more prepared to mother a son and no less butch-mother, though her position as biological mother compels her to take up the task, as it also in some sense legitimates her womanhood, sanctions, and protects. With health stable enough during his first week of life, Rafael and Moraga are flown to a hospital in the San Francisco area for the majority and duration of Rafael's attaining of health. While Moraga follows Rafa without question as his biological mother, bureaucratic red tape makes Ella's admittance to the neonatal intensive care unit more difficult. The nurses accommodate Moraga and Ella's relationships to each other and to Rafael, but not without a marked change in perception and treatment, some experiencing discomfort initially and others not overcoming this discomfort at all. She and Ella enter a public realm in which the uncomplicated fusion of sexuality and maternity experienced in private homeplace is complicated by heterosexist policies and perceptions.

Whenever Ella and Moraga come to visit Rafael outside of designated visiting hours, they must check in with security at the doors of the hospital, enduring harassment permitted by the "immediate family only" regulation. In recounting the experience, Moraga captures the rage and simultaneous fatigue involved: "I just want to get in there and see my baby. But each night we go through the same interrogation. . . .

The same old ritual, the same harassment night after night. Then he [the security guard] can't help himself, and a grin begins to crack the professional façade. 'You say you're both the moms!' He eyes his buddies, his co-workers, and the street gang begins to form around us" (75). Moraga depicts the threat, the violence inherent in the response to her and Ella. Her response is visceral, fueled by fear for Rafaelito and by the end of patience:

> *Don't fuck with me tonight, boys.* We had already filed our complaints over earlier harassment, called their supervisor who always seemed to enjoy the joke as much as they did. . . . Pero, para nada. Nobody really gives a damn that two women have their baby in a hospital for over three months, not knowing if he is going to live or die, and they still have to endure insults from testosterone-driven homophobes with no power acting like they got some. (My class and race analysis don't do shit for me when the brothers are standing in the way of my child.) (75–76)

In this context, Moraga not only rages against, castigates, a system that does not recognize her family, but also rages in her own impotence to effect change. Resorting to the harshest of language, Moraga reveals the depth of emotion as well as the toughness central to her sense of lesbian self. Moraga also wonders what difference it would make were it she, instead of more feminine Ella, who was not the biological mother. She mediates upon the politics of butch/femme subjectivity, having long been the more identifiable lesbian in their relationship and, thus, having experienced the discrimination that accompanies visibility. Her sympathy with Ella is limited, and she finds a bittersweet, if problematic, sense of satisfaction in being accepted through biological motherhood: "I can't protect her from the pain she experiences each time they make her the outlaw. I'm the dyke in the matter, I tell myself. I'm the one who's supposed to be on the outside. But not now. As Rafael's biological mother, I am surrounded by acceptance at the hospital, until Ella walks in and we are again the lesbian couple, the queer moms—exoticized and eroticized" (76). Clearly, any facet of pleasure in Moraga's sense of proprietary power as biological mother is fleeting, eradicated by queer identity and relationship.

Isolated, Moraga and Ella only once see another lesbian couple mothering—on their way out of the hospital with a healthy, if small, Rafaelito in arm. Vulnerable and harassed, she and Ella have had to fight their way into joint motherhood. As they leave the hospital, then, they experience a sense of freedom—the insulated freedom of being and reinforcing family within constructive and safe homespace, where butch-motherhood is not the aberrance.

A year later, Moraga's butch subjectivity resurfaces in another reminder of butch-motherhood as defiance of expectation. While spending time with Ella's mother in Massachusetts, all take a walk through Provincetown, Moraga pushing Rafael in his stroller and Ella following, arm in arm with her mother. Ella, more femme in identity and affect, comments as they walk about how differently others perceive them when Moraga walks with the grandmother figure and Ella pushes the stroller (110). When Ella pushes the stroller, no one looks twice, childlessness the presumption that follows butch Moraga. Despite how natural and solid her maternal subjectivity is to Moraga, others are jolted by her butch-mother-self.

Lover-Mother/Co-Mother

Foregrounding her relationship with Ella, sexual and emotional, Moraga continues to exemplify Driver's call for a richer conceptualization of maternal subjectivity. Moraga writes forthrightly of the strain that motherhood places upon her relationship with Ella, of exhaustion, absorption in the infant, of adapting to new schedules, and of setting new priorities, all of which impact relationships between parents, regardless of sexual orientation. Yet, Moraga and Ella, as queer parents, defining and creating family, as Moraga says, "from scratch" (14),[7] with more fluid parameters, legal and otherwise, certainly struggle differently than heterosexual parents and as both individuals and partners in determining maternal/parental roles and responsibilities. As each adapts to parenthood, their intimacy ebbs and flows.

Moraga very clearly articulates to her partner, Ella, that she alone will be the mother of the child she bears, despite the support she requests from Ella. The uncertainty in her request centers on the flexibility of roles, not the fact that Moraga will be *the* mother: "In the beginning I didn't know how much mother Ella would be to our child. Neither did she. I didn't know how much I wanted to share motherhood. I didn't know how soft and hard it is—that letting go—to entrust another human being in the raising of your child" (16). Even as Moraga clearly owns her decision to become a mother, she as clearly voices that she would not have made the decision without sure knowledge of support. And, even as she recognizes the selfishness of asking merely for Ella's support, she insists upon her maternal primacy. She does not leave any doubt that it could be any other way for her, and does so without ambivalence.

Ella is included in the process of Rafael's conception, which Moraga describes with candor—Pablo, the donor of sperm, in the bathroom with a mason jar and Ella with syringe in hand—and in contrast with the spiritual peace she experiences as the possibility of life begins within her. The first attempt at conception successful, Moraga characterizes Rafael's genesis as "homemade," redefining the concept of the "natural." Immediately, being pregnant inspires maternal subjectivity, a clear sense of a new being in whom she will endow a part of herself.

During the initial months of Moraga's pregnancy, her connection to Ella intensifies as she recognizes the stability and companionship she provides: "I cling to Ella in a way I never imagined" (38). Moraga adds depth to this deepening of their commitment in a journal entry: "*Seeing Ella's goodness to me in my pregnancy has opened my heart to her in a way I know cannot be reversed. She has allowed me to depend on her. And, for the first time in my life, I do*" (41). Witnessing life in process of becoming, the two reach a new level of intimacy.

This intimacy continues to intensify when Ella and Moraga together attend to Rafael during his three-month hospitalization. They pray together. They hope and fear together. They rely upon one another in ways neither had imagined were possible before the crisis of Rafael's premature delivery. Moraga recognizes Ella's capacity for unfaltering strength, sees in her body a safe place to surrender her grief and exhaustion. Also, as they take shifts with Rafael, and, together, watch him repeatedly approach and retreat from death he becomes more solidly *their* child, and Moraga's repeated use of the pronoun "our" replaces her use of "my."

Once Rafael's health is more stable and the family begins to construct a home life, the intimacy between Ella and Moraga begins to ebb. As Rafael's needs dominate, Moraga wonders about the impact on her relationship: "*I worry, what does this mean? The child has moved my woman and me into separate beds*" (87). As baby care becomes the center of homeplace, Moraga and Ella are also impatient with one another and at odds about priorities dictating time at home and at work as artist and activist, respectively. The rigid order Moraga has imposed upon the household, a mechanism for exercising control in response to the powerlessness of witnessing Rafael at the brink of death for so many weeks, compounds interpersonal distance (88). She writes of the detachment that has come to characterize their relationship since Rafael's arrival:

> *We go about our live in separate orbits. I want the distance. I must confess that in some of my imaginings of the future, I do not see her clearly formed there. I only know my son's constant presence. . . . Maybe "lover" has been replaced with mother these days, but it does not satiate. At times I miss la passion, fear how remote it has become between Ella and me. Worse, fear it no longer matters to me, which I know is a lie, a camouflage waiting in the bushes to jump out and fall on some other woman's bones.* (109)

As mother-self takes precedence, lover-self diminishes, is displaced. Moraga struggles to understand the shift in intimacy and the growing distance is not without pain, and a wistful sadness, as the recognition of the inevitable dissolution of the relationship sets in.

Finally, home-space conflates with writing-space, reinforcing Moraga's compulsion to control environment, and to resent sharing space and control of that space with Ella. "*My home has become my fiercely guarded sanctuary*" (110). As response to this exclusivity, Ella ultimately moves out of the home, though not out of the family. In transforming family definition, Moraga conveys that Ella's move to an alternate physical pace has positive impact on their family life, that Ella still functions centrally in Moraga's perception and construction of family for Rafael.

Writer-Mother

Moraga does not at any point relinquish her artist identity, nor allow the creative power of maternity to overshadow artistic impulse.[8] Even when pregnant, Moraga feels her writer-self profoundly: "*My body now taking on the full shape of creation does not lessen my need for art*" (44). Yet, the sheer energy-sapping physicality of pregnancy at times keep her from the inspired state that is familiar, leaving a craving she characterizes as hunger (47).

Caring for her son, she describes writing at odd hours of the first year of motherhood. The balance of mother-self and writer-self is hard-won as Moraga struggles to return to some routine once Rafael's health is stable: "*My writer's heart feels stolen by the struggle for my baby's survival. . . . I miss the immersion into my writing terribly, fear I will not be able to resurrect that impassioned momentum*" (86). She "sneaks" journal time (87), and wonders when and if she will write as profusely and with the inspiration she knew before motherhood. The relentless and immediate demands of motherhood, compounded by the emotional drain of months of hanging on Rafael's every breath as he secured his hold on life, leave Moraga exhausted of creative energy. She grapples with discouragement, even depression, and her dreams are rampant with dark images and nightmarish possibilities.

Responding not solely to the reality of the limited hours in a day and the ways an infant's needs take priority, Moraga also writes about the conflicting emotions that accompany this conflict: "*I want to smother a slowly surfacing guilt that my concern has shifted from baby to work so suddenly . . . I need to know I am more than these tasks of motherhood, more than mother. I need to remember that I am a writer*" (88). She insists upon the primacy of her writer-self and exhaustion gives way to reconciliation that she may not be the same writer she once was, but she *will* write. She realizes that becoming mother has altered her writer-self: "The writing isn't any less challenging, but now a hole has been created through which my child passed. . . . Now the work—the art—passes through me differently" (95). Ultimately, Moraga reconciles the confluence of selves: "*I am trying to be a mother who writes well. I am trying to be a writer who mothers well*" (96). She claims the subjectivity of "*mother-writer*" (96) and attributes to writing a reciprocity with mothering, as it is through writing that she re-members becoming mother (99).

Queer Familia: Coalescence in Evolution

Not able to imagine herself as mother throughout her twenties and thirties, Moraga nevertheless mothered, mothered both lovers and their children. In her prologue, then, Moraga writes of a significant catalyst in her realization of desire to carry and bear a child—the experience of raising a young boy, whom she grew to consider a son, with a former lesbian partner. Despite her mothering, when her relationship with this partner dissolved, so, too, did the relationship with her son, Joel. Remembering Joel, Moraga recognizes the depth of her capacity to be mother and mourns her powerlessness to maintain that bond with this child, not hers biologically nor legally. Her love for this "(almost) son" (22, 77) painfully accentuates the precariousness of queer family and is foundational motivation for her desire to create and nurture a revolutionary family, a queer familia.

Moraga traces the process of creating queer familia from its initial intellectual conception to the physical challenge and act of conception to establishing roles and deciding how to parent and what to teach. She illustrates the complexities and paradoxes of lesbian motherhood and constructing a family both queer and Mexican, for she considers Rafael Angel an extension of queer family, but, just as, or, perhaps, more crucially, Mexican family. As Tatonetti describes, Moraga portrays "the sometimes intertwined, sometimes disparate interactions of ethnic and sexual politics with the politics of queer motherhood" (242). Queer familia unifies the two realms of Moraga's understanding of family—through her "blood familia" and through her lesbian identity and experiences. It is from this place within the duality of being Mexican and lesbian, then, that Moraga constructs maternal subjectivity.

Moraga describes with love and trepidation the composition of her chosen family: "A gay man. A queer contract. . . . A whitegirl lover with lovely cullud girl curls and a butt to match and Spanish that don't make a fool outta her. This is my home. For now. I don't know what the future will bring. We try to get what we can on paper, to protect ourselves against pain, against loss, but the papers don't protect us" (39). The love is clear in the language, as is the knowledge that they form family against the odds. She speaks of this family—herself, Ella, Rafael, and his biological father, Pablo—as family in evolution: "[We] work out our evolving roles and our evolving consciousness in the midst of an evolving child" (38).

The challenges within the process of evolution, the mapping of uncharted territory, manifest in two distinct ways: Moraga's candid admission of vulnerability and insecurity within her mother role and her inscription of coming to terms with possible reasons for Rafael's precarious start in life. *Waiting in the Wings* lays bare Moraga's insecurities and anxieties. She recounts sin verguenza the complicated emotions that accompany pregnancy, birth, and the first months of her son's precarious hold on life. She is unabashed in confessing her anxieties during early pregnancy. Experiencing bleeding throughout, she lives with the fear of miscarriage, of loss (30, 39). Fear of loss even in the early stages of pregnancy is, more broadly, manifestation of anxiety and fear about the tenuous nature of queer familia in process.

Rafa's premature arrival affects Moraga's maternal subjectivity profoundly. She feels unprepared for his arrival. Uncertain about motherhood before Rafael's birth, these uncertainties continue in his first months at home and are exacerbated by the fear and worry that have become habit during his hospital stay. "*I am a mother now and I do not yet know how to fully inhabit that place in the world*" (86). This thought is less about insecurity and more about imagining herself into maternal subjectivity. Again, the difficulty of this task represents the necessity of carving a space for queer familia, queer Chicana motherhood.

Additionally, amidst uncertainty, Moraga experiences anger and confusion about when, where, and upon whom to assign blame for Rafael's frighteningly early entrance into the world. Moraga first accepts his premature birth as her own failure, and his clinging to life as solely a product of her faith (58). While she then looks outward to the medical practitioners who ignored her relentless allergies and sinus trouble (67), she still feels responsible for, and mourns, the time both she and Rafael were deprived: "*What is hardest to write about is the loss I feel in not having brought Rafael to full term. At times I think it is loss, then wonder if it's really guilt I feel that my son had to go through so much suffering outside the womb because I couldn't protect him inside*" (98). Her prominent sense of isolation and lone responsibility for Rafael's health and well-being reflects the maverick position, the fighter stance, she believes she must adopt to create and sustain queer familia.

Yet, Moraga also clearly sees the negative impact of those outside of her familia on her own health and the health of her family. For example, significantly, Moraga emphasizes that her role as caretaker in the family (ignoring her instinctual desire to rest, she has instead listened to the imminent ex-brother-in-law explain the dissolution of his marriage to her sister) may have been a factor in the onset of her untimely labor. And, even as her relationship with Ella dissolves, Moraga sees pressure from the outside as a primary cause: "*We are best just the three of us, no world pressing down upon us. Is it the world that divides?*" (112) Supported socially or merely not discriminated against, left to construct and nurture their own homeplace, perhaps their family could thrive.

Moraga aptly concludes *Waiting in the Wings* with an epilogue that centers on the sweet persistence of and deep love within the queer familia that she builds for Rafael. Cuddling with Ella, Rafa with an arm around each, Moraga writes, "No accounting for what finally makes a family, except love. I remain awed by this mystery of how love and blood and home and history and desire coalesce and collide to construct a child's sense of self and family. I know blood quantum does not determine parenthood any more than it determines culture. Still, I know blood matters. It just does not matter more than love" (125).

Within this statement, Moraga simplifies the construction of family, but without loss of the mysterious balance that she has negotiated through the text and continues to negotiate each day. Her family is queer, is Mexican by culture and blood, and is sustained by the confluence.

Notes

1. It is interesting that Moraga finds it necessary to include the note "On Naming, Genre, and Language" as an informal preface to her text. Within the note, she explains decisions to alter chronology "for dramatic storytelling" and to change the names of "characters" to protect privacy. This note carries generic implications. Clearly, Moraga observes the overlap between autobiographical "truth" and fiction.

2. In accordance with Moraga's decision, I do not italicize Spanish within quotations I include from her text, nor do I italicize my own Spanish language inclusions.

3. Among many such unifying mechanisms, one might include epigraphs, chapter, and section titles, and the content of recorded dreams. However, the title of the text and the cover art are significant examples worth explicating as models for the kind of explication other mechanisms could support. Moraga's title is multivalent, a communication of several aspects of her perception of self. She speaks of Rafael as "waiting in the wings" to enter life, particularly life within the family Moraga builds for him and of herself. "Waiting in the Wings" also clearly resonates with Moraga's sense of herself as playwright, her sense of "wings" as liminal space, points just beyond the curtains of the life's stage. Additionally, Rafael "waits in the wings," the arms, of those who have passed before him, his ancestors; this meaning reflects Moraga's perception of family as well as her sense of the permeable boundary between the living world and the spirit world. Rafael's middle name, Angel, also resonates with the image of wings, as well as speaking his connection to those who have passed before him. Not only has Rafael been "waiting in the wings," but Moraga's maternal subjectivity, too, has been "waiting in the wings," a latent potential for much of her womanhood. Significantly, then, the imagery of the frontispiece reflects these several layers of meaning. A black-and-white portrait of Moraga, relaxed, smiling and holding Rafael, a serious expression furrowing his young brow rides above her subtitle: *Portrait of a Queer Motherhood*. The image rests at a slant upon the right lower corner of the electric lavender of a very blurred photo of a large extended family, faces unidentifiable. The sense of Moraga's own queer motherhood—she and her son—resting upon, if peripherally, extended family speaks in image Moraga's sense of her unique construction of family yet somehow in full agreement and reliance upon the presence and concept of longstanding traditional family. The blurred faces signify both the death of this sense of extended family as well as the transformation Moraga applies through her queer motherhood.

4. La Malinche, also known as Malintzin Tenépal, Doña Marinal, or Malinali, was translator for Hernan Cortés, as well as his mistress and mother of his son. She is both historical figure and cultural icon. While Chicana feminists reclaim and revise her maligned history (e.g., recognizing her status as daughter traded into slavery in the service of patriarchal favoring of her brother, celebrating her role as mother of La Raza, iden-

tifying her agency and foresight in realizing that many more lives would be lost were she not to act, and acknowledging her linguistic ability to mediate between cultures), La Malinche is yet dominantly viewed as traitor. Even linguistically, in Spanish malinche connotes betrayal.

5. My translation: "For his first day of Lupita, may our beauty, struggle, and culture fill you always." Día de Lupita is December 12, the day of Catholic recognition of the Virgen de Guadalupe and her appearance to Juan Diego in the sixteenth century. La Virgen de Guadalupe is a figure who surpasses the confines of religious worship and has historically been and continues to be an iconic figure in Mexican culture.

6. For a second time within this short prologue, Moraga utilizes rhetoric of war directly, connecting on another level to her *Loving in the War Years*.

7. The epigraph for her first chapter, from which this term is taken, is a passage from Moraga's dramatic work, *Giving Up the Ghost*.

8. Certainly, Moraga's balancing of writer-self with mother-self, except as it is woven into the network of mother-self subjectivities she embodies is not innovative (i.e., Margaret Atwood, Maya Angelou, Marge Piercy, Anne Lamotte, Louise Erdrich are a handful of women who have written about this balancing act). See essays in Brenda O. Daly and Maureen T. Reddy, eds. *Narrating Mothers: Theorizing Maternal Subjectivities*.

Works Cited

Chandler, Mielle. "Queering Maternity." *Mother Matters: Motherhood as Discourse and Practice; Essays from the Journal of the Association for Research on Mothering*, 2004. 179–91.

Daly, Brenda O., and Maureen T. Reddy, eds. *Narrating Mothers: Theorizing Maternal Subjectivities*. Knoxville: University of Tennessee Press, 1991.

Driver, Susan. "Can Queer Theory Radicalize 'the Mother's' Body?" *Canadian Women's Studies* 16, 2 (1996): 30–32.

———. "Feminist Sublimations, Queer Disidentifications: Losing Touch of Maternal Subjectivity." *Tessera* 25 (1998): 25–37.

hooks, bell. "Homeplace: A Site of Resistance." In *Yearning: Race, Gender, and Cultural Politics*. Boston, MA: South End Press, 1990. 41–49.

Moraga, Cherríe. *Giving Up the Ghost: Teatro in Two Acts*. Los Angeles, CA: West End Press, 1986.

———. *Loving in the War Years: lo que nunca pasó por sus labios*. 2nd ed. Boston, MA: South End Press, 2000.

———. *Waiting in the Wings: Portrait of Queer Motherhood*. Ithaca, NY: Firebrand Books, 1997.

Tatonetti, Lisa. "'A Kind of Queer Balance': Cherríe Moraga's Aztlán." *MELUS* 29, 2 (2004): 227–47.

Babies and Boundaries: Mother-Speaking in Rachel Cusk's *A Life's Work*

Celia Shiffer

ANYONE WHO PULLS RACHEL CUSK'S *A LIFE'S WORK: ON BECOMING A Mother* from the "Parenting" shelf at the local mega-bookstore risks disappointment for, despite its label as "Gen Childcare" and its unassuming position amid the Cs of parenting manuals, the book refuses to instruct. In fact, as the subtitle states, the book is not about "parenting" but about "becoming"; it is not about instruction but about comprehension; and, most importantly, it is not about raising a child but about being a Mother. Cusk is haunted by the word "mother"—its certainty and its cultural meaning. She knows, as many women do, that "mother" makes "woman," and she knows that being a mother must be an experience that is both natural and completing. Nonetheless, she acknowledges that such certainty, such totality, is suspect. Her experience tells her so: she writes, "Birth is not merely that which divides women from men: it also divides women from themselves, so that a woman's understanding of what it is to exist is profoundly changed" (7). Cusk's experience as a new mother exposes the narrated altruistic and all-encompassing "mother" as painful, divisive, and traumatic.

Such notions as "all-encompassing" and "divisive" are conflicted because the terms themselves derive meaning from a culture that values individualism and privileges the "I." But motherhood, as Cusk reminds us, is not about the one (as we've come to live as, more or less, to the point of pregnancy), nor can it be entirely about the other (as it is suddenly supposed to be). In fact, motherhood cannot recognize such a logic of binaries and separations. And so, rather than accept the cultural mythologies surrounding motherhood, which say "mother" and conjure images of selflessness, nurturance without end, uncomplicated love, and a painless—and silent—disappearance of identity, Cusk speaks up. She fights her sublimation by "mother" and she resists obedience to—she refuses to be gagged by—the "expertise" of doctors and the mandates of how-to manuals, for such instructions and mythologies are based in a fantasy that pits self against other as they set the stage for trauma and conflict. Standing resolute in a tedious row of parenting how-to's, *A Life's Work* is important as much for Cusk's refusal to instruct as for her acknowledgment of—and her giving voice to—a (traumatized) maternal subject. By breaking from traditional narratives of motherhood, which remain individualistic and ultimately destructive as they promote both sacrificing an individual self to an other and obliterating the mother's "I," she argues for an alternative view of self that is grounded in the relational.

Language and the Maternal

Despite their centrality to our cultural stories (the idealized Virgin Mother/the Bad Mother), mothers remain strangely silent. Speaking is the means by which we keep ourselves intact and make our way to living—it is the means by which we assert some kind of self and exist in the world beyond ourselves—yet mothers are expected to speak primarily for their children and to assert the child's existence rather than their own. The mother's voice, then, may be robbed by her children, by doctors and other "experts," by cultural stories, and often by psychoanalysis, which is structured by the father's word. As Susan Rubin Suleiman explains of psychoanalytic theory, "Just as motherhood is ultimately the child's drama, so is artistic creation. In both cases the mother is the essential but silent Other, the mirror in whom the child searches for his own reflection, the body he seeks to appropriate, the thing he loses or destroys again and again, and seeks to recreate" (117).

The mother, then, is paradoxically conceived as always producing—she is always being the material from which the child creates—but she is never creating. Beyond the stories themselves, though, the mother is silenced—or, perhaps more accurately, submerged—by language itself, which Jacques Lacan names the Symbolic, the realm of the Law and of the Father. Yet the mother is not entirely silent, and she certainly exists. According to Julia Kristeva, she exists in the semiotic, the material, maternal realm, which cannot be heard in the words themselves but rather in the rumblings and ruptures beneath and between.

I mention these theories about language as a way to color Cusk's work as theory made "real" by a mother's experience, for she has both exposed the impossibility of cultural narratives of motherhood and ruptured those narratives by her material and maternal narrative. Her story conjures the symbolic and semiotic realms as it opposes the language of doctors, experts, culture, and community to her experience of motherhood; moreover, her story insists that we recognize the split as not only between word/experience and Father/Mother but also between privileged "I"/relational self. To explore Cusk's construction of such a relational—fluid and maternal—self, I begin by sketching her concern with narrative. I then explore of the relationship between pain and mothering and analyze Cusk's creation of a new subjectivity. Finally, I turn to a consideration of what it means to narrate—or speak—as a mother.

Mothers, Subjectivity, and Narrative

Cusk opens her autobiographical story with a passage from psychologist James Hillman's "The Bad Mother": "As child is equivalent with imagination, the mother's language becomes unimaginative, imperative, abstract. . . . And her language loses its emotion and incantational power; she explains and argues" (qtd. in Cusk). The passage introduces a central concern of Cusk's narrative, while highlighting the doubleness of this concern. On one hand, Hillman claims that the mother has a conflicted relationship with language and that she in fact becomes less tied to or embodied in language as her child somehow grows fuller and more living; as the child comes to be recognized as separate, the mother comes to inhabit the barren space of abstractions and imperatives. In the psychologist's narrative of motherhood, the mother is negated as she becomes increasingly alienated from her child—and perhaps from the world. The discourses that work to name an experience (motherhood) or identity (mother) also create that experience or identity. Yet Cusk is not as much concerned with what Hillman claims as with the fact that Hillman speaks at all. As her project in autobiography insists, and as any such project would, "becoming" is bound to language. Cusk argues that "becoming a mother" is excruciatingly difficult precisely because the language by which to do so—because the stories available to mothers—is the language of the institutional, the patriarchal, the symbolic.

Adrienne Rich's *Of Woman Born* is recognized by Cusk and others concerned about the creation of mothers' subjectivities as the first work to call attention to motherhood as a patriarchal institution. Cusk deliberately builds on Rich's oft-cited distinctions "between two meanings of motherhood, one superimposed on the other: the *potential* relationship of any one woman to her powers of reproduction—and to children; and the *institution*—which aims at ensuring that that potential—and all women—shall remain under male control" (Rich, 13). The potential relationship can be imagined as chosen and as always in-process or in-creation; it is multiple, unprescribed, shared, and continuous. But, as Rich argues and Cusk illustrates, the institution of motherhood produces the mothering recognized as "good" in Western cultures; "good" mothers treat pregnancy as a fragile and near-holy state, closely following medical advice and monitoring their bodies and their selves, and engage in a motherhood of self-sacrifice. As mothers, many women can't help but to measure themselves against this ideal from time to time; as children, we must certainly have felt short-changed, at least in the most "unfair" of childhood moments, without one. The institution of motherhood, then, produces subjects that act as vessels for new bodies and as capsules of patriarchal ideology; as "mother" is idealized, the mother herself is negated, made absent and silent.

As poststructuralism has made clear, institutions are simultaneously created and maintained by discourses, and discourses create/maintain/are power; therefore, the stories we tell and are told construct our experiences of mothers and of mothering. Moreover, the ability to speak, to tell one's own story, is essential to the process of subjectivity. The problem faced by many mothers is that the dominant narrative has left no room for them to speak and has thereby effectively sublimated or even erased the subject who is called, and who calls herself, a "mother." For Cusk, this process of erasure is acutely painful and its attendant reconstruction is mystifying, and so she turns to writing "with the aim of answering the larger question of what it is to turn from a woman into a mother" (8). Cusk recognizes that subjectivity—for anyone—means to claim one's own language, to stake out one's own "self." Yet this act—the telling of one's own story—is particularly difficult for women who become (who simply *are*) mothers, for the contradictions that structure the discourses of patriarchy (male/female; self/other; one/multiple; mind/body; good/bad) are amplified in motherhood, when the self and body are simultaneously gouged and extended and there is no language with which to render this experience as anything but oppositional.

Pain and Mothering

Much of Cusk's story is concerned with the trauma of motherhood, which is a trauma registered both on the body and in the mind. First, references to the work of motherhood on the body drive the narrative; as Cusk explains in her introduction: "I could imagine those other things [love, work]; giving birth to a child I could not" (1). Love, career, and motherhood are imaginable, for they have been amply shaped by the stories we're told and tell ourselves as we grow. Childbirth, however, is a physical moment, one that is finite and that erupts through the body rather than the mind and, because of its fundamental physicality, childbirth—the moment one technically becomes a mother—cannot make its way to the real nor can it be imagined.[1] The fact of this moment haunts Cusk and, before ever having given birth, she looks with awe and terror at women's bodies in locker rooms and remembers that "as a child, from the moment I gained some understanding of what it entailed, I worried about childbirth . . . the promise of a future violence" (12). The reality of childbirth and its accompanying pain characterizes the opening chapters of Cusk's narrative, and it is imagined only as an abstract, though perhaps tinged with blood and tearing, "violence."

In order to make the moment manageable, Cusk seeks out stories of childbirth. As she moves closer to the event of birth, she looks to doctors, nurses, parenting manuals, and other women to reveal the mystery. Nevertheless, it becomes ever more elusive and obscured by narratives structured by silence, cloaked in medical abstractions, and made "real" by the case histories of women akin to the Stepford Wives. She begins to suspect a "secret female history . . . conspiratorially concealed" (17) and can only imagine a woman's experience of pregnancy to mirror that of a character in *Invasion of the Body Snatchers*; the woman becomes merely a casing, a copy, forever at a distance from the real: "[There is] an additional horror surrounding the mystery: that somehow, during those tortured hours, some fundamental component of oneself is removed, so that afterwards even though one looks and sounds more or less exactly as one did before, one is in fact a simulacrum, a brainwashed being programmed not to bear witness to the truth" (18).

Cusk imagines childbirth as a trauma, consisting of a painful ripping apart and dislocation of self; recovery requires the piecing together of the image of the former self. In this depiction of childbirth, what was once whole is now incomplete, structured by a void, and a truth too painful to be recalled or narrated is the root of the trauma.² Without its own stories, childbirth becomes a dark secret, kept under the watch of doctors and in the control of their language. In the midst of such silence, the experience becomes at once too large and too annihilating for mothers to claim ownership of the experience and to have agency. The secret terror will keep mothers in line, following doctors' orders.

The pain that terrorizes Cusk is not only bodily pain. While a significant portion of her story focuses on the ravages of motherhood on the body, particularly in such chapters as "Forty Weeks" and "A Valediction to Sleep," this bodily pain necessarily works in conjunction with the psychic pain of becoming a mother. In fact, the two cannot be separated, for to become a mother—to engage in the practices of mothering—is to be both bound to and inhabited by an other in complex and overlapping ways. Upon noticing her newborn daughter's linea negra, a shared, faint line halving their bodies, Cusk recalls reading that a mother and her newborn ought to be referred to as one, as "mother-and-baby" or "motherbaby." She writes, "I find this claim unnerving, even threatening, in spite of the fact that it perfectly describes the profound change in the co-ordinates of my being that I experience in the days and weeks after my daughter's birth" (93–94). These early weeks send Cusk—and probably her daughter—into shock, for there are suddenly two and the world is ungrounded. She tries to describe what she's become: "I feel like a house to which an extension has been added" (94); "a person now exists who is me, but who is not confined to my body" (95); "I cohabit uneasily with myself" (97); and, finally, "I have no subjectivity" (97). Suddenly, she is two—or one-plus, or perhaps two-plus—her subjectivity has been shattered and reassembled to make a whole that is unrecognizable as such.³

The emotional or psychic pain that characterizes the early months of motherhood takes shape in daily, material events. With every midnight cry for milk, with every struggle to transport baby, diaper bag, and stroller through public space, and with every interrupted conversation, Cusk feels a loss of self. She becomes bored with her role as her daughter's "kidney," processing and discarding her waste (134), she becomes worn out by her own and her daughter's lack of sleep, and she longs to escape for a few hours with friends. The days, hours, and minutes of motherhood are filled with heavy work; motherhood is not an abstract state but rather an overwhelming and constant job. The reality of motherhood as it takes shape daily must come as a shock to many new mothers, for it contrasts sharply with the idealization of motherhood. As narrated in western cultures at least, motherhood is a blissful, honorable, and natural state. It is the means to wholeness, for we learn that children make women true women. Motherhood is the ultimate mark of a woman's success; it translates her identity into terms of reverence and abundance. When the fantasy comes into contact with the material, day-to-day world, however, the mother is faced with the fact of her erasure.

Other Subjectivities

Cusk's earliest responses to the experience of motherhood are characterized by pain because she can imagine and understand it only in terms of self/other, independence/dependence, or freedom/confinement. To become a mother within such a discursive system is to be robbed of one's own life and to be left without options, and to survive requires not only a negation of self but also total sacrifice of the self. To give completely is to—perhaps—become a good mother. Cusk refuses this option. She certainly wants to be a good mother, but she recognizes that it must be on other terms. She understands that there is something wrong, "conspiratorial" even, with the narratives available to her; and while she never openly questions the privileging of the individual self, her autobiographical project nevertheless allows her to reformulate the structure of identity.

In her article "Emancipated Subjectivities and the Subjugation of Mothering Practices," Mielle Chandler challenges the notion that to be an individual, to be independent and answerable only to oneself, is to be emancipated. The "I" required to work, to author, to "live," according to Chandler, is not the only kind (or even the best kind) of subjectivity, nor is it the kind of subjectivity available to mothers. She explains:

> To write a paper is to leave mothering, or, rather, it is to leave the type of subjectivity I engage in while mothering . . . The process is one of traveling between an individuated and separated subjectivity which allows me to write, and an actively in-relation subjectivity (if it can be called a subjectivity) which is born of mothering. It is an existence

fraught with tension, for while each site demands my attention, the former requiring quiet sustained concentration, the latter an alertness of a catcher behind home plate, neither allows me to inhabit the other equally. (271)

To be a mother is to be a self in-relation, a subject position that is denied entrance to the larger (public, legitimate) world. The public world respects autonomy, authority, and independence; its relations are often hierarchical and its subjects are distinctly delineated. But, as Chandler claims, there are other ways of being, ways that must be recognized and written in order to name, legitimize, and prescribe—enable—a more complete and fulfilling kind of mothering (and kind of subjectivity). If such stories were told, the trauma of motherhood as described by Cusk would be lessened; motherhood would not mark the disappearance of the self but rather the expansion or branching out of selfhood.

The subject in-relation construct recognizes that to "be" a subject is to be always in-relation with other subjects, and being always in-relation means also to inhabit malleable space. A subject is not a fixed entity, a self permanently inscribed in mind and flesh, but rather a subject is always becoming. Judith Butler's theory of performativity allows for an understanding of subjectivity as such a process and practice. She explains: "Performativity is thus not a singular 'act,' for it is always a reiteration of a norm or set of norms, and to the extent that it acquires an act-like status in the present, it conceals or dissimulates the conventions of which it is a repetition" (Butler, 12). In other words, if we think of selfhood, of subjectivity, as a performance, to "be"—which is to be recognized by others as well as by oneself as existing, as "being," as having an identity—is to be reiterating norms, to be inscribing a self through continuous, and repetitious, acts. Certainly, motherhood can be construed as performance; in fact, the barrage of parenting manuals and the insistent instruction of others—doctors, nurses, health visitors, teachers, other mothers, strangers—makes clear the extent to which motherhood must be carefully practiced and precisely performed. As Chandler contends, "It is my position that 'mother' is best understood as a verb, as something one does, a practice which creates one's identity as intertwined, interconnected and in-relation. . . . To be a mother is to enact mothering" (273–74). "Mother," then, offers a model of subjectivity antithetical to the individualistic and hierarchical patriarchal model, for it is always becoming and its structure is in-relation (as opposed to autonomous). To enact the subject-position "mother" could very likely mean to opt out of the public realm by default, for there is still little room in the "working" world for a person whose body does not mark the boundaries of the self (in-relation) and whose time cannot be requisitioned free and clear.

Narrating "Mother"

Not only is such a multiplicitous and amorphous subjectivity not recognized, valid, or privileged in the public world, but it is also negated by the discourse of patriarchy. Lacan spoke of "Woman," constructing women as lack and maintaining our absence from language:

> when any speaking being whatever lines up under the banner of women it is by being constituted as not all that they are placed within the phallic function. It is this that defines the ... the what?—the woman precisely, except that *The* woman can only be written with *The* crossed through. There is no such thing as *The* woman, where the definite article stands for the universal. There is no such thing as *The* woman since of her essence—having already risked the term, why think twice about it?—of her essence, she is not all. (Lacan, 144)

Lacan asserts that the notion of a whole self is a fiction but that language—the symbolic—acts as a stand-in for wholeness. Still, the compensatory realm of language is available to the male speaking subject as it replicates the "Law of the Father"—the law of the one. The symbolic, then, simultaneously negates the female speaking subject and creates itself over and on top of itself. Language promises wholeness, power, an "I," yet it takes shape as an ever-more final interdiction to the female speaking subject.

I offer this cursory discussion of Lacan's notions of language and subjectivity in order to draw a parallel to Cusk's dilemma as both a mother and a writer and to explore her narration/enactment of subjectivity. First, Cusk's entrance to the institution of motherhood is eerily delineated by the voice of the father, and her project to write her own story is equally mired in the impossibilities and silences of the symbolic. Her pregnancy is marked by the father's law, which is articulated by every parenting book, every hospital pamphlet, and every doctor's visit. Cusk searches for other stories about motherhood—mothers' own narratives, stories about their experiences—rather than those prescribing and mapping out a mother's narrative (precluding the possibility that she write her own). Yet she continues to come up against the same stories. She explains,

> modern pregnancy is governed by a regime breathtaking in the homogeneity of its propaganda, its insignia, its language.... I long to receive some signal of subterfuge, some coded reference to a resistance. My sex has become an exiguous, long-laid, lovingly furnished trap into which I have inadvertently wandered and from which now there is no escape. I have been tagged, as if electronically, by pregnancy. My womanly movements are being closely monitored. (24–25)[4]

As Cusk makes clear, the stories she finds are monolithic and dictatorial; she is not the subject of these stories but rather she is subject to them. Like Lacan's symbolic realm, which is dependent upon the absence of The Woman, the institution of motherhood is dependent upon the absence of the mother and, in the stories of motherhood, her presence is designated by her lack. The mother's absence is described by Cusk as she notes, with growing alarm, "the population of my privacy" (34); mothers, it seems, are colonized and thereby created through the word of the father.

Cusk's longing for "some coded reference to a resistance" is a longing for other stories, which are stories told in a feminine code, able perhaps to fracture the law and to nourish new grounds of experience. She recognizes that language is the means to making mothers' experiences real, public, and valid and, even moreso, that it is the means to becoming a mother on one's own terms. Yet if, as Lacan claims and as the "propaganda" encountered by Cusk indicates, "woman is excluded *by* the nature of words" (Rose, 49), then to tell or write a story as a mother is an exceptionally problematic task, for she must use a language dependent upon her lack to assert her "being."

I do not wish to argue that Cusk has written in/a new language; she has, however, written a new story of motherhood.[5] Moreover, this new story is important because it both recognizes and enacts a kind of subjectivity that is healthy not only for mothers but also for communities and cultures. Her story is new, not in that it is the first or only of its kind, but in that it breaks from the traditional narrative of motherhood. This break is signified by the very act of writing from the (m)other's speaking position, and it is foregrounded by the start of the narrative, where Cusk chooses to open with a quotation from "The Bad Mother." Her story, then, is structured by a split between a mother's story and the story of the father or the institution; by juxtaposing the two narratives throughout the book, Cusk insists that the oppressive gaps between mothers' experiences and patriarchal institution be heard, seen, and felt. The story constructs wholeness as necessarily gaping, fragmented, and contradictory, as it is simultaneously figured as moving across boundaries, flowing in and out. For example, she writes: "We are still so close to our sundering that neither of us seems entire: the painful stump of our jointness, livid and fresh, remains" (51). This is early in her mothering, and so Cusk's use of "entire" is uncertain; as her story is written, however, "entire" comes to include a simultaneous and eternal sundering and jointness. As she is becoming a mother, she recasts what it means to be a whole, complete, subject.

The "newness" of Cusk's narrative also stems from its grounding in the body and its acknowledgment of pain. Women's bodies are central to this story and motherhood is sketched as both psychological and bodily work. Cusk places descriptions of the physical experience of motherhood against the sterile (and subject-less) language of the institution, exposing the master narrative as fraudulent while reiterating the fragmentedness of subjectivity. The women's bodies she feared and revered as a child become sites of agency rather than vessels of mystery. Through linguistic reckoning with the pain of childbirth, breast-feeding, and sleeplessness, for example, Cusk exhumes a story in which the lived, felt experience of motherhood coincides with—or even gives heft to—the more miraculous, beyond-the-body, beyond-the-self depictions of mothering. The experiences of the body—its joy and its pain, its tearing, leaking, and aching—are signposts that remind Cusk of her humanity: "Threads of association hang from me, as if I were unraveling, entangling themselves in the world's weakness. I see elderly people, people in wheelchairs, people begging for money or crying in the street, and they tug at my fibres" (97). The mother's body has made two and it knows pain; by regarding this pain, and by writing about it, Cusk constructs a subject that is not only in-relation but that is also necessarily in-the-body.

By telling a story about motherhood that insists on its trauma and by confronting the individual, day-to-day, bodily experience of motherhood, Cusk illustrates that becoming a mother is an experience that threatens to break apart and consume the self while also offering the greatest potential for new connections, new intimacies, and new conceptions of selfhood. The self becomes both more and less; subjectivity is practiced as the subject interacts, expanding and losing boundaries, and constructs her own story. Writing and mothering are creative acts that enable the expansion of subjectivity beyond the body while simultaneously insisting on its corporeality, on the page and in the flesh. As becoming a "mother" crystallizes for Cusk, she describes its shape:

> I miss my daughter's babyhood already. In her growing up I have watched the present become the past. . . . I understand that it means that I am standing still. Motherhood sometimes seems to me like a sort of relay race, a journey whose purpose is to pass on the baton of life, all work and heat and hurry one minute and mere panting spectatorship the next; a team enterprise in which stardom is endlessly reconfigured, transferred. I see my daughter hurrying away from me, hurtling towards her future, and in that sight I recognise my ending, my frontier, the boundary of my life. (206)

For Cusk, subjectivity is predicated on loss, on pain, but it does not require an ever-reaching for wholeness. Instead, she comes to value a subjectivity that recognizes loss as one aspect of experience and that is also structured by the doubleness of living: the being a self in-relation, where the self is repeated in others and created by others; the experiencing of joy and pain, of mind and body intermingled; the enacting of subjectivity in daily life and in our words; the standing still while still becoming. She does not presume to be "all," but rather claims that "all" exists only by encompassing, and being, others.

Importantly, Cusk's refiguring of subjectivity and her "becoming a mother" grew out of writing. In a study of autobiography, Sidonie Smith tells us that "There is no essential, original, coherent autobiographical self before the moment of self-narrating" (108). To enter into an autobiographical project is to see the pieces of our lives slip and slide apart; the narrated-ness of our lives emerges, and we may go scrambling for the solidity of our fathers' stories or we may "story" our selves. As Cusk shows, the materiality involved in becoming a mother mirrors the writing process of autobiography: the self is reproduced in flesh and in words. It is rewritten and extended, made whole but always incomplete and beyond. As more mothers begin to narrate their own lives, the myth of the "original, essential, coherent" mother will disintegrate, making room for stories—and lives—that are grounded in relatedness, fed by incongruence, and driven by agency.

Conclusion

We live in a culture that privileges the "I," equating identity, contentment, and even freedom with the ability to speak an autonomous self. We also idealize mothers, insisting that a good mother is one whose "I" disappears in the face of her child. To be a good mother, then, is to give up a piece of oneself, to sublimate one's voice, and to deny one's own act of creation while affirming the life of an other. Moreover, to be a good mother is to listen to the father, to step in time with the mandates of how-to manuals and of neighborhood moms. This very structure, though, as Cusk insists, annihilates and numbs mothers, for it simultaneously takes away the privilege of autonomy and denies the self. Maternal experience, which is most "real" in its materiality and pain, is subsumed by theoretical and prescriptive language. Cusk reminds us, certainly, that we still live in the father's world; however, by refusing the father's mandates and by grounding language in experience, she succeeds in telling a new story of motherhood and speaking a new kind of "I."

Notes

1. For Lacan, the real is the realm in which the symbolic and imaginary meet. It is an impossible point; nothing can exist in the real. My use of the term is not nearly as pure. I imagine the real to be a visceral realm, where something is known in the body and in something like the intuitive mind to be (real). To try to put the real into language would be to remove it from the real; however, as in the case of childbirth as feared by Cusk, language and stories may help to bring us at least somewhat closer to knowing—or perhaps theorizing—the real.

2. Cusk ends up having a cesarean section, which leads her to question the realness of the birth and the legitimacy of her identity as a mother. She writes, "It is as if I am unable to find any connection between my physical implication in the fact of her existence, and the emotional world I had imagined would automatically accompany it, a world in which I would as automatically be included . . . Or perhaps it is the clinical, hospital-appointed nature of the birth itself that has caused me to lose the thread of things, for in truth my experience of birth was more like the experience of having an appendix removed than what most people would understand by 'labour.' Without its connecting hours, the glue of its pain, the literalness of its passage, I fear that I will not make it to motherhood; that I will remain stranded as someone who merely had an operation, leaving the baby with no more sense of how she came to be here than if she had been left on the doorstep by a stork" (53–54).

3. As Sharon Abbey and Andrea O'Reilly explain in their introduction to *Redefining Motherhood*, "Subjectivity shifts synchronically and diachronically. In any given day, a

mother will move from one identity to another. At any given moment several selves will be complementary and conflicted" (14).

Cusk often refers to this monitoring of mothers, which hangs like a shadow over a mother's daily living. In her article "Across the Divide," O'Reilly cites Sara Ruddick's construct, "the gaze of others," to illustrate the "policing" of mothers within the institution of motherhood (74). O'Reilly summarizes feminist arguments about the role of mothers within the institution of motherhood, explaining that mothers enforce the rules found in parenting books and in doctors' offices; in other words, a mother's role is to institute the rules of patriarchy, a system that works to deny her a voice while privileging the one and sublimating the body. While the discourse surrounding motherhood denies the voice or stories of the subject in-relation, the "gaze of others" is simultaneously enacted by others and internalized by the mother in a process by which she learns to police herself. Cusk resists this internalization, as the very act of writing her own narrative demonstrates, and she returns to what she calls "the population of my privacy" (34) throughout her story. She remarks, "The baby plays a curious role in the culture of pregnancy. It is at once victim and autocrat . . . It is not, I feel sure, the baby who exerts this watchful pressure: it is the baby's meaning for other people, the world's sense of ownership stating its claim" (30, 35).

4. "New language" echoes earlier calls, begun by French feminists of the 1970s and 1980s, for a "women's language." Such a language would be grounded in the female body, in its multiplicities and doubleness, and would, as imagined by Hélène Cixous, "laugh" at the law of the father. Julia Kristeva looked to the maternal body in particular as the means to fracturing the symbolic. While the possibility of a new or different language is perhaps a stretch, as Cusk insists, "other" stories need to be told, and their telling will happen in different ways. In *A Life's Work*, therefore, we find stories that are grounded in the maternal body, in both content and structure (nonlinear, repetitive or cyclical, driven by rhythms rather than by climax and resolution). This isn't exactly a new language, though it certainly calls the old into question.

5. In her article "Written on the Body," Rishma Dunlop argues for the "emancipatory process that is writing" (119) connecting, as Cusk does, the act of writing to the act of becoming. She explains, "If I am 'storied' by my society and my culture as well as my own particular pleasures and desires, breaking free from the 'texts' of my culture challenges me to stretch beyond these scripts by rethinking the assumptions that structure societal codification" (119). The confining scripts offered to Cusk by doctors and health visitors are the impetus to recast subjectivity so that she eventually overturns her own assumptions about the meaning/value of "independence."

Works Cited

Butler, Judith. *Bodies That Matter: On the Discursive Limits of "Sex."* New York and London: Routledge, 1993.

Chandler, Mielle. "Emancipated Subjectivities and the Subjugation of Mothering Practices." In *Redefining Motherhood: Changing Identities and Patterns*. Edited by Sharon Abbey and Andrea O'Reilly. Toronto: Second Story Press, 1998. 270–86.

Cusk, Rachel. *A Life's Work: On Becoming a Mother*. New York: Picador USA, 2001.

Dunlop, Rishma. "Written on the Body." In *Redefining Motherhood: Changing Identities and Patterns*. Edited by Sharon Abbey and Andrea O'Reilly. Toronto: Second Story Press, 1998. 103–24.

Lacan, Jacques. "God and the *Jouissance* of Woman." In *Feminine Sexuality*. Edited by Juliet Mitchell and Jacqueline Rose. New York and London: W.W. Norton, 1985. 137–48.

O'Reilly, Andrea. "Across the Divide: Contemporary Anglo-American Feminist Theory on the Mother-Daughter Relationship." In *Redefining Motherhood: Changing Identities and Patterns*. Edited by Sharon Abbey and Andrea O'Reilly. Toronto: Second Story Press, 1998. 69–91.

Rich, Adrienne. *Of Woman Born: Motherhood as Experience and Institution*. New York: W.W. Norton, 1976.

Rose, Jacqueline. "Introduction—II." In *Feminine Sexuality*. Edited by Juliet Mitchell and Jacqueline Rose. New York and London: W.W. Norton, 1985. 27–57.

Smith, Sidonie. "Performativity, Autobiographical Practice, Resistance." In *Women, Autobiography, Theory: A Reader*. Edited by Sidonie Smith and Julia Watson. Madison: University of Wisconsin Press, 1998. 108–15.

Suleiman, Susan Rubin. "Writing and Motherhood." In *Mother Reader: Essential Writings on Motherhood*. Edited by Moyra Davey. New York: Seven Stories Press, 2001. 113–37.

Maternal Subjectivity: A Kristevan Reading of Anne Enright's Memoir, *Making Babies: Stumbling into Motherhood*

Heather Ingman

THIS CHAPTER EXAMINES THE RECENTLY PUBLISHED AUTOBIOGRAPHical account of motherhood, *Making Babies: Stumbling into Motherhood*, by the Irish writer Anne Enright. It will argue that, by dwelling on the physical aspects of childbirth and early motherhood, Enright reintroduces what has traditionally been repressed in the Irish Catholic discourse of maternity, namely the female body. It aims to show that Enright's memoir lends itself to being read in the light of Julia Kristeva's theories on motherhood and that, in the context of the lengthy silencing of the mother's voice in Irish culture and writing, such a reading highlights Enright's courageous reclamation of the subjectivity of Irish motherhood.

If, as Mary Mason says, women's autobiography is not so much about the self as about "self-realization and self-transcendence through the recognition of *another*" (Olney 1992, 235) and if, as Jessica Benjamin argues, mothers are changed through their experience of recognizing the child as other (Benjamin 1988/1990, 23), we might expect there to be numerous maternal autobiographies, especially in Ireland where, for a long time, women were defined by their maternal function. In reality, the idealization of the mother figure by Irish Roman Catholic and nationalist ideologies silenced Irish mothers twice over. Not only were women relegated to the private, domestic sphere but, by placing little emphasis on the physical realities of maternity and providing little practical help for mothers, such idealizations resulted in Irish mothers being too burdened by domestic responsibilities to make their voices heard. Indeed they were actively discouraged from doing so. One bishop exhorted Irish women in the following terms to abandon the public sphere: "Do not forget that you are Irish mothers, do not forget your glorious traditions. . . . Appear seldom on the promenade, and sit oftener by the cradles; come down from the platform and attend to the cot" (Hayes and Urquhart 2001, 155).

Some understanding of the silencing of the mother's voice in the life of the Irish nation is necessary in order to appreciate the significance of Anne Enright's memoir. For much of the twentieth century Irish mothers labored under religious and political discourses which connected motherhood with self-sacrifice and, by association with the Virgin Mary, with sexual purity. Though praised in poetry and oratory as symbols of the Irish nation in such figures as Mother Ireland and Kathleen Ni Houlihan, in practice, Irish mothers were denied access to contraception, decent allowances, and free health care, and struggled to raise large families. As Áine McCarthy puts it in her article, " 'Oh Mother Where Art Thou?' Irish Mothers and Irish Fiction in the Twentieth Century": "A surface rhetoric about the ideal of motherhood . . . co-existed with an underbelly of muted maternal reality, forced adoption, illegal abortions, infanticides, incarcerations in Magdalene laundries or lunatic asylums" (McCarthy 2004, 100).

Even in twenty-first-century Ireland there remains a grave lack of provision for the needs of mothers (Kennedy 2002, 2). These practical pressures have meant that few Irish women have found the energy or the confidence to speak as mothers in popular culture, the church or the state. One notable exception to this silencing of the mother's voice is Kathleen Behan's autobiography, *Mother of All the Behans*, published in 1984. A comparison of Behan's autobiography with Enright's memoir highlights the latter's openness and daring in the context of Irish writing about motherhood. *Mother of All the Behans* was not written by Behan herself but is the result of several conversations with her son, Brian, who performed the task of inscribing (and perhaps editing) their conversations and the book was published under his name. The voice of the Irish mother is thus still coming to us not entirely at firsthand but mediated through another, male, voice.

Kathleen Behan recalls raising her children in Dublin tenements and she paints a vivid picture of the political and economic realities of Irish working-class mothers' lives during the early decades of the twentieth century. However, Behan was a committed socialist and a nationalist and it is politics rather than personal emotion that dominates her autobiography, leading to significant gaps. For example, Behan censors all physical descriptions of childbirth and early motherhood and her account reveals a distaste for the body that, it has been argued, was widespread in Ireland at the time. In "The Family and The Female Body in the Novels of Edna O'Brien and Julia O'Faolain," Lorna Rooks-Hughes argues that the idealization of motherhood in Ireland led to a desexualization of the female body which was damaging to women's sense of self (Rooks-Hughes 1996, 83–97). Cheryl Herr's article, "The Erotics of Irishness," concurs and argues that the various ideologies which have held Ireland in their grip during the twentieth century have been responsible for a general suppression of the body in Irish society (Herr 1990, 1–34). Behan's upbringing in a convent orphanage apparently left her ignorant of the facts of life until she was seventeen and she confesses that she never much enjoyed sex and knew nothing about contraceptives till her sons were grown up. Behan's reticence about the body was typical of her time and contrasts, as we shall see, with Enright's frankness.

There are other silences in the book. The autobiography is called *Mother of All the Behans* but in reality Behan concentrates on her three sons, Brendan, Brian, and Dominic, whose various literary and political activities brought them into the public domain. Her daughter, Carmel, is a significant silence in the book. Nor does Behan dwell very much on her relationship with her own mother. This relationship was disrupted when Behan was five by her father's death which left the family in poverty and forced her mother to place her daughters in an orphanage run by nuns. Behan recalls her sense of shame when her mother came to visit and she had to watch the nuns pressing money into her mother's hand. The weakness of the mother is paramount in this portrayal but, surprisingly, her daughter does not explore the political reasons behind it, namely the poor employment prospects for Irish women and the lack of support for widows which was not remedied until second-wave feminists started campaigning on their behalf in the 1970s.

These gaps and silences in Behan's account suggest that the kind of Republican politics she espoused came at the price of suppressing certain truths about the body, femaleness and the mother-daughter relationship. A parallel may be drawn with Maud Gonne MacBride's autobiographical memoir, *A Servant of the Queen: Reminiscences* (1938), which, though written from a very different perspective from Behan's, is again remarkable for its subordination of motherhood to political concerns. There is little mention of Maud Gonne's daughter, Iseult, in *A Servant of the Queen* and where she is mentioned, her relationship to Gonne is never made clear. At one point, Gonne even refers to her daughter as "the charming child I had adopted" (MacBride 1938/1994, 288). Iseult, born in 1894, was in fact the illegitimate daughter of Maud Gonne and the French radical, Lucien Millevoye. In their 1994 introduction to *A Servant of the Queen*, the editors point out that Gonne came under pressure to keep silent about Iseult from her son, Séan MacBride, who was worried about the damage revelations of the existence of an illegitimate half sister might do to his political career. Like *Mother of All the Behans*, Maud Gonne's autobiography subordinates motherhood to social and political concerns.

It is against this background of the silencing of the mother's voice that Anne Enright endeavors in *Making Babies* to bring the semiotic maternal body into Irish writing. I will first examine Julia Kristeva's writing on motherhood and then demonstrate how a Kristevan reading underlines the originality of Enright's memoir in the context of Irish writing on motherhood. In Kristevan theory, abjection is the underside of the symbolic, what society must reject, cover over and contain, usually involving repudiation of our link with animality, sexuality, and mortality. As Kristeva explains in *The Sense and Non-sense of Revolt* defilement is present when the border between two identities becomes blurred: the corpse which is both human and nonhuman and thus points up the fragility of identity, is an example of the abject, as are filth, waste, excrement, blood (especially menstrual blood), nail clippings, hair, all of which blur the body's boundary and for that reason may figure in ritual acts of purity (Kristeva 2000, 21–22).

In Kristevan theory, abjection also functions as a necessary part of the acquisition of language and the setting up of a stable sexual and psychical identity in the life of an individual. Thus the first object of abjection is the pre-Oedipal mother (Kristeva 2000, 21). The infant must learn to abject the maternal body in order to achieve the separation necessary for individual identity. As Kristeva argues in *Powers of Horror*, before abjection, the infant is immersed in the *chora*, a nonspatial, nontemporal receptacle of drives where being is undifferentiated. Abjection precipitates the process by which subject and object are produced. I give birth to myself through the exclusion of not-I. Fear of dependence on the mother, of our materiality and inevitable death remains nevertheless, forever threatening the subject with dissolution and engulfment (Kristeva 1982, 9–15).

In *Powers of Horror*, Kristeva extends the theory of the abject from the individual to cultural, religious and national identity constructed against the exclusion of maternity and the feminine and in *The Sense and Non-sense of Revolt* she makes clear that what has to be expelled from national life is the maternal abject: "if we look at the question in religious terms, we see that the social and symbolic pact . . . is a transversal link that is constituted by the evacuation of the maternal: in order to establish the symbolic pact, one has to get rid of the domestic, corporal, maternal container" (Kristeva 2000, 21).

She returns to the subject in *The Feminine and the Sacred* where she argues in her correspondence with Catherine Clément that "what is fundamentally warded off is maternal power" (Kristeva 2001, 95). According to Kristevan theory, in both the life of the nation and of individuals, the abject is never fully obliterated but hovers at the borders of a subject's or a nation's identity, simultaneously fascinating and terrifying, a constant threat to stable identity. In *"Stabat Mater,"* Kristeva's reflections on her own bodily experience of motherhood break up her analysis of the historical development of the cult of the Virgin Mary by emphasizing what that cult has suppressed or ignored, namely the pain, tears, sweat of childbirth and the sleeplessness, milk, and eroticism of motherhood.

In the same way as Kristeva shows that Jewish purity rituals arose from a desire to distinguish Judaism from the maternal cults by which Judaism was surrounded so, it has been argued, in Ireland hypermasculinized nationalism evolved as a reaction against the feminization of Ireland in colonial discourse (Cairns and Richards 1988, 42–57). In this hypermasculinized Irish nationalism maternal subjectivity featured as the abject, that which had to be suppressed in order for identity to form. Even in writing by women, the Irish mother is frequently presented as an object of horror that the daughter must outgrow in order to claim her identity (Weekes 2000, 100–123). By writing out of her own experience of motherhood and by dwelling, like Kristeva in *"Stabat Mater,"* on the blood, sweat, shit, and milk of childbirth and early motherhood, Anne Enright challenges her nation's relegation of maternal subjectivity to the abject and seeks to reclaim the voice of Irish motherhood.

The comparison with Kristeva is all the more appropriate since Anne Enright herself refers to the French writer in her account: "As Julia Kristeva says, quoting Mallarmé, 'What is there to say concerning childbirth?' I find that question much more pungent than Freud's well-known 'What does woman want?' Indeed, what does it mean to give birth to a child? Psychoanalysts do not talk much about it" (Enright 2004, 11).

Though Enright does not give the source of this quotation, it comes from Kristeva's essay "A New Type of Intellectual: The Dissident" (1977). Enright may also be familiar with Kristeva's well-known essay on motherhood, *"Stabat Mater,"* since Enright's description of pregnancy as a time "underwater, where there are no words" (Enright 2004, 20) echoes Kristeva's description in *"Stabat Mater"* of matriarchal civilization as a place of "an underwater, trans-verbal communication between bodies" (Kristeva 1997, 324).

Making Babies begins by noting Enright's reluctance to speak as a mother: "Speech is a selfish act, and mothers should probably remain silent" (Enright 2004, 1). Later she reflects on "this new drama of being a mother . . . about which so little has been written. Can mothers not hold a pen?" (Enright 2004, 42). She suggests that the reason why mothers do not write is "because motherhood happens in the body, as much as the mind" (Enright 2004, 47). The body, however, has traditionally been censored in Ireland. Breast-feeding, for example, "though general all over Ireland, was absolutely hidden" (Enright 2004, 43). Or else iconized in pictures of the Madonna and Child or usurped by the Sacred Heart: "The closest the culture came to an image of actual nursing was in the icon of the Sacred Heart, endlessly offering his male breast, open and glowing, and crowned with thorns" (Enright 2004, 43).

Enright suggests, therefore, that the silencing of mothers is due both to the censoring of the body in Irish culture and to the way in which Catholicism has sought to usurp, and thereby control, the maternal function. In this respect, her argument resembles that of Kristeva in *"Stabat Mater"* where Kristeva argues that Catholic societies contain the threat from the maternal body and its *jouissance* through the cult of the Virgin Mary which she terms: "a masculine appropriation of the Maternal" (Kristeva 1997, 310).

Unlike earlier child psychologists and object relations theorists such as Donald Winnicott and John Bowlby who stressed that it was the mother's task to listen to her child (see Ingman, 199, 11–12), in *"Stabat Mater"* Kristeva puts the focus back on the mother when she urges women both to explore their own experiences of motherhood and to attend to what other women have to say about motherhood: "There might doubtless be a way to approach the dark area that motherhood constitutes for a woman; one needs to listen, more carefully than ever, to what mothers are saying today, through their economic difficulties and . . . their discomforts, insomnias, desires, pains, and pleasures" (Kristeva 1997, 326).

This kind of dialogic listening, Kristeva believes, will open the way to an understanding of mothers based not on idealization, as in the cult of the Virgin Mary, but on recognition of their individuality. Dialogic listening is, in effect, what Anne Enright attempts in *Making Babies* where she intersperses her own experience of motherhood with anecdotes about other mothers she has encountered. The numerous references to the bodily changes surrounding childbirth and early motherhood represent Enright's attempt to write the female body into Irish literature against a background of suppression and reticence such as we saw in Kathleen Behan's account. Like Kristeva in *"Stabat Mater"* for whom pregnancy "extracts woman out of her oneness" (Kristeva 1997, 382), Enright portrays her attempts to come to terms in the early days of her pregnancy with the fact that she is no longer one, but "a peculiar, mutant, double self—motherandchild" (Enright 2004, 20). Both Kristeva and Enright depict pregnancy as something which "happens" to a woman's body rather than being under her control. In her essay, "Motherhood According to Giovanni Bellini" (published originally in 1975), Kristeva writes: "Cells fuse, split, and proliferate; volumes grow, tissues stretch, and body fluids change rhythm, speeding up or slowing down. Within the body, growing as a graft, indomitable, there is an other. And no one is present within that simultaneously dual and alien space, to signify what is going on. 'It happens, but I'm not there.' 'I cannot realize it, but it goes on.' Motherhood's impossible syllogism" (Kristeva 1997, 301). Similarly, Enright says: "We do not choose, sometimes, to be occupied by this other creature, and this is one reason why women find pregnancy unsettling. It is assumed that our bodies will 'know', even if we don't, what pregnancy is like and what it is for; that we are, on some cellular level, wise, or even keen on the reproductive game. But I do not know how such cellular knowledge might happen, or where it might inhere" (Enright 2004, 11).

Both writers dwell on the sensual experience of pregnancy and the early days of motherhood in remarkably similar terms: "Scent of milk, dewed greenery, acid and clear, recall of wind, air, seaweed" (Kristeva 1997, 317). "Amniotic fluid smells like tea. . . . There is a little something extra in there, sharp and herbal—green tea maybe, or gunpowder tea. Pregnancy smelt like grass" (Enright 2004, 26).

Both writers present pregnancy as a time out of time, "a non-place, a suspension" as Enright puts it (Enright 2004, 20). For both women, pregnancy and the early days of motherhood are a moment when the semiotic disrupts the chronological linear time of the symbolic, equated by Kristeva in "About Chinese Women" with the time of the father (Kristeva 1986, 152–53). In *Making Babies*, Enright portrays herself as a mother living to the semiotic rhythm of her baby's wail. Indeed Enright's attempt to reproduce the semiotic chant of a baby's cry runs to three pages in her account (Enright 2004, 127–30). In the semiotic, the mother loses all sense of her boundaries as an individual: "No identity holds up" says Kristeva (Kristeva 1997, 323). Similarly, Enright feels the borders of her self spill over as she experiences the urge to nurse strangers, a tree, a passing child: "This occasional incontinence is terrifying" (Enright 2004, 46). Yet both also emphasize the joy of motherhood: "Motherhood condemns us to a demented *jouissance*" says Kristeva (Kristeva 1997, 323). "I am extravagantly happy," writes Enright, "messy, creaky, bewildered, exhausted and in pain, but happy, hopeful, and immensely refreshed by it all" (Enright 2004, 53).

In *"Stabat Mater,"* early motherhood is described as a time when a daughter discovers her mother: "Recovered childhood, dreamed peace restored, in sparks, flash of cells, instants of laughter, smiles in the blackness of dreams, at night, opaque joy that roots me in her bed, my mother's, and projects him, a son, a butterfly soaking up dew from her hand, there, nearby, in the night. Alone: she, I, and he" (Kristeva 1997, 318).

Rather than a physical reunion (since Kristeva's mother was still in Communist Bulgaria), this passage is describing Kristeva's psychological reconciliation with her mother with whom she had often had a difficult relationship. "By giving birth, the woman enters into contact with her mother," she writes in "Motherhood According to Giovanni Bellini" (Kristeva 1997, 303). Enright experiences a similar psychological reunion with the mother as she ponders what piece of advice she would leave to her baby in the event of her death: "I open my mouth and . . . my own mother comes falling out of it. But of course" (Enright 2004, 75).

Watching their babies, both writers find themselves probing their own earliest memories: "Concerning that stage of my childhood, scented, warm and soft to the touch, I have only a spatial memory. No time at all. Fragrance of honey, roundness of forms, silk and velvet under my fingers, on my cheeks. Mummy" (Kristeva 1997, 323).

Similarly, Enright's earliest memories concern shape and texture: a pot stand, pulling wallpaper off a wall: "The plaster underneath it was pink and powdery, and I imagine now that I can remember the shivery taste of it. I also remember the shape of the tear on the wall" (Enright

2004, 66–67). And now for her baby daughter, "The world is all colour, light and texture" (Enright 2004, 67). Both writers express the separation between mother and child. However close the mother may feel to her baby, it is still a separate being:

> Then there is this other abyss that opens up between the body and what had been its inside: there is the abyss between the mother and the child. What connection is there between myself, or even more unassumingly between my body and this internal graft and fold, which, once the umbilical cord has been severed, is an inaccessible other? My body and . . . him. No connection. Nothing to do with it. And this, as early as the first gestures, cries, steps. . . . The child, whether *he* or *she* is irremediably an other. (Kristeva 1997, 322–23)

Despite the fact that Kristeva insists that such separation would occur regardless of the sex of the child, it may be significant that Enright expresses this sense of separation from her baby only when she is describing the birth of her second child, a son: "I have the strongest feeling that he is his own person—a person I don't know yet, and may never actually know. This is the thrill of separation, and there is bleakness to it, too" (Enright 2004, 96). If the gender of the child is significant to such moments of separation, it would bear out those theorists who argue that Western culture encourages mothers to keep their daughters close but to push their sons away (see, for example, Chodorow 1978, 169).

There is an even more intriguing parallel between Kristeva and Enright: in the course of writing on maternity, both writers touch on the subject of death. In Kristevan theory, it is not only the pre-Oedipal mother which functions as the abject; the abject functions also as an avowal of the death drive, an acknowledgment of the nearness of dissolution of identity. Hence the terror it holds for us, reminding us of our mortality. In *Powers of Horror*, she says: "The corpse, seen without God and outside of science, is the utmost of abjection. It is death infecting life. Abject. It is something rejected from which one does not part, from which one does not protect oneself as from an object. Imaginary uncanniness and real threat, it beckons to us and ends up engulfing us" (Kristeva 1982, 4).

In Kristeva's theory of the abject, both the maternal body and death alternately fascinate and terrify us because both threaten us with the dissolution of our individual boundaries. Interestingly, Enright's account also links maternity with that other abject, death, when, in her final chapter titled "Oh, Mortality," she describes a suicide attempt she made in her twenties. The links between maternity and death begin early on in *Making Babies*. Three pages in, Enright describes childbirth as feeling "like dying, pulled inside out" (Enright 2004, 3). At one point, as she was giving birth, she had the feeling that, unless she received pain relief immediately: "I would go under—in some spiritual and very real sense, I would die" (Enright 2004, 31). In the early days of motherhood, when the reader might have expected her to focus on the experience of birth, she describes how the sight of German tourists dying on the Concorde caused her milk to flow (Enright 2004, 45). Mortality is never far out of sight in this maternal narrative.

In the final chapter of *Making Babies*, Enright's suicide attempt is dated precisely to Easter Monday 1986. There must have been personal reasons for her attempt but she does not give these. Instead she sets her suicidal instincts, as earlier she had set motherhood, in their sociocultural context: "The older I get the more political I am about depression, or less essentialist—it is not because of who you are, but where you are placed. Ireland broke apart in the eighties, and I sometimes think that the crack happened in my own head. . . . The country was screaming at itself about contraception, abortion, and divorce. It was a hideously misogynistic time" (Enright 2004, 186–87).

One factor she highlights in particular is the influence of Catholicism on her childhood and her subsequent loss of faith: "I fell out of the world, temporarily, on Easter Monday 1986—so maybe it was just a Catholic hangover, the remnant of spending my early life praying to a dead body on a stick" (Enright 2004, 186). Likewise, in her account of the sources of melancholy in *Black Sun: Depression and Melancholy* (1987), Kristeva implicates loss of faith: "There is nothing more dismal than a dead God, and Dostoyevsky himself was disturbed by the distressing sight of the dead Christ in Holbein's painting, contrasting with the 'truth of resurrection.' The periods that witness the downfall of political and religious idols, periods of crisis, are particularly favorable to black moods" (Kristeva 1997, 184).

After the failure of her suicide attempt, telling almost no one about it, Enright resumed her usual routine: "except that I always had this, like a sweet in the bottom of an old pocket, a little yearning something—the desire to die" (Enright 2004, 188). Similarly, in Kristeva, the depressed person becomes attached to her sadness, it is "that impossible love, never reached, always elsewhere, such as the promises of nothingness, of death" (Kristeva 1997, 187).

Eventually Enright was hospitalized with severe depression. The treatment she received led, like Kristeva's abject, to loss of her boundaries as an individual: "For six months, the medication turned all my thoughts into symptoms, and made me question everything about who I was. It dismantled my personality" (Enright 2004, 193). Even after she had been sent home, she had to be careful: "There is a certain ruthlessness about a recovering depressive, and like alcoholics we are never cured. It takes rigour. . . . Every choice you make leads in a straight line to life, or to death" (Enright 2004, 193). In Kristeva's account in *Black Sun*, the melancholic "is ready at any moment for a plunge into death" (Kristeva 1997, 181).

Only after the birth of her children does Enright realize that her attitude to death has changed: "I had got into such a habit of gratitude, and a mother's worry for the future, that I didn't, I found, want to die at all, not for a very long time" (Enright 2004, 195–96). In *"Stabat Mater,"* after the birth of her son, Kristeva asks: "Death, then, how could I yield to it?" (Kristeva 1997, 314). In Enright's account, maternity succeeds in canceling out her former death wish and this would seem to support Kristeva's suggestion in *"Stabat Mater"* that "man overcomes the unthinkable of death by postulating maternal love in its place" (Kristeva 1997, 325). For Enright, as for Kristeva, maternal "herethics is undeath" (Kristeva 1997, 330).

To conclude: Anne Enright's maternal narrative gains in being read against Kristeva's reconceiving of the figure of the mother for such a reading brings out, not only what is personal in this account, but also its sociocultural context. As Patricia Kennedy argues in her introduction to *Maternity in Ireland: A Woman-Centred Perspective* (2002), far from being a personal, private experience, motherhood is inevitably shaped by the society in which the mothering takes place: "Motherhood is both personal and political. Mothers live their lives where the public and private meet. Their everyday lives are influenced by public expectations, prescribed roles, social, political, economic and cultural constraints and circumstances while on a parallel level private, biographical, emotional, physical and physiological experiences have to be coped with by these same mothers" (Kennedy 2002, 1–2).

In the context of the lengthy suppression of maternal subjectivity in the life of the Irish nation, Enright's determined emphasis on her personal experience of the physical realities of motherhood may be said to form a political strategy. Elspeth Probyn, writing about Latin American women's testimonies, calls autobiography "a conjectural document of the self and of the times . . . which arises from the situation as it comments upon it" (Probyn 1993, 98). Discussing Probyn's statement, Linda Anderson has said: "The question is recast, therefore, in relation to autobiography, becoming not 'what is it' but instead 'what does it *do*' " (Anderson 2001, 91). In this context, what Enright's narrative does is resist idealizations of motherhood prevalent in Irish nationalist and religious discourse and form the beginnings of the emergence of maternal subjectivity in Irish writing. It is to be hoped *Making Babies* will encourage other Irish mothers to make their voices heard.

Works Cited

Anderson, L. *Autobiography*. London and New York: Routledge, 2001.

Behan, B. *Mother of All the Behans: The Autobiography of Kathleen Behan as Told to Brian Behan*. Dublin: Poolbeg, 1994 (1984).

Benjamin, J. *The Bonds of Love: Psychoanalysis, Feminism, and the Problem of Domination*. London: Virago, 1990 (1988).

Cairns, D., and S. Richards. *Writing Ireland: Colonialism, Nationalism and Culture*. Manchester: Manchester University Press, 1988.

Chodorow, N. *The Reproduction of Mothering: Psychoanalysis and the Sociology of Gender*. Berkeley and Los Angeles: University of California Press, 1978.

Enright, A. *Making Babies: Stumbling into Motherhood*. London: Jonathan Cape, 2004.

Hayes, A., and D. Urquhart. *The Irish Women's History Reader*. London: Routledge, 2001.

Herr, C. "The Erotics of Irishness." *Critical Inquiry* 17, 1 (1990): 1–34.

Ingman, H. *Mothers and Daughters in the Twentieth Century: A Literary Anthology*, Edinburgh: Edinburgh University Press, 1999.

Kennedy, P. *Maternity in Ireland: A Woman-Centred Perspective*. Dublin: Liffey Press, 2002.

Kristeva, J. *The Feminine and the Sacred*. New York: Columbia University Press, 2001.

———. *The Kristeva Reader*. Edited by T. Moi. Oxford: Basil Blackwell, 1982.

———. *The Portable Kristeva*. Edited by K. Oliver. New York: Columbia University Press, 1997.

———. *Powers of Horror: An Essay on Abjection*. New York: Columbia University Press, 1982.

———. *The Sense and Non-sense of Revolt: The Powers and Limits of Psychoanalysis*. Translated by J. Herman. New York: Columbia University Press, 2000.

MacBride, M. G. *A Servant of the Queen: Reminiscences*. Edited by A. N. Jeffares and A. MacBride. Gerrards Cross: Colin Smythe, 1994 (1938).

McCarthy, A. "'Oh Mother Where Art Thou?' Irish Mothers and Irish Fiction in the Twentieth Century." In *Motherhood in Ireland: Creation and Context*. Edited by P. Kennedy. Dublin: Mercier Press, 2004. 95–107.

Olney, J., ed. *Autobiography: Essays Theoretical and Critical*. Princeton: Princeton University Press, 1992.

Probyn, E. *Sexing the Self: Gendered Positions in Cultural Studies*. London and New York: Routledge, 1993.

Rooks-Hughes, L. "The Family and the Female Body in the Novels of Edna O'Brien and Julia O'Faolain." *The Canadian Journal of Irish Studies. Special Edition. Edna O'Brien* 22, 2 (1996): 83–97.

Weekes, A. O. "Figuring the Mother in Contemporary Irish Fiction." In *Contemporary Irish Fiction: Themes, Tropes, Theories*. Edited by L. Harte and M. Parker. Basingstoke: Macmillan Press, 2000. 100–23.

The Motherhood Memoir and the "New Momism": Biting the Hand that Feeds You

Andrea O'Reilly

AFTER READING AND REREADING A DOZEN OR MORE MOTHERHOOD memoirs and many more articles on the subject matter, I, in a frustrating moment of writer's block, decided to Google the subject to see if someone else's insight on the subject matter would facilitate my own. While "motherhood memoir" yielded 545 hits, and "memoir" another 8,900, the phrase "mommy lit" resulted in a staggering 33,400 entries (October 16, 2006). It seems that while I may have been at a loss for words, plenty had been written on the subject matter of "mommy lit." While, to my knowledge, the genre eludes a precise definition, there seems to be some agreement on its characteristics. In her recent article "You are not Alone: The Personal, the Political, and the 'New' Mommy Lit," Heather Hewett explains that "the only requirement seemed to be that it explores the 'real' experience of motherhood honestly, without sentimentality or idealization or judgment from the point of view of the mother. And more often than not, it circled around the issues of work, identity and motherhood" (121). In addition, all agree that "mommy lit" is a very recent literary genre, emerging only within the last six years, at the turn of the millennium.

Stephanie Wilkinson and Jennifer Niesslein, editors of *Brain, Child*, open their 2005 article on "Motherhood in Book Publishing" referring to the initial mission statement of their magazine. "Motherhood," they wrote in their inaugural 2000 issue, "is worthy of literature." "It seemed an outrage to us," they go on to say, "that there were probably as many literary books on bull-fighting as there were on the near-universal experience of raising kids" (1). Now, five years later, they concede that "anyone can go into a decent bookstore and find volumes of thought-provoking writing about motherhood. In addition to the advice books and lite humor, you can find a smorgasbord of serious books about motherhood" (1). In particular, the mother-lit trend that began in the mid-1990s is, they note, "if not exactly a flood, seems a healthy stream" (3). Faulkner Fox, author of the best-selling *Dispatches*, explains that when she started her book project in the fall of 2001, a book like hers didn't exist: "If it had," she says, "I would have just read it, not written it" (as quoted in Wilkinson and Niesslein, 4). Fast-forward five years and Heather Hewitt writes: "As my due date quickly approached, I became more and more apprehensive. I found myself craving books on the subject of motherhood, but not books that made me feel worse.... I wanted something else: the stories of other mothers, their collective wisdom, and the bigger picture of motherhood in America. Fortunately, there were plenty of books to choose from" (121). Indeed a Google search of the words "motherhood," "mothering," "mothers" yields 438,000 hits. This is indeed light-years away from what was available to mothers ten to twenty years ago. In 1983, when I first became pregnant, you would be lucky to come across a copy of Rich's *Of Woman Born* (1976) or Jane Lazarre's *The Mother Knot* at a used bookstore, that is, if they had not gone out of print. What's more, we certainly could not turn to the estimated 8,500 parenting blogs for comfort and community. Again, if we were fortunate we had a mother-friend from the same apartment block who we could meet in the playground after dishes were done and weather permitting.

Numerous explanations have been offered to account for the explosion of mothering literature and, in particular, motherhood memoirs, over the last fifteen years and most notably in the last six years. Wilkinson and Niesslein point to several factors, one of which is feminism. They explain:

> This generation of mothers is the first to have grown up with the women's movement of the seventies in progress. At least some of us were told from the get-go that our opinions matter, that our experiences are valid. Growing up with the same sense of entitlement as our brothers played out in all sorts of well-documented ways. One less documented way that today's women's sense of entitlement has played out is in publishing. If football coaches and fishing enthusiasts could pen books about their experiences, why not mothers? (5).

Related to this, as Wilkinson and Niesslein note, is the purchasing power of women: they buy 68 percent of all books and read 56 percent of all literary works (6). Another reason, not discussed by Wilkinson and Niesslein, is demographics. In 2000 the first group of third-wave feminists turned thirty-five and began having children; while some third-wave writers and activists had their children at a relatively young age, notably Ariel Gore, most did not become mothers until their mid to late thirties at the turn of the millennium. Indeed, a review of current feminist third-wave writings reveals a baby boom among third wavers. These women, who were thinking and writing about other feminist issues in the 1980s and '90s, turned their attention to motherhood as they became mothers themselves and, as a result, we have seen the appearance and appeal of "mommy lit" over the last five to six years.

This paper will suggest reasons other than feminism, purchasing power and demographics to account for the emergence of "mommy lit" at the turn of the new millennium. (These three factors, however, do contribute to and support the explanation I develop below.) I argue that this literary genre was born from a new ideology of motherhood, what Sharon Hays has termed intensive mothering and Susan Douglas and Meredith Michaels call the "new momism." More specifically, I contend that, as this new ideology made possible a public voice on motherhood, it simultaneously limited what that voice could say about motherhood. Beginning with a discussion of intensive mothering and the "new momism," the essay will go on to highlight several themes of the motherhood memoir from the perspective of this new discourse on motherhood. In particular, I will argue that, as this discourse makes a critique of patriarchal motherhood possible, it simultaneously censors what can be said in that very same critique. More specifically, I argue that this discourse ultimately reinscribes or, more accurately, naturalizes and normalizes the very patriarchal conditions of motherhood that feminists, including the motherhood memoir writers themselves, seek to dismantle. At the turn of the last century maternal feminists relied upon the belief in innate gender difference, particularly the alleged moral superiority of mothers, to lobby for and make legitimate their claims for female suffrage. Similarly, be it consciously or otherwise, motherhood memoir writers today draw upon the ethos of the "new momism" to value and validate a public literature on motherhood; in particular, the assumption that children are the all-consuming focus and purpose of a mother's life. This use of maternal feminism and the "new momism" did make possible significant gender change: female suffrage in the last century and a deprivatization of motherhood in this century. However, it also serves to reify gender difference and hence reinforce traditional and patriarchal notions of womanhood and motherhood, most notably, the private/ public divide and the feminine/nurturer and masculine/producer gender dichotomy. This chapter will examine the motherhood memoir's compliance and complicity with the new momism philosophy of mothering to argue that real challenge and change becomes possible only when this genre confronts and counters this discourse of motherhood.

INTENSIVE MOTHERING AND THE "NEW MOMISM"

Intensive mothering is characterized by three interconnected themes. The first defines mothering as *natural* to women and essential to their being which, as Pamela Courtenay Hall notes, conveyed the belief that "women are *naturally* mothers, they are born with a built-in set of capacities, dispositions, and desires to nurture children [. . . and that this] engagement of love and instinct is utterly distant from the world of paid work . . . " (337). Second, the mother is to be the central caregiver of her biological children, and thirdly, children require full-time mothering, or in the instance where the mother must work outside the home, the children must always come before the job. This model of mothering, as Sharon Hays explains in *The Cultural Contradictions of Motherhood*, "tells us that children are innocent and priceless, that their rearing should be carried out primarily by individual mothers and that it should be centered on children's needs, with methods that are informed by experts, labor intensive, and costly" (21). She emphasizes that intensive mothering is "a historically constructed *cultural model* for appropriate child care" (21, emphases in original). "Conceptions of appropriate child rearing," she continues, "Are not simply a random conglomeration of disconnected ideas; they form a fully elaborated, logically cohesive framework for thinking about and acting toward children. . . . We are told that [intensive mothering] is the best model, largely because it is what children need and deserve. This model was not developed overnight, however, nor is intensive mothering the only model available to mothers" (21).

Sharon Hays argues that intensive mothering emerged in the postwar period. Conversely, I contend that while the origins of intensive mothering may be traced back to this time, intensive mothering, in its fully developed form, came about in the early 1990s. Hays argues, as noted above, that intensive mothering is characterized by three themes: "first, the mother is the central caregiver"; second, "mothering is regarded as more important than paid employment"; and third, that such mothering requires "lavishing copious amounts of time, energy, and material resources on the child" (8). I would suggest that while the first two characterize mothering from postwar to present day, only mothering of the last fifteen years can be characterized by the third theme.

The postwar discourse of good motherhood demanded that mothers be at home full time with their children, however, this did not necessitate the intensive mothering expected of mothers today. Today, the ideology of good motherhood demands more than mere physical proximity of mother-child: contemporary mothers are expected to spend what the discourse of the experts call "quality time" with their children. Mothers are told to play with their children, read to them and take classes with them. While the children in the fifties and sixties would jump rope or play hide-and-seek with the neighborhood children or their siblings, today's children dance, swim and "cut and paste" with their mothers in one of many "moms and tots" programs. Likewise, today children as young as one-month-old are enrolled in a multitude of classes from water-play for infants, French immersion for toddlers, karate for preschoolers, and competitive skiing, skating, or sailing for elementary-school-age children. (An article I read recently also recommended reading and singing to your child in utero.) Though they have fewer children and more labor-saving devices—from microwaves to take-out food—today's mothers spend more time and energy (and I may add money) on their children than their mothers did in the 1960s. And the majority of mothers today, unlike forty years ago, practice intensive mothering while engaged in full-time employment. Mothering today, as in the postwar era, is "expert driven." However, mothering today is also, under the ideology of intensive mothering, more child-centered than the "children should be seen but not heard" style of mothering that characterized the postwar period. Indeed, as Susan Douglas and Meredith Michaels observe in *The Mommy Myth*, "Intensive mothering [has become] the ultimate female Olympics" (6).

Douglas and Michaels term this contemporary discourse of motherhood the "new momism": "The insistence that no woman is truly complete or fulfilled unless she has kids, that women remain the best primary caretakers of children, and that to be a remotely decent mother, a woman has to devote her entire physical, psychological, emotional, intellectual being, 24/7, to her children. The new momism is a highly romanticized view of motherhood in which the standards for success are impossible to meet" (4).

However, as Douglas and Michaels go on to explain, "The new momism involves more than just impossible ideals about women childrearing, it redefines all women, first and foremost, through their relationships to children. Thus, being a citizen, a worker, a governor [and so forth] are suppose to take a backseat to motherhood" (22). "The new momism," Douglas and Michaels continue, "insists that if you want to do anything else, you'd better first prove that you're a doting, totally involved mother before proceeding. The only recourse for women who want careers, or to do anything else besides stay at home with the kids all day, is to prove they can 'do it all'" (22). A crucial dimension of the "new momism," which has particular relevance to the motherhood memoir, is the concept of choice. Douglas and Michaels explain:

> Central to the new momism is the feminist insistence that women have choices, that they are active agents in control of their own destiny, that they have autonomy. But here's where the distortion of feminism occurs. The only truly enlightened choice to make as a woman, the one that proves, first, that you are a "real" woman, and second, that you are a decent, worthy one, is to become a "mom" and to bring to child rearing a combination of selflessness and professionalism.... Thus the new momism is deeply contradictory: It both draws from and repudiates feminism. (5)

Moreover, in its assertions of female agency and autonomy, the "new momism" denies and distorts the fact that most mothers have little or no choice in the making of their lives. The concept of choice, as feminist theory has shown us, is a liberal fiction that serves to disguise and justify social inequities, particularly those of gender.

The Motherhood Memoir

The contemporary motherhood memoir both draws from and disputes the new momism. As noted above, the emergence of this discourse on motherhood gave women permission to talk publicly on motherhood: in the vein that "motherhood is so important and central to women that, of course, they can and must discuss it." At the same time, memoir writers critique many aspects of intensive mothering that make contemporary motherhood limiting to women. However, the motherhood memoir, because it is informed, if not created by, the discourse of the new momism, also often reinscribes the very gender roles that cause mothering to be oppressive to women and that are at the heart of the author's critique of patriarchal motherhood.

To use the vernacular, motherhood memoirs are concerned with "telling it like it is." In Susan Maushart's words, memoir authors examine "the mismatch between the expectations and the experiences [of motherhood]" (xi). Maushart uses a metaphor to signify what I term the cognitive dissonance between the reality and ideology of motherhood. To be masked is "to deny and repressed what we experience, to misrepresent it, even to ourselves" (1–2). "The realities of motherhood," Maushart writes, "are kept carefully shrouded in silence, disinformation, and outright lies" (5). The mask of motherhood, she continues, "keeps women from speaking clearly what they know, and from sharing truths too threatening to face" (7). "It is not an emperor who is walking naked through the streets," writes Wendy Le Blanc in *Naked Motherhood: Shattering Illusions and Sharing Truths*, "it is our Mothers. All of us collude with the conspiracy by pretending we can see her fully clothed in all her mythological finery" (1). In *Mother Shock*, Andrea Buchanan asks "Why did no one tell me what motherhood is really like? Why had I never bothered to ask?" (xi). Each motherhood memoir, in one way or another, seeks to "unmask" motherhood: to speak honestly and authentically about what it means to become and be a mother.

Unquestionably, motherhood memoirs should be required reading for all mothers-to-be. We could begin a revolution in motherhood if we gave these books as shower gifts instead of the usual blankets and nappies. The motherhood memoir prepares women for the truths of mothering and enables mothers to feel less guilt, anxiety, and stress about being a mother. In this, they are indeed revolutionary. However, I sense a hesitation in this mission of unmasking motherhood: Is it enough to identify and detail the differences between our expectations of motherhood and its realities, or to simply catalogue and critique the gender inequities of current family arrangements without seeking to change them? To be sure, to say that the boredom, exhaustion, ambivalence, guilt, loneliness, anxiety, and self-doubt mothers feel is normal and common—indeed more real than the contented, calm, and composed mother found in magazines—is therapeutic, indeed liberating. Likewise, documenting the day-to-day work of mothering makes real and public the second and third shifts of women's domestic labor and confirms the gender inequities of most households. Nonetheless, I think we need to be asking more difficult questions: Why is there such a discrepancy between myth and reality? What purpose socially, economically, psychologically does the ideology of perfect motherhood serve? Or more pointedly, in terms of the discussion of this paper, why are we content with only unmasking motherhood; should our aim not be to challenge and change patriarchal motherhood? It is my belief that while most motherhood memoirs do expose motherhood as a patriarchal institution, they do not ultimately denounce or transform this institution. This is because the motherhood memoir critique is ultimately contained and constrained by the discourse of the new momism that creates and informs it.

In her highly perceptive article, "Mommy Memoirs: Feminism, Gender and Motherhood in Popular Culture," Ivana Brown argues that the motherhood memoir is characterized by three themes: "Emphasis on gender dualism and gender difference in parenting; the significance of the bodily experience of motherhood; [presence] of the 'natural mother' myth, which assumes women's superiority and ability as natural caregivers" (202). Examples of such gender essentialism pervade the motherhood memoir. Naomi Wolf, for example, writes: "We looked at the results [of the pregnancy test] and gazed at each other. Then we reacted very differently. My husband needed to run—and think; and I needed to sit still and not think. Male and female . . . we reacted spontaneously, like different elements" (15). And Susan Cheever writes: "For months and months . . . it felt as if my daughter and I were rejoined in our bodies as well as in our souls. Any separation was indescribably painful. When I was with her I was whole—my two parts were reunited." In *Breeder*, the natural mother myth is expressed in the valorization of attachment parenting. As one writer notes, "Ben and I hold Ember all of the time, until she freaks and needs her space. The first time I recognized that her crying meant she just wanted to be put down, I was both heartbroken and relieved" (Gore, 113).

What Brown does not develop in her article, and what is the focus of my research on the motherhood memoir, is that these three themes are precisely the underpinning assumptions of the new momism discourse; namely, that mothering is a highly gendered and embodied experience that women are naturally drawn to and prepared for. While memoir authors do critique the *consequences* of these assumptions—i.e., women do all the work of mothering with little or no support—they do not challenge the assumptions themselves; thus, their challenge remains at the level of criticism and not change. This is most evident in the authors' views on childcare. Of the memoirs I have read thus far, none of the authors consider childcare as a possible option for allowing women to develop a selfhood outside of motherhood. For some the reason is financial, though for most it is because they subscribe to the new momism belief of the necessity of full-time, natural and attachment mothering. They believe that they must be at home 24/7 for the benefit of the child for at least the first three to five years, and to do otherwise would be unwise, if not unnatural, to both child and mother. Indeed, as Ivana Brown notes in her research paper: "While some authors challenge parts of the 'natural mother' myth, all of them are the primary caregivers of their children" (56). She goes on to explain: "Mothers are the main caretakers of the children and fathers are more or less absent, appearing at the time of birth and then having a role in the background in financially supporting the family and helping the mother with certain tasks and responsibilities. The absence of fathers from the daily parenting tasks remains mostly unexplained" (56). "This approach," as Brown notes, "contributes to the categorical differentiation between men and women [in the motherhood memoir]" (45). Interestingly but not surprisingly, in earlier motherhood memoirs, most notably *The Mother Knot, American Mom* and *The Mother Zone*, ones that predate the rise of the new momism discourse, childcare is a central theme.

For me the most worrisome part of the new momism, particularly as it is manifested in the motherhood memoir, is that being a stay-at-home mother is constructed as the mother's choice. Again, to return to Douglas and Michael's discussion of choice, they write:

> The mythology of the new momism now insinuates that, when all is said and done, the enlightened mother chooses to stay at home with the kids. Back in the 1950s mothers stayed home because they had no choice. Today having been to the office, having tried a career, women supposedly have seen the inside of the male working world and found it be the inferior choice to staying home, especially when her kids' future is at stake. It's not that mothers can't hack it (1950s thinking). It's that progressive mothers refuse to hack it. The June Cleaver model, if taken as a *choice*, as opposed to a requirement, is the truly modern fulfilling forward-thinking version of motherhood. (23)

While many of the authors expose the concept of choice for what it is—a fiction and a fallacy—they nonetheless see their full-time mothering as inevitable and necessary. However, other memoir writers do deflect and disguise the very real structural and familial inequities mothers face by way of a narrative of choice. A writer in the collection *Breeder*, who practices attachment parenting as a college student, for example, explains that she decided to quit school when pregnant with her second child because "I was tired every day, tired all over, and the prospect of spending the next several months so impossibly tired was too much for me" (Gore, 83). So, as she goes on to explain, "Feeling that I faced a *choice* between my future and my present, I *withdrew* from my classes" (84, emphases added). Later she writes, "My education has not been put on hold; on the contrary, I am a full-time student in an accelerated toddler studies program. My three-year-old is experimenting with wet-on-wet watercolours, and the baby will be walking soon. Now that's what I call progress" (85). As someone who gave birth to three children in five years while an undergrad and later a grad student, I can certainly understand being "impossibly tired," but the reasons for such tiredness are as much the result of her adherence to the new momism discourse, which requires her to be the main caretaker of the children 24/7 via attachment parenting as they are of the demands of academia. Had she used some childcare, insisted upon shared parenting (her partner is mentioned only once), and renounced or reduced her "natural" and intensive mothering practices, she would have had, in all likelihood, the time and energy to combine motherhood with her studies. (This is not to minimize the real need for structural change in education/workplace to enable women to combine work with motherhood.) But because of her adherence to the new momism philosophy of mothering, she simply cannot see these as possibilities, and thus must accept societal and familial gender inequities as both inevitable and natural. More troublesome is that all of this is narrated and justified in the language of choice and, even more problematically, as a feminist choice: i.e., when she proclaims: "now that's progress."

Most motherhood memoirs, because of their identification with the new momism, can not discern, let alone critique, the root causes of mothers' oppression: thus the genre remains one of complaint and not change. Some memoir authors, most notably Faulkner Fox and Marrit Ingman, do challenge. Not surprisingly, these authors also offer a critique of the new momism. We need more such memoir writers if we hope to move the genre from a rant to a revolution. But to do so, we must do away with the new momism, and its naturalization of gender inequities. Indeed, memoir authors must bite the hand that feeds them.

Work Cited

Blakely, Mary Kay. *American Mom.* Chapel Hill, N.C.: Algonquin Books, 1994.

Brown, Ivana. "Mommy Memoirs: Feminism, Gender and Motherhood in Popular Culture." *Journal of the Association for Research on Mothering* 8, 1 & 2 (Winter/Summer 2006): 200–12.

Buchanan, Andrea. *Mother Shock: Loving Every (Other) Minute of It.* Seattle, WA: Seal Press, 2003.

Cheever, Susan. *As Good as I Could Be.* New York: Washington Square Press, 2001.

Douglas, Susan, and Meredith Michaels. *The Mommy Myth: The Idealization of Motherhood and How It Has Undermined All Women.* New York: Free Press, 2004.

Fox, Faulkner. *Dispatches from a not-so-perfect life: on how I learned to love the house, the man, the child.* New York: Harmony Books, 2003.

Gore, Ariel, and Bee Lavender. *Breeder: Real-Life Stories from the New Generation of Mothers.* Seattle, WA: Seal Press, 2001.

Hall, Pamela Courtenay. "Mothering Mythology in the Late Twentieth Century: Science, Lore, and Celebratory Narrative." *Canadian Woman Studies* 18, 1 & 2 (Summer/Fall 1998).

Hays, Sharon. *The Cultural Contradictions of Motherhood.* New Haven: Yale University Press, 1996.

Hewett, Heather. "You Are Not Alone: The Personal, the Political, and the 'New' Mommy Lit." In *Chick Lit: The New Woman's Fiction.* Edited by Suzanne Ferriss and Mallory Young. New York: Routledge Press, 2006.

Ingman, Marrit. *Inconsolable: How I Threw My Mental Health Out with the Diapers.* Berkeley: Seal Press, 2005.

Jackson, Marni. *The Mother Zone: love, sex, and laundry in the modern family.* New York: Holt, 1992.

Lazarre, Jane. *The Motherknot.* New York: Dell Books, 1976.

Le Blanc, Wendy. *Naked Motherhood: Shattering Illusions and Sharing Truths.* Sydney, Australia: Random House, 1999.

Maushart, Susan. *The Masks of Motherhood: How Becoming a Mother Changes Everything and Why We Pretend It Doesn't.* New York: New Press, 1999.

Wilkinson, Stephanie, and Jennifer Niesslein. "Tales From The (Mother) Hood: Motherhood in Book Publishing." *Brain, Child* (Spring 2005).

Wolf, Naomi. *Misconceptions: Truth, Lies and the Unexpected on the Journey to Motherhood.* New York: Random House, 2003.

Contributors

SILVIA CAPORALE-BIZZINI, PhD, is associate professor in the department of English at the University of Alicante where she teaches English literature and cultural theory. Among other many publications she has coedited *Reconstructing Foucault: Essays in the Wake of the 80s* (1994), *Historia Crítica de la Novela Inglesa Escrita por Mujeres* (2003) and edited *Discursos teóricos en torno a la(s) maternidad(es)* (2004) and *Narrating Motherhoods, Breaking the Silence: Other Mothers, Other Voices* (2006). She has also published a number of articles and essays in international journals. She is currently working on the praxis of autobiographical and memoir writing in the (self) definiton of difference in a context of cultural hybridity within the experience of immigration.

SONYA CORBIN DWYER is an associate professor in psychology at Sir Wilfred Grenfell College, Memorial University of Newfoundland. She is also a registered psychologist. She received her PhD from the University of Calgary.

R. JOYCE Z. L. GARAY is an assistant professor in the English Department at New Mexico State University. She specializes in modern and contemporary American literatures, teaching courses in Latina/o literatures, Black U.S. literatures, women writers and autobiography.

LYNN GIDLUCK is director of the Saskatchewan office of the Canadian Centre for Policy Alternatives. Together with her partner, she also owns and operates a public relations firm in Regina, Saskatchewan. She received her MA from the University of Regina.

HEATHER INGMAN is a member of the School of English, Trinity College, Dublin. She has published widely on women's writing, including women's interwar fiction and Irish women's writing. Her publications include *Women's Fiction Between the Wars: Mothers, Daughters and Writing* (1998) and *Mothers and Daughters in the Twentieth Century: A Literary Anthology* (1999). Her most recent book is *Twentieth Century Fiction by Irish Women: Nation and Gender* (2007).

JENNIFER A. JONES is the married mother of three young adult children as well as a doctoral student within the Humanities Program at Queensland University of Technology. Her research project engages with narratives of mothers of young adult children in order to articulate the ontological reality of this phase of mothering. She is a member of the Association for Research on Mothering and is currently treasurer of the Australian branch of the association.

SUE KENTLYN is a research member of the faculty of Social and Behavioural Sciences of the University of Queensland.

CAROLINA NÚÑEZ PUENTE is a post-doctoral fellow and lecturer at the Department of English, Universidade da Coruña, Spain. She holds an MA in Women's and Gender Studies (Rutgers University) and a PhD in English Philology (Universidade da Coruña). She is author of *Feminism and Dialogics: Charlotte Perkins Gilman, Meridel Le Sueur, Mikhail M. Bakhtin*. Valencia: PUV, 2006. She has published articles both in Spain and abroad. She has been a visiting scholar in Germany, the UK, and the USA. Her current book project focuses on American women writers, etnicity, and ethics.

ANDREA O'REILLY, PhD, associate professor in the School of Women's Studies at York University, is coeditor/editor of twelve books on including *Mother Outlaws: Theories and Practices of Empowered Mothering* (2004), and *Maternal Theory: The Essential Readings* (2007). Recently she was invited to serve as general editor for the first-ever *Encyclopedia of Mothering*. The three-volume work will be published in 2010. O'Reilly is author of *Toni Morrison and Motherhood: A Politics of the Heart* (2004) and *Rocking the Cradle: Thoughts on Motherhood, Feminism, and the Possibility of Empowered Mothering*, (2006). She is founder and director of the Association for Research on Mothering (*ARM*). Founded in 1998, *ARM* is the first feminist research association on the topic of mothering-motherhood and has more than five hundred members worldwide. Dr. O'Reilly is also founder and editor-in-chief of the *Journal of the Association for Research on Mothering*, the first, and still only, scholarly journal on motherhood. Both ARM and its journal are recognized worldwide as the leading research center/journal on Motherhood. In 2005 she launched Demeter Press, the first feminist press on motherhood. Dr. O'Reilly has presented her research at more than seventy conferences in over twenty-three countries and was a keynote speaker at the *National Women's Studies Conference* in 2006. She has also given numerous talks at universities across North America and Europe. In 1998 she was the recipient of the universitywide Teacher of the Year award at York University, and in 2007 she was granted the dean's award for Outstanding Research.

BETH OSNES is an assistant professor of theater at the University of Colorado in Boulder. She is author of *Acting: An International Encyclopedia* and many chapters and articles on both mothering and theater. She was a Fulbright Scholar in Malaysia where she conducted field research on the traditional performing arts. She is cofounder of Mothers Acting Up (MAU), a movement to inspire and engage mothers in advocating for the world's children. With MAU she is now touring a theater program, The (M)other Tour, to locations around the world.

LESLEY PATTERSON is a sociologist with research interests spanning family life, welfare reform, gender, and work. Her PhD explored lone mothers' narratives in the context of neoliberal welfare reform discourses that constructed lone mothers as problematic women, mothers, and citizens. She is currently working on two qualitative longitudinal studies. One is exploring low-income lone mothers' experiences over time, with a focus on both income adequacy and security, and familial and intimate relationships. The other is investigating how first-time parents negotiate both the division of labor and their parental identities in the five years following the birth of their first child. In addition, Lesley has an interest in narrative, and recently completed a narrative analysis of how young people imagine their lives might turn out, especially in regard to family life, friendship and intimacy across the life course.

MARTHA SATZ is the white mother of children of color—one now a law professor, the other a young adult. She has written about this experience, "Trans-Racial Mothering: Double-Edged Privilege," in the *Journal of Social Distress and the Homeless: Adoption Across Race, Culture and Class*: Special Issue 18, 1–2 (February 2008); "Should Whites

Adopt Black Children: One Family's Phenomenological Response," in *Imagining Adoption: Adoption in Literature and Culture*, ed. Marianne Novy (2001), 267–76; "Adopting a Set of Assumptions: Memoirs of an Unconventional Mother," *Philosophy and Everyday Life: Narrative and Philosophy*, ed. Laura Duhan Kaplan (2001); and "Confessions of a Witch with Limited Powers," in *Everyday Acts Against Racism: Mothers' Stories*, ed. Maureen Reddy (1996). As an assistant professor in English at Southern Methodist University, she teach courses in women's studies, minority literature, and ethics and literature. She is currently at work on a book-length manuscript on adoption in literature and culture.

NÓRA SÉLLEI is associate professor at the department of British Studies at the Institute of English and American Studies, University of Debrecen, Hungary. She gained her PhD (1996) and "habilitation" (2002) from the same university. Her publications include four books *Katherine Mansfield and Virginia Woolf: A Personal and Professional Bond*, (1996); a monograph in Hungarian on nineteenth-century British women writers' novels—*Lánnyá válik, s írni kezd* (1999); one on early twentieth-century autobiographies by women writers—*Tükröm, tükröm . . .* (2001); and a monograph on the state of Hungarian feminist literary criticism—*Mért félünk a farkastól?* (2007). She is the series editor of the Hungarian feminist book series Artemis Books (Artemisz Könyvek), a coeditor of the *Hungarian Journal of English and American Studies*, a member of the advisory board of *Gender Studies*, and the translator of Woolf's *Moments of Being* (1999), Jean Rhys's *Smile Please* (2001), and Woolf's *Three Guineas* (2006).

CELIA SHIFFER, Ph.D. is an Assistant Professor of English at Bucks County Community College, Pennsylvania, where she teaches courses in writing, women's studies, and British literature.

MARY WEARN serves as Assistant Professor of English at Macon State College, where she teaches American literature and writing. Her research interests include nineteenth-century women writers, abolitionist texts, representations of motherhood, and religion in literature. Her book *Negotiating Motherhood in Nineteenth-Century American Literature* (2008), examines the critical debate about family, womanhood, and motherhood that was waged in the heart of the sentimental era.

ANN ELIZABETH WILLEY is an Associate Professor and the Director of Undergraduate Studies in the Department of English at the University of Louisville. She is also the single mother of two children, a 5-year-old boy and a 2-year-old girl. Her main research interests are modernity and the state in African literature but lately she has found herself thinking more and more about the discourses of mothering, especially in how they intersect with American discourses of consumerism, the free market, and personal responsibility.

Index

Abbey, Sharon, 222–23 n. 3
abjection, 228–29, 233. *See also* negation
"About Chinese Women" (Kristeva), 232
Achebe, Chinua, 188
"Across The Divide" (O'Reilly), 223 n. 3
adoption, 71–83. *See also* adoptive mothers; transracial families
adoptive mothers, 17, 74, 76, 77
advertising. *See* media
advice. *See* experts
African-Americans, 24, 183–93. *See also* slavery
age, 62, 90, 240
agency: female, 20; in slavery, 22, 152; lesbian, 119; maternal, 38, 63–64, 220. *See also* authority; autonomy; power; voice
Aid to Families with Dependent Children, 67 n. 8
Aird, Enola, 136
alienation. *See* negation
Ambert, A., 75–78
American Mom (Blakely), 246
Americans, 75
Anderson, Linda, 12, 16, 236
"Annunciation" (Le Sueur), 22, 156, 161–65
Arendt, Hannah, 27
Asia, 71. *See also* China
Aston, Elaine, 137
At the Protest for Charlton Heston (Osnes), 129–30
attachment mothering, 246, 247. *See also* intensive mothering
Australia, 115–18

authority, 106
Autobiographical Narratives of Transformation (Barros), 43
Autobiography (Anderson), 12
autobiography, 10, 12–23, 27–28, 42–45, 46 n. 6, 161, 181 n. 1, 221, 225, 235–36; African-American, 185, 192; in theater, 124–38; of mother-in-mourning, 170–81. *See also* biography, maternal; memoir; narratives, maternal; voice
autonomy, 107–9, 243

Babies and Boundaries: Mother-Speaking in Rachel Cusk's A Life's Work (Shiffer), 24–25
babies, 215, 223 n. 3, 228, 232–33; shopping for, 92. *See also* childbirth; linea negra; motherhood: early days of Babies R Us, 92
'bad' mothers, 19. *See also* blame
"Bad Mother" (Hillman), 212, 219
Baker, Bobby, 125–26
Bakhtin, Mikhail, 159, 162, 167 n. 8; and chronotopes, 163, 165, 167 n. 5; and dialogics, 156–57, 166, 166 n. 1; on individuality, 164; on language, 161
Barros, Carolyn, 43
Bartels-Rabb, L. M., 73–74
Barthes, Roland, 28
Bauer, Dale M., 166 n. 2
Behan, Kathleen, 226–27, 231
benefits, maternity, 52–53, 73. *See also* welfare
Benjamin, Jessica, 225
Benjamin, Walter, 16, 42

255

256　INDEX

Beyond the Whiteness of White: Memoir of a White Mother of Black Sons (Lazarre), 23–24, 184–93
biography, maternal, 57–60, 67 nn. 9 and 10. *See also* autobiography; narratives, maternal; writing
biological essentialism. *See* essentialism, biological
biracial families. *See* transracial families
Birth Control Review (Sanger), 47 n. 8
birth. *See* childbirth
birth control, 43, 47 n. 7, 226. *See also* pregnancy: strategies
birth, premature, 207
Bizzini, Silvia Caporale, 16
Black Looks (hooks), 187
Black Sun: Depression and Melancholy (Kristeva), 234, 235
Blacks. *See* African-Americans
blame, 76, 102. *See also* 'bad' mothers
Blatch, Harriot Stanton, 138
Bock, Jane D., 62–63
body, maternal, 126, 163, 223 n. 4; effects of childbirth upon the, 220, 229; terror of the, 214, 233; in relation to the infant, 228, 231; suppression of the, 227, 230. *See also* breast-feeding; childbirth
Boesing, Martha, 125
books, 239–40; child-rearing, 106. *See also* literature
Bordo, Susan, 40–41
boredom, 215, 244–45
Bowen, J., 75
Bowlby, John, 230
Brain, Child, 238
breast-feeding, 230. *See also* milk
Breeder (Gore), 245, 247
Brown University, 184
Brown, Ivana, 245, 246
Brown, Wendy, 41
Bruner, J, 110
Buchanan, Andrea, 244
Buci-Glucksmann, C, 42, 46 n. 5
butch identity, 198–202. *See also* lesbians
Butler, Judith, 121

Butler, Octavia, 191
Byrne, Anne, 59

"Can" (Driver), 199
Canada, 71, 73, 82
capitalism, 50. *See also* consumerism
Capo, Beth Widmaier, 47 n. 7
caring, maternal, 9, 189–90
career, 76, 90, 97, 243. *See also* work, paid
Case, Sue Ellen, 125
Catholicism, 25, 225, 230, 234. *See also* Virgin Mary
celebrity mothers, 40, 76
cesarean section, 222 n. 2
Chandler, Mielle, 12, 200, 216–17
Charleston, S.C., 183–84
Charlesworth, M., 107
Cheever, Susan, 245
Cherniavsky, Eva, 148
Chicanas, 45, 195–209
Child, Lydia Maria, 192–93
childbirth, 25, 214–15, 222 n. 2, 229, 231, 232, 234; natural, 167 n. 7; and pain, 214–16. *See also* birth, premature; body, maternal; cesarean section; doula
child-centered. *See* attachment mothering; intensive mothering
children, 241, 242, 243; adult, 101–12; separation from, 233, 245. *See also* babies; cuteness; daughters; sons
China, 71, 78, 82
Chinese children, 77
Chodorow, Nancy, 159, 200
choice: to adopt, 76; motherhood as, 62, 65, 87–88, 243, 246–47; not to mother, 74, 76. *See also* autonomy; pregnancy: strategies
chora, 228
Christianity, 118, 173, 174, 179
chronotopes, 162–65, 167 n. 5
Cixous, Hélène, 163, 179, 223 n. 4
citizen-worker model, 54–55, 65
Clegg, Stewart, 59
Clément, Catherine, 229
clinics, fertility. *See* fertility
Clinton, Bill, 67 n. 8

"Coalescence in Evolution: Queer Familia in Cherríe Moraga's *Waiting in the Wings*" (Garay), 24
Coleman, Linda, 19–20
"Compulsory Heterosexuality and Lesbian Existence" (Rich), 114
Comstock Act, 47 n. 7
consumerism, 92–94
contraception. *See* birth control
Corbin, Sonya, 16, 17
Cosslet, Tess, 39
cryobank. *See* sperm donors
Cultural Contradictions of Motherhood (Hays), 241
cultural materialism, 46 n. 4
culture, 38–39, 41, 42; popular, 76. *See also* Catholicism; celebrity mothers; Christianity; Judaism; patriarchy
Cusk, Rachel, 24–25, 210–23
cuteness, 130

Dalmiya, Vrinda, 189–90
Daly, Brenda O., 10, 11
Daughter's Cycle Trilogy, The, 126
daughters, 10, 109, 126, 180–81, 229, 232, 233
de Lauretis, Teresa, 121
death, 175, 233–35; child, 14, 108–9, 170–81
dependence, 22, 101–12, 159, 179, 188, 228
depression, 234–35; postpartum, 157
"Dialogics of the Sexual-Maternal: Multiple Births in Gilman and Le Sueur" (Puente), 22
dialogics, 156, 166 n. 1, 166–67 n. 2
Diamond, Elin, 157
Dion, Celine, 76
discourse, dominant, 39, 46 nn. 4 and 5, 86, 213
Dispatches (Faulkner), 239
divorce, 61, 117
doctors. *See* hospitals; medical institutions
Dolan, Jill, 125, 126, 137–38
Domestic Purposes Benefits, 52, 53, 55, 66 n. 1

Douglas, Ann, 149
Douglas, Sharon, 26, 40, 240, 242–43, 246
doula, 86–87
Doyle, Catherine, 106
Drawing on a Mother's Experience (Baker), 125–26
Dread Road, The (Le Sueur), 167 n. 7
Driver, Susan, 198–99, 202
DuBois, W. E. B., 184
DuCille, Ann, 193
Dunlop, Rishma, 223 n. 5
DuPlessis, Rachel Blau, 12

Eakin, Paul John, 42
"Emancipated Subjectivities and the Subjugation of Mothering Practices" (Chandler), 216–17
employment. *See* work, paid
Enright, Anne, 25, 225–36
"Erotics of Irishness" (Herr), 227
essentialism, biological, 38, 77. *See also* natural mothering; 'real' mothers
ethics, maternal, 180. *See also* caring, maternal
eugenics, 47 n. 8
experts, 83, 106–7, 211, 242. *See also* books

faith, loss of, 234
"Family and The Female Body in the Novels of Edna O'Brien and Julia O'Faolain" (Rooks-Hughes), 227
family, 74, 78, 196
fathers, 95, 103–4, 117, 167 n. 3, 246. *See also* husbands
Felman, Shoshanan, 12
Feminine and the Sacred, The, (Kristeva), 229
feminine écriture, 161, 162. *See also* autobiography; mommy lit; writing
femininity, 179, 200
feminism, 15, 125, 126, 167 n. 7, 227, 243. *See also* feminists; psychoanalytic theory, feminist; suffrage, women's; women

Feminism, Bakhtin and the Dialogic (Bauer, McKinstry), 166–67 n. 2
"Feminist Sublimations, Queer Disidentifications: Losing Touch of Maternal Sexuality" (Driver), 198
Feminist Theatre Practice: A Handbook (Aston), 137
feminists, 40, 75, 136. *See also* feminism
fertility, 75, 76–77, 89–90. *See also* sperm donors; sterilization
Fetterley, Judith, 13
Flood, M., 117
Fo, Dario, 126
Foucault, M., 38, 41, 46 n. 5
Fox, Faulkner, 239, 247
Fraser, Nancy, 64
Freud, Sigmund, 160, 173, 176, 179, 180, 229

Garay, R. Joyce Z. L., 24
"Garden of Babies, The" (Gilman), 167 n. 3
Gardiner, Janice, 67 n. 9
gaze of others, 223 n. 3
gender: binaries, 61, 198; discrimination, 159–60; equality, 55; inequalities, 26, 240–41, 247. *See also* butch identity; femininity; lesbians; sexuality
Geographies of Learning (Dolan), 137
Gergen, M., 75
Gibson, Donald, 147
Gidneck, Lynn, 16–18
Gilman, Charlotte Perkins, 22–23, 156–61, 165–66, 167 nn. 3 and 4
Girl, The (Le Sueur), 167 n. 7
Giving Up the Ghost (Moraga), 209
GLBTTIQ community, 120
Glenn, Evelyn Nakano, 127
globalization, 39, 54
Goldman, Alvin, 189, 190
Good Flirt, The, (Osnes), 131
'good mother,' 18, 38, 74, 108, 213, 216, 222, 242. *See also* idealized mother; intensive mothering; "real" mothers
Gore, Ariel, 240
Gramsci, Antonio, 41–42, 46 n. 5
grandmothers, 145–47

Greenhalgh, Jill, 125, 126
Grieving Self, The (Doyle), 106
Gusdorf, Georges, 174, 181 n. 1

Haiti, 82
Hall, Beth, 79, 81
Hall, Pamela Courtenay, 241
Hamilton, C., 117
Hansen, Elaine Tuttle, 19
Haraway, Donna, 50
Hartnett, Sonya, 105
Hayes, Alan, 226
Hays, Sharon, 26, 40, 106, 240–42
He Left plot, 59–61, 63
Heddon, Deidre, 134
Hegemony and Socialist Strategy (Laclau, Mouffe), 46 n. 2
hegemony, 39, 41, 46 n. 5
Heilbrun, Carolyn, 26
Henke, Suzette, 42
Herland-Ourland (Gilman), 167 n. 3
Herr, Cheryl, 227
heterosexuality, 74, 114, 116, 119, 200. *See also* sexuality
Hewett, Heather, 238, 239
Higginbotham, J. S., 81, 82
Hilborn, R., 81
Hill, Anita, 189
Hillman, James, 212
Hinings, D., 109
Hirsch, Marianne, 11, 20, 26–27, 172–73, 179
history, 46 n. 4
home-space, 204
Homeless: Us Against 'Us Vs. Them' (Osnes), 131–32
homophobia, 117–18, 122, 201
homosexuality. *See* GLBTTIQ community; homophobia; lesbians
hooks, bell, 187
Horniblow, Molly, 145, 147, 152
"Horse, The" (Le Sueur), 167 n. 7
hospitals, 200–201, 222 n. 2. *See also* medical institutions
Howe, D. P., 109
husbands, 60–61, 64. *See also* fathers

idealized mother, 10, 127, 225, 227. *See also* 'good mother'; "real" mothers
identity, 46 n. 5, 64, 137; autobiography and, 19, 42, 58, 181 n. 1; maternal, 15, 37, 41, 59, 64, 75, 104, 222 n. 2, 228. *See also* individuality; selfhood; subjectivity, maternal
Ikemoto, Lisa, 38
"Implicated in a Color Change: Darkening the Picture of Jane Lazarre's Maternal Transracial Memoir" (Satz), 23–24
incest, 96
Incidents in the Life of a Slave Girl (Jacobs), 21–22, 143–54, 185–86
individuality, 25, 164, 172, 216–17; maternal loss of, 232, 235. *See also* autonomy; identity, selfhood, voice
industrialization, 106
infants. *See* babies
infertility. *See* fertility
infidelity, 60–61, 64
Ingman, Heather, 25
Ingman, Marrit, 247
institution of motherhood. *See* motherhood, as institution
insurance, 89–90
intensive mothering, 26, 241–43. *See also* attachment mothering; 'good mother'; responsibility, maternal; sacrifice; selflessness
internet, 91–94
interracial marriage, 188
Ireland, 25, 225–31, 234–36
IRS, 87
Italy, 126

Jackson, Marni, 26–27
Jacobs, Harriet, 21–22, 143–54, 185–86, 192–93, 193 n. 1
Jagose, A., 121
Jameson, Fredric, 39
Jelinek, Estelle C., 174, 181 n. 3
Johnson, Miriam, 10–11
Johnston, D., 74
Johnston, P., 72, 73

Jones, Jenny, 18
Judaism, 229

Kennedy, Patricia, 235
Kentlyn, Susan, 18–19
Kids Aren't Cute (Osnes), 130
Kindred (Butler), 191
Kittay, Eva, 188, 190
Kitzinger, Sheila, 106, 108, 109, 115
Kristeva, Julia, 170, 172–73, 175, 179, 211, 223 n. 4, 225–36

La Malinche, 208–9 n. 4
labor. *See* childbirth
Lacan, Jacques, 211, 218, 219, 222 n. 1
Laclau, Ernesto, 39, 46 n. 2
Lakoff, R. T., 75
language, 161, 218; and adoption, 71, 75–77, 81–83; maternal, 173, 211–12, 219; and single mothers, 86–99; women's, 223 n. 4
Lanser, Susan S., 166
Latina. *See* Chicana
Lazarre, Jane, 23–24, 183–93
Le Blanc, Wendy, 244
Le Sueur, Meridel, 22–23, 156, 161–66, 167 nn. 6 and 7
Lee, Robert E., 186
Lehmann, Rosamond, 23, 170–81
lesbian: coming out as, 116–17, 196–97; mothering, 24, 44–45, 74, 114–23, 195–209; sexuality, 199. *See also* lesbians
lesbians, 160, 161; children of, 117–22. *See also* GLBTTIQ community; homophobia; lesbian
Levander, Caroline, 145
liberalism, 172, 181 n. 1, 243; neo–, 51–67
Life's Work, A (Cusk), 210–23
linea negra, 215
literature, 13, 238; parenting, 40, 42, 78, 162. *See also* autobiography; books; feminine *écriture*; mommy lit; writing
Living of Charlotte Perkins Gilman, The (Gilman), 157
loss, 206, 221. *See also* death: child

Loving in the War Years: lo que nunca pasó por sus labios (Moraga), 195
low-income families, 65, 66. *See also* poverty; welfare
Lugones, Maria, 191

MacBride, Maud Gonne, 227–28
Magdalena Symposium, 125
Making Babies: Stumbling into Motherhood (Enright), 25, 225–36
Malin, Jo, 44
Mallarmé, 229
Marcus, Laura, 13, 42
Marxism, 46
Mason, Mary, 225
Massey, D., 109
masturbation, 160
mater dolorosa, 23, 173, 179
Maternal Thinking (Ruddick), 9
Maternity in Ireland: A Woman-Centred Perspective (Kennedy), 235
matrifocality, 10–11
Maushart, Susan, 244
McCarthy, Áine, 226
McKinstry, Jaret, 166 n. 2
McNally, David, 163, 167 n. 8
McRae-McMahon, Dorothy, 116, 118
media, 41. *See also* celebrity mothers
medical institutions, 87, 157. *See also* hospitals
Melina, L. R., 82
memoir, 183–93, 238–48. *See also* autobiography
memory, 42, 46 n. 3
men. *See* fathers; husbands; sons; sperm donors
Mexicans, 196, 197. *See* Chicana
Michaels, Meredith, 26, 40, 240, 242–43, 246
milk, 146, 173, 229, 234
Millevoye, Lucien, 228
Mitchell, Silas W., 157
mommy lit, 238–40. *See also* narratives, maternal
Mommy Memoirs: Feminism, Gender and Motherhood in Popular Culture (Brown), 245

Mommy Myth, The (Douglas, Michaels), 242
Moosnick, Nora Rose, 79
Moraga, Cherríe, 24, 41, 42, 44–45, 195–209
Mother Journeys: Feminists Write About Mothering (Reddy, Roth, Sheldon), 44
Mother Knot, The (Lazarre), 246
Mother Load, The (Osnes), 124–38
Mother of All the Behans (Behan), 226, 228
Mother Shock (Buchanan), 244
Mother Zone, The (Jackson), 246
mother: becoming a, 212, 220–21, 230; definition of 210, 217. *See also* idealized mother; matrifocality; motherhood; mothering; 'real' mothers; single mothers; subjectivity, maternal; wife role
Mother's Day Parade, 136
Mother-Daughter Plot: Narrative, Psychoanalysis, Feminism (Hirsch), 20
Motherhood According to Giovanni Bellini (Kristeva), 231, 232
motherhood as institution, 11, 104–5, 118–19, 213, 223 n. 3. *See also* "good mother"; patriarchy; silence; subjectivity, maternal
Motherhood in Bondage (Sanger), 43
"Motherhood in Book Publishing" (Wilkinson, Niesslein), 238
"Motherhood Memoir and the 'New Momism': Biting the Hand That Feeds You" (O'Reilly), 26
motherhood, 9–28, 38, 39, 210, 216; early days of, 231, 232, 233; hierarchy of, 16, 17, 72–75; movement, 136. *See also* motherhood as institution; mother
Mothering (journal), 92–93
mothering. *See* attachment mothering; mother; motherhood; intensive mothering; work, mother; political mothering; responsibility, maternal

Mothers Acting Up, 126–27, 134, 136
Mothers: A Loving Celebration (Shields), 108
Mouffe, Chantal, 39, 46 n. 2
Muldoon, Robert, 53
Murdoch, Iris, 188

Nakano, Glenn, 42
Nakazawa, D. J., 79, 80
Naked Motherhood: Shattering Illusions and Sharing Truths (Le Blanc), 244
Narrating Maternity: Theorizing Maternal Subjectivities (Daly, Reddy), 10
narratives, maternal, 9–28, 51, 56–57, 60, 75, 212, 221, 223 n. 3. *See also* autobiography; biography, maternal; voice; writing
narratives, dominant, 18, 102–112, 220. *See also* patriarchy
Native Americans, 163
natural mothering, 11, 38, 93, 105, 164, 241, 245. *See also* essentialism, biological
negation, 212, 213, 216. *See also* silence
new momism, 26, 238–48
"New Thoughts on 'the Oldest Vocation': Mothers and Motherhood in Recent Feminist Scholarship" (Ross), 13
New Type of Intellectual: The Dissident, A, (Kristeva), 230
New Zealand, 50–67
Niesslein, Jennifer, 238–40
Northrup, Christine, 109
nursing. *See* breast-feeding

O'Reilly, Andrea, 26, 105, 222–23 n. 3
Of Woman Born (Rich), 9, 11, 213
"'Oh Mother Where Art Thou?' Irish Mothers and Irish Fiction in the Twentieth Century" (McCarthy), 226
Osnes, Beth, 19, 124–38

Paddock, D., 74, 78
Parkes, C. M., 110

patriarchy, 103, 156, 159, 163, 218–19, 222, 240. *See also* "good mother"; motherhood as institution; narratives, dominant; silence
Patterson, Lesley, 16–17
performativity, 217
"Performing the Self" (Heddon), 134
"Persephone" (Le Sueur), 167 n. 7
Plummer, Ken, 56
political mothering, 13, 16, 21, 27–28, 39–40, 44, 126–28, 131, 135–38
Porter, M., 105
Post, Amy, 144
poverty, 43, 53. *See also* low income families; welfare
power, 41, 42, 229. *See also* authority; autonomy; political mothering; voice
Powers of Horror (Kristeva), 173, 228–29, 233
pregnancy, 77, 163, 219; early, 206, 213, experience of, 214, 231; and the good; mother; and sexuality, 203–4; strategies, 97, 136; tests, 62; unplanned, 61–63. *See also* birth control; sterilization
Price, R., 83
Price-Herndl, Diane, 161
Probyn, Elspeth, 15–16, 235–36
psychoanalytic theory, 172, 198, 211
Puente, Carolina Núñez, 22
purity, 228, 229. *See also* Virgin Mary

queer: consciousness, 24; motherhood, 195–209; theory, 18–19, 121–22, 198. *See also* GLBTTIQ community; lesbian; lesbian mothering
"Queering Maternity" (Chandler), 200

race, 24, 183–93; and mothering, 74, 78–80. *See also* interracial marriage; racism; transracial families
racism, 78–79, 185, 187–90, 192. *See also* slavery
Radin, Margaret, 93
Rame, Franca, 126

"real" mothers, 17, 39, 40, 72, 73, 79, 82, 222 n. 1, 222, 238. *See also* idealized mother; mother
Reddy, Maureen T., 10, 11
Redefining Motherhood (Abbey, O'Reilly), 222–23 n. 3
Register, C., 72, 81
religion. *See* Catholicism; Christianity; faith, loss of; Judaism
"Reproducing the Working Class: Tillie Olson, Margaret Sanger, and American Eugenics" (Roche), 47 n. 7
Reproduction of Motherhood (Chodorow), 200
responsibility, maternal, 62, 102, 106, 110–11, 178
Rich, Adrienne, 9, 11, 21, 75, 83, 114, 118–119, 213
Richardson, D., 105
Roche, Claire M., 47 n. 8
Rogus, Caroline, 77
Rooks-Hughes, Lorna, 227
Ross, Ellen, 13–14
Ruddick, Sara, 9, 11, 21, 27, 102, 108, 188, 190, 223 n. 3

sacrifice, 146, 213, 216, 226. *See also* attachment mothering; 'good mother'; intensive mothering; responsibility, maternal; selflessness
Sanger, Margaret, 43–44, 47 nn. 7 and 8
Satz, Martha, 23–24
Sawbridge, P., 109
Sawicki, Jana, 15
selfhood, 22, 25, 40–41, 98, 111, 163, 188, 191, 215, 217–18, 220–21; autobiography and, 15, 37, 42–43, 64, 225. *See also* identity; individuality; negation; subjectivity, maternal; voice
selflessness, 90, 243. *See also* intensive mothering; sacrifice
Séllei, Nóra, 23
Sense and Non-sense of Revolt (Kristeva), 228–29

"Sequel to Love" (Le Sueur), 167 n. 7
Servant of the Queen, A: Reminiscences (MacBride), 227–28
sexuality, 115, 121, 160–61; maternal, 22, 118, 131, 156, 159, 198, 227. *See also* heterosexuality; infidelity; lesbian; purity
Shields, Carol, 108
Shiffer, Celia, 24–25
Shumaker, Conrad, 157
silence, 13–14, 211, 226, 228, 230, 244. *See also* negation; patriarchy; voice
simulation theory, 189, 191
Single Mother plot, 59–63
single mothers, 16–18, 50–67, 77, 86–99
Single Mothers By Choice, 87–88, 99 n. 2
slavery, 21–22, 143–54, 183, 185–87, 193 n. 1. *See also* racism
Smith, 115–16
Smith, Sidonie, 20, 221
Smith, Stephanie, 150, 151
Snitow, Anne, 14
sons, 120, 190, 199–200, 233
"Sorties" (Cixous), 179
Spelman, Elizabeth V., 193 n. 1
sperm donors, 18, 91–96, 120, 203
"Spring Story" (La Sueur), 167 n. 7
"Stabat Mater" (Kristeva), 23, 170, 179, 229–32, 235
Steedman, Carolyn, 37
Steinberg, Gail, 79, 81
sterilization, 163, 167 n. 7
Stories of No Intent, 60, 61, 63
Story of a Mother II, The (Boesing), 125
Stowe, Harriet Beecher, 144, 149
Strong Mothers, Weak Wives (Johnson), 10–11
subjectivity, maternal, 12, 179, 213, 221, 222–23 n. 3, 225–36. See also identity; mother; motherhood; selfhood
suffrage, women's, 181 n. 2, 240
suicide, 234
Suleiman, Susan Rubin, 211

Surrey, J., 107
Swan in the Evening: Fragments of an Inner Life (Lehmann), 23, 170–81
Swanson, D., 74
Swindells, Julia, 13

taboo, 172, 173, 175
Taming of the Mother Mind, The, (Osnes), 130–31
Tatonetti, Lisa, 45, 196, 206
Tatum, Beverly, 79
theater, 124–38
Tompkins, Jane, 149
Tougaw, Jason, 44
"Transitions from Heterosexuality to Lesbianism" (Kitzinger, Wilkinson), 115
transracial families, 23–24, 71–83, 183–93
trauma, 25, 43–44, 214, 215
True Story, 14
"Turned" (Gilman), 167 n. 3
Tutta casa, letto e chiesa (Rame, Fo), 126
Tuttle Hanson, Elaine, 39

Uncle Tom's Cabin (Stowe), 149
"Unnatural Mother, The" (Gilman), 167 n. 3
Uses of Autobiography, The (Swindells), 13

validation stories, 17, 50–67. *See also* He Left plot; narratives, maternal; Single Mother plot
van Gulden, H., 72–74, 82
Veeder, William, 159
Venn-Brown, Anthony, 118
Victoria, Queen, 171, 181 n. 2
Victorian motherhood, 144–45, 149, 150, 161, 171
Virgin Mary, 118, 173, 229, 231
Voice of the Mother: Embedded Maternal Narratives in Twentieth-Century Women's *Autobiographies* (Malin), 44
voice, 165; maternal, 13, 14, 26, 41, 44, 111, 171–73, 211. *See also* agency; autobiography; biography, maternal; identity; memoir; selfhood; silence; subjectivity, maternal; writing

Waiting in the Wings: Portrait of Queer Motherhood (Moraga), 24, 44–45, 195–209
Walker, Bert, 53
Wallbank, Julie 17
Wardrop, Daneen, 152
Watson, Julie, 20
Waugh, Patricia, 159
Wearn, Mary McCartin, 21
welfare, 17, 50–67. *See also* low-income families; poverty
What Diantha Did (Gilman), 167 n. 3
Whites, 23–24, 74, 78, 183–84
Why Children? (Snitow), 14
"Why Should a Knower Care?" (Dalmiya), 189
widows, 66 n. 1
wife role, 104
Wilkinson, Stephanie, 115, 238–40
Willett, Cynthia, 180
Willey, Ann Elizabeth, 17–18
Wilson, Scott, 39
Wilton, 119, 121, 122
Winant, H., 81
"Wind" (Le Sueur), 167 n. 7
Winnicott, Donald, 230
Wittig, Monique, 114
Wolf, Naomi, 245
women, 104–5, 198, 218, 223 n. 4, 243. *See also* daughters; feminism; lesbians; mothers; young women
Women, Autobiography, Theory: A Reader (Smith, Watson), 20
Woolf, Virginia, 172
work: mother, 102, 216, 245; paid, 65, 125, 242. *See also* benefits, maternity; career
Writing a Woman's Life (Heilbrun), 26
writing, 42, 129, 161, 223 n. 5; maternal, 27, 37–49, 204–5, 213, 216–17, 219, 221, 230. *See also* autobiography; biography, maternal; literature; mommy lit; narratives, maternal; voice

"Written on the Body" (Dunlop), 223 n. 5

Yellin, Jean Fagan, 151
"Yellow Wallpaper, The" (Gilman), 22, 156–62, 165, 167 n. 3

You Are Not Alone: The Personal, the Political, and the "New" Mommy Lit (Hewett), 238
young women, 53, 61, 63

Žižeck, 46 n. 4